D1719845

V&R unipress

ZEITGESCHICHTE

Ehrenpräsidentin:
em. Univ.-Prof. Dr. Erika Weinzierl († 2014)

Herausgeber:
Univ.-Prof. DDr. Oliver Rathkolb

Redaktion:
em. Univ.-Prof. Dr. Rudolf Ardelt (Linz), ao. Univ.-Prof.[in] Mag.[a] Dr.[in] Ingrid Bauer (Salzburg/ Wien), SSc Mag.[a] Dr.[in] Ingrid Böhler (Innsbruck), Dr.[in] Lucile Dreidemy (Wien), Dr.[in] Linda Erker (Wien), Prof. Dr. Michael Gehler (Hildesheim), ao. Univ.-Prof. i. R. Dr. Robert Hoffmann (Salzburg), ao. Univ.-Prof. Dr. Michael John / Koordination (Linz), Assoz. Prof.[in] Dr.[in] Birgit Kirchmayr (Linz), Dr. Oliver Kühschelm (Wien), Univ.-Prof. Dr. Ernst Langthaler (Linz), Dr.[in] Ina Markova (Wien), Univ.-Prof. Mag. Dr. Wolfgang Mueller (Wien), Univ.-Prof. Dr. Bertrand Perz (Wien), Univ.-Prof. Dr. Dieter Pohl (Klagenfurt), Univ.-Prof.[in] Dr.[in] Margit Reiter (Salzburg), Dr.[in] Lisa Rettl (Wien), Univ.-Prof. Mag. Dr. Dirk Rupnow (Innsbruck), Mag.[a] Adina Seeger (Wien), Ass.-Prof. Mag. Dr. Valentin Sima (Klagenfurt), Prof.[in] Dr.[in] Sybille Steinbacher (Frankfurt am Main), Dr. Christian H. Stifter / Rezensionsteil (Wien), Priv.-Doz.[in] Mag.[a] Dr.[in] Heidemarie Uhl (Wien), Gastprof. (FH) Priv.-Doz. Mag. Dr. Wolfgang Weber, MA, MAS (Vorarlberg), Mag. Dr. Florian Wenninger (Wien), Assoz.-Prof.[in] Mag.[a] Dr.[in] Heidrun Zettelbauer (Graz).

Peer-Review Committee (2021–2023):
Ass.-Prof.[in] Mag.[a] Dr.[in] Tina Bahovec (Institut für Geschichte, Universität Klagenfurt), Prof. Dr. Arnd Bauerkämper (Fachbereich Geschichts- und Kulturwissenschaften, Freie Universität Berlin), Günter Bischof, Ph.D. (Center Austria, University of New Orleans), Dr.[in] Regina Fritz (Institut für Zeitgeschichte, Universität Wien/Historisches Institut, Universität Bern), ao. Univ.-Prof.[in] Mag.[a] Dr.[in] Johanna Gehmacher (Institut für Zeitgeschichte, Universität Wien), Univ.-Prof. i. R. Dr. Hanns Haas (Universität Salzburg), Univ.-Prof. i. R. Dr. Ernst Hanisch (Salzburg), Univ.-Prof.[in] Mag.[a] Dr.[in] Gabriella Hauch (Institut für Geschichte, Universität Wien), Univ.-Doz. Dr. Hans Heiss (Institut für Zeitgeschichte, Universität Innsbruck), Robert G. Knight, Ph.D. (Department of Politics, History and International Relations, Loughborough University), Dr.[in] Jill Lewis (University of Wales, Swansea), Prof. Dr. Oto Luthar (Slowenische Akademie der Wissenschaften, Ljubljana), Hon.-Prof. Dr. Wolfgang Neugebauer (Dokumentationsarchiv des Österreichischen Widerstandes, Wien), Mag. Dr. Peter Pirker (Institut für Zeitgeschichte, Universität Innsbruck), Prof. Dr. Markus Reisenleitner (Department of Humanities, York University, Toronto), Dr.[in] Elisabeth Röhrlich (Institut für Geschichte, Universität Wien), ao. Univ.-Prof.[in] Dr.[in] Karin M. Schmidlechner-Lienhart (Institut für Geschichte/Zeitgeschichte, Universität Graz), Univ.-Prof. i. R. Mag. Dr. Friedrich Stadler (Wien), Prof. Dr. Gerald J. Steinacher (University of Nebraska-Lincoln), Assoz.-Prof. DDr. Werner Suppanz (Institut für Geschichte/Zeitgeschichte, Universität Graz), Univ.-Prof. Dr. Philipp Ther, MA (Institut für Osteuropäische Geschichte, Universität Wien), Prof. Dr. Stefan Troebst (Leibniz-Institut für Geschichte und Kultur des östlichen Europa, Universität Leipzig), Prof. Dr. Michael Wildt (Institut für Geschichtswissenschaften, Humboldt-Universität zu Berlin), Dr.[in] Maria Wirth (Institut für Zeitgeschichte, Universität Wien).

Alle Hefte dieser Zeitschrift sind peer-reviewed.

zeitgeschichte
49. Jg., Sonderheft (2022)

Authoritarian Regimes in the Long Twentieth Century.
Preconditions, Structures, Continuities – Contributions to European Historical Dictatorship and Transformation Research

Edited by
Florian Kührer-Wielach and Oliver Rathkolb

With 11 figures

V&R unipress

Vienna University Press

Gefördert von:

Die Beauftragte der Bundesregierung
für Kultur und Medien

Institut für deutsche Kultur
und Geschichte Südosteuropas
an der LMU München

FSC MIX
Papier aus verantwor-
tungsvollen Quellen
FSC® C083411
www.fsc.org

Bibliografische Information der Deutschen Nationalbibliothek
Die Deutsche Nationalbibliothek verzeichnet diese Publikation in der Deutschen
Nationalbibliografie; detaillierte bibliografische Daten sind im Internet über
https://dnb.de abrufbar.

**Veröffentlichungen der Vienna University Press
erscheinen bei V&R unipress.**

Gedruckt mit freundlicher Unterstützung des Zukunftsfonds der Republik Österreich,
der Kulturabteilung der Stadt Wien (MA 7) und der Historisch-Kulturwissenschaftlichen Fakultät
der Universität Wien.

In Zusammenarbeit mit dem Institut für deutsche Kultur und Geschichte Südosteuropas (IKGS)
an der LMU München.

Vandenhoeck & Ruprecht Verlage | www.vandenhoeck-ruprecht-verlage.com

ISSN 0256-5250
ISBN 978-3-8471-1502-1

Contents

Florian Kührer-Wielach / Oliver Rathkolb

Introduction

This special issue of the journal *zeitgeschichte* presents the results of the doctoral theses written within the context of the Doctoral College (DC) "European Historical Dictatorship and Transformation Research" (2009–2013) in the form of selected scholarly essays. Within the framework of this project, jointly conducted by the Institutes of Contemporary History, Political Science, East European History, and Byzantine and Modern Greek Studies of the University of Vienna, and funded by the Faculty of Historical and Cultural Studies of the University of Vienna, doctoral students from various disciplines devoted themselves to the study of authoritarian regimes of the 20th century in Austria, Belarus, Greece, Hungary, Italy, Latvia, Lithuania, Poland, Portugal, Romania, Spain, and the Soviet Union. Taking a comparative approach to socio-historical transformation research, the theses examined different aspects of dictatorships, particularly "small" ones: the conditions of their emergence; structures; continuities; and preceding and subsequent processes of political and social transformation. The various regional, methodological, and professional approaches of the respective projects are represented in the diversity of the contributions assembled in this volume. They reflect the results of the research training group from a certain temporal distance, and the current state of research has been included wherever possible. Common to all the essays is the historical perspective, which has been combined with approaches rooted in social and political science.

Florian Kührer-Wielach analyzes Romania's transformation and integration process in the years 1918–33 from a regional perspective and the associated path to an authoritarian regime. Katharina Ebner uses a transfer-historical approach to examine the spread of Mussolini's fascist ideology via the "transmission belts" of Vienna and Budapest. Florian Wenninger subjects historiographical interpretations of the end of the first Austrian republic to critical analysis and proposes an updated reading on the basis of new findings. Linda Erker's study of the University of Vienna in the years 1933–38 considers a wealth of sources in her examination of what remains an underresearched period in the history of this institution. Nathalie Soursos compares visual representations of Metaxas' dictatorship in Greece with that of Mussolini in Italy, using press photographs. Kathrin Raminger also takes a comparative approach by examining art exhibitions of the dictatorships of Salazar in Portugal and Franco in Spain with regard to their political instrumentalization. Petitions, complaints, and statements are the focus of Inga Paslavičiūtė's contribution, in which she examines this form of communication between the regime and society in terms of its functions as an outlet and instrument of control and traces the volatile boundaries of permissive discourse. Eleni Kouki uses the example of the Greek military dictatorship of April 21 (1967–74) to address the question as to what the analysis of monuments and ceremonies can contribute to an understanding of the mechanisms of authoritarian regimes. Florian Musil examines the transformation of Spanish society from Franco's military regime to a modern liberal democracy beginning in 1976, focusing on civil society in the Barcelona metropolitan region. The long shadow of the interwar period is addressed in Lucile Dreidemy's essay, which reflects on the Dollfuss myth and its persistence in Austrian postwar discourse, and Filip Zieliński's, which deals with the topos of a Polish "Golden Age" between the world wars after the fall of the Iron Curtain. Finally, Johannes Thaler proposes how central theories of fascism can be made productively combined despite their partly opposing approaches.

The fellows were supervised in their work by scholars at the participating institutes. The framework of the research training group also enabled regular and intensive exchange both between its researchers and with renowned experts from various disciplines in the humanities and social sciences in addition to joint publications and international conferences on European dictatorship and transformation research. The chronicle in the appendix lists the persons involved and documents the research training group's manifold activities.

Florian Kührer-Wielach

Habsburg Revenants on Victory Road. Greater Romania's Integration Process 1918–33

The time had finally come to make Romania a "fertile and flourishing garden", as the Romanian Foreign Minister Alexandru Vaida-Voevod wrote in London's renowned *Slavonic and East European Review* in January 1929.[1] His National Peasant's Party had just taken over the government with an overwhelming election victory, turning the political situation in Romania upside down. It had won with a program that drew heavily on the already legendary unification of the eastern Hungarian territories of Transylvania, the Banat, and the Partium with the Kingdom of Romania. Hence we go back ten years to that 1 December 1918 and travel from London to Alba Iulia in Transylvania – German Karlsburg or Hungarian Gyulafehérvár.

1.   A Vision for a New Country

While the Romanian army had already taken the southeastern part of the region, war still raged in the Banat and just a few weeks after the last Habsburg emperor, Karl (from the Hungarian perspective King Karl IV) had officially renounced all participation in the affairs of government, tens of thousands of delegates had gathered there to proclaim the annexation to and a democratic vision for the new, coming Romania. On the one hand, they had the national emancipation of the Romanians living in Hungary in mind, but on the other hand, they were aware of

---

1 Vaida-Voevod, "Ten Years of Greater Roumania," *The Slavonic and East European Review* 7 (1929) 20, 261–267. This scientific essay is based on the results of my dissertation: Florian Kührer-Wielach, *Siebenbürgen ohne Siebenbürger? Zentralstaatliche Integration und politischer Regionalismus nach dem Ersten Weltkrieg* (München: De Gruyter Oldenbourg, 2014). (Südosteuropäische Arbeiten 153) as well as on my chapters Florian Kührer-Wielach, "A fertile and flourishing garden. Alexandru Vaida-Voevod's Political Account Ten Years after Versailles," in "Romania and the Paris Peace Conference (1919). Actors, Scenarios, Circulation of Knowledge", *Journal of Romanian Studies*, Special Issue edited by Svetlana Suveica, 1 (2019) 2 (Stuttgart: ibidem, 2019): 135–52.

the politically and economically comparatively backward conditions in the "Old Kingdom" of Romania. The authors of the resolution organized themselves in a "Great National Assembly" (*Marea Adunare Naţională*). With the voice of the Greek Catholic Bishop Iuliu Hossu and under the eyes of his Orthodox colleague Miron Cristea, they demanded "provisional autonomy" for the territories annexed by Hungary as well as

1. Full national liberty for all peoples living together. Each people shall be educated, administered, and judged in its own language by individuals from its own midst, and each people shall have the right of representation in the legislative bodies and in the country's government in proportion to the number of individuals constituting it.
2. Equal rights and full confessional autonomy for all confessions in the state.
3. The perfect establishment of a pure democratic regime in all spheres of public life. Universal, direct, equal, secret, proportional, suffrage in the communities for both sexes aged 21 and over, for representation in communes, counties, and parliament.
4. Complete freedom of the press, association and assembly, free expression of all human thought.
5. A radical agrarian reform. [...]
6. Industrial workers are guaranteed the same rights and benefits that are provided in the most advanced industrial states of the West.[2]

However, if we revisit Vaida-Voevod's portrayal to an international audience in early January 1929, developments in the first decade after the end of the Danube Monarchy seem to have followed a different, less utopian path: the emergence of so-called Greater Romania "born from military glory and the wisdom of the Romanians from the old kingdom and the new provinces", as Vaida-Voevod put it, was quickly followed by "ten years of fear, disillusion and experience".[3]

Vaida-Voevod, the spin doctor of the predominantly Transylvanian-led National Peasant's Party (*Partidul Naţional-Ţărănist*, PNŢ), was – in the spirit of political storytelling – very interested in portraying the period before the opposition's victory as a dark decade. All the greater was the impression of a

---

2 "The Resolution of the National Assembly in Alba-Iulia on the 18th of November/the 1st of December", <http://www.cimec.ro/Istorie/Unire/rezo_eng.htm> (13 December 2018). (Translation edited by the author.)
3 Alexandru Vaida-Voevod, "Ten Years of Greater Roumania," *The Slavonic and East European Review* 7 (1929) 20, 261.

"redemption" which, given the election results of 1928, was shared by a large part of the electorate.[4]

2. Hope: 1928

The advent of the so-called National-Peasant government about a decade after the disintegration of the Danube Monarchy and the emergence of "Greater Romania" thus represented an extraordinary moment of hope for the Romanian people. A 'redeemer figure' was found in the earnest personality of Iuliu Maniu (1873–1953), a lawyer who had studied in Vienna and Budapest and had previously acted as an attorney for the Greek Catholic Church.[5] Maniu stood for the desire for change, supported by the broader masses: the "change" eagerly awaited since 1918 now finally seemed possible, the "fruitful and flourishing garden" within reach.

However, the period of national-peasant governments was to end less gloriously in 1933: the shooting of striking railway workers by the executive and the murder of the recently installed liberal Prime Minister Ion G. Duca by fanatical fascists marked – synchronously with European developments – the beginning of an era of radicalization and authoritarianism. In this essay, I will try to answer the question as to why the potentially "fertile and flourishing garden" ended up becoming something of a graveyard.

We will approach this question in several steps: First, we will consider the months after 1918, since examination of the situation in this liminal moment shows how little people were prepared for the actual collapse of the Danube Monarchy and what a daunting task the inhabitants of the enlarged Romania faced. Secondly, I will outline the most important aspects of the Romanian integration process and thus show how a power struggle for dominance in the state unfolded, encompassing all areas of public life down to the private, personal sphere. Thirdly, I show how the 'neo-Romanian' opposition reacted to the transformation of Greater Romania, actually managed to gain power, and ultimately failed due to its own pretensions. Fourthly, I show the development in the 1930s before finally providing an outlook on the further developments.

Our companion on this journey will be Alexandru Vaida-Voevod, a Vienna-educated doctor and scion of an ennobled Greek Catholic landowning family since his biography and political actions demonstrate the significance of the

---

4 Sextil Puşcariu, "Regionalismul constructiv," *Societatea de Mâine* 2 (1925) 6, 83–86, 85: "Ardealul era arbitrul situaţiei politice în România"; Kührer-Wielach, "Siebenbürgen ohne Siebenbürger," 252.
5 Kührer-Wielach, "Siebenbürgen ohne Siebenbürger," 375.

after-effects of the Danube Monarchy in an almost ideal-typical way. This structural and cultural echo of the Habsburg Empire is an essential component of my perspective on the Romanian transformation after 1918: the consciousness of the national unity of the Romanians from all the merged regions could not conceal the different historical imprints. These disparities were instrumentalized and intensified in an increasingly violent political contest. Hopes for improvement in the overall social situation were dashed several times, leading to further destabilization and disavowal of a democracy that was fragile from the outset and practiced partly just for show. However, I do not set out from a bipolar analytical scheme that only distinguishes between factors of continuity and ruptures or success and failure. Rather, I would like to understand the actions of the actors after World War I as a form of *adaptation*.[6] Collective visions and the struggle to realize them have just as much of a place in this interpretive scheme as contingency management, spontaneous reactions to change, and interest-driven speech and action. In order to create synchronous as well as diachronic contexts, I will allow myself to deviate from the classical chronological account at times. So, back once more to 1918.

3.   1918 – a Decisive Moment without a Decision

The national master narrative presented the emergence and existence of Greater Romania up to the present day as an unstoppable process without any alternative and the unification of almost all territories inhabited by Romanians as the only logical, just, and sensible outcome – in other words, as a typical *Risorgimento* narrative in which one's own nation takes center stage. Consequently, the interwar period is presented as a golden age of Romanian national becoming,[7] which is not entirely illogical in view of everything that came afterwards (dictatorship, world war, communism). However, this idealizing view does not do justice to the erratic developments in the two decades after World War I, which were sometimes driven by political arbitrariness and violence as well as the international economic crisis.

   "1918" came rather unexpectedly because, in fact, only a few months earlier hardly anyone could have imagined the extent of the geopolitical upheaval – that is, the complete dissolution of Austria-Hungary, the shrinking of Germany, and

---

6 Florian Kührer-Wielach and Sarah Lemmen, "Transformation in East Central Europe. 1918 and 1989 – a Comparative Approach," *European Review of History* 23 (2016) 4, 573–579, 577.
7 Lucian Boia, *Geschichte und Mythos. Über die Gegenwart des Vergangenen in der rumänischen Gesellschaft* (Wien – Köln – Weimar: Böhlau, 2003), 10.

the end of the Tsarist Empire – regardless of whether one was loyal to the dynasty, a nationalist, or both.

4.   A Look Back at the Late Danube Monarchy

The thin but energetic layer of Romanian intellectuals under the Habsburg crowns had actively contributed to the vision of overcoming the Austro-Hungarian dualism established in 1867. We owe one of the best-known plans for a federal Danube monarchy to Banat-born Aurel Popovici with his work *Die Vereinigten Staaten von Groß-Österreich* (The United States of Greater Austria).[8] Alexandru Vaida-Voievod (then Vajda von Felső-Orbó[9]) reported in his memoirs how the Romanian students in Vienna, of which he was one, hung on the lips of Professor Popovici, then in Café Wien.[10] A few years later, Vaida-Voevod found himself in the wider circle of advisors to the heir apparent, Franz Ferdinand, in which such ideas about abolishing the hated Austro-Hungarian dualism were developed and discussed.

In 1916, when the small kingdom of Romania entered the war on the side of the Entente, Vaida-Voevod published an article in the *Österreichische Rundschau* calling for the unconditional loyalty of the Hungarian Romanians to the Habsburgs.[11] He was not alone in this attitude guided by pragmatism, realism, and the lack of alternatives – as demonstrated by a declaration of loyalty to the Hungarian Crown written a few months later and signed by some 200 Romanian politicians, church leaders, and intellectuals from Hungary.

Loyalty to the dynasty and national emancipation were thus not contradictory, especially since a vehement Magyarization policy was pursued by the governments while the nominally apolitical Emperor or King Franz Joseph was seen as "above things". Thus the Romanian National Party in Hungary founded in the 19th century – with Maniu and Vaida-Voevod among its leaders – had fought for its seats in the Budapest parliament at the turn of the century. Aligned as an "ethno-party", it strove for a monopoly position in the representation of Hungarian Romanians. This experience and attitude were to continue to have an effect after 1918 under the new auspices.

---

8 Aurel Popovici, *Die Vereinigten Staaten von Groß-Österreich. Politische Studien zur Lösung der nationalen Fragen und staatrechtlichen Krisen in Österreich-Ungarn* (Leipzig: B. Elischer Nachfolger 1906).

9 "Vaida-Voevod (Vajda von Felső-Orbó), Alexandru (1872–1950), Politiker," <https://www.biographien.ac.at/oebl/oebl_V/Vaida-Voevod_Alexandru_1872_1950.xml> (7 May 2022).

10 Alexandru Vaida Voevod and Alexandru Şerban, *Memorii*, Vol 1, edited by (Cluj-Napoca: Editura Dacia, 1994), 68.

11 A. von Vajda, *Österreichische Rundschau*, 15.9.1916.

In the last months of the war, the representatives of the Hungarian Romanians then saw that their chance had come to take over the leadership in the areas of eastern Hungary inhabited by a Romanian majority – with or without the Habsburgs at the helm. Thus it was Vaida-Voevod who, on behalf of the Executive Committee of the Romanian National Party, announced the the Hungarian Romanians' secession in the Budapest Reichstag in October 1918. This short but rapid development led to the union of eastern and southeastern Hungary with the Kingdom of Romania.

5.   A Look Back at the "Old Kingdom" of Romania

The small Romanian kingdom on the lower Danube, known as the "Old King-dom" (*Vechiul Regat*) in historiography, had come into being in several steps: to create facts, within a few weeks in 1859 the estates of the two Romanian Danubian principalities of Moldavia and Wallachia elected Alexandru Ioan Cuza as their respective head. This process, which initially met with resistance from the High Porte and the Habsburg Empire, is remembered as the "small unification" (*mica unire*). In 1862, however, an institutional unification between the two entities took place, in 1866 they gave themselves a constitution, and in 1878 Romania formally gained independence in the wake of the Congress of Berlin. In 1881, Romania became a kingdom. As in Greece and Bulgaria, a member of a foreign dynasty was placed on the throne: thus, from 1866 to 1947, members of the House of Hohenzollern-Sigmaringen were to wear the Romanian crown. In 1885, the Orthodox Church achieved autocephaly, that is, administrative and canonical autonomy vis-à-vis the patriarch of Constantinople, and consolidated its posi-tion as the Romanian "national church", which it was de facto, for demographic reasons alone. The political landscape was very monotonous in that the census electoral law, which was only gradually relaxed, favored a constant, very thin layer of boyars and excluded most of the population from political and economic participation. Two clans organized in parties dominated: the Conservatives, whose success depended on a high electoral census, which plunged them into relative insignificance after its final abolition after 1918, and the Liberals, grouped around their first leader, Ion C. Brătianu, whose family would also dominate the political sphere in the interwar period.

6.   The "Great Unification" in Figures

In 1918, the "Unification King" Ferdinand and his wife Queen Maria not only saw Hungarian, that is, Transleithanian territories growing into their small kingdom. Around the same time, the parliament of the Austrian, i. e. Cisleithanian *Kronland* Bukovina also decided to secede to Romania, albeit without a spectacular march. This was an "unconditional annexation" declared in the provincial capital of Czernowitz by only a rump parliament in which by no means all representatives of the various groups or estates were present. The situation was similar in Bessarabia, whose provincial council had already renounced its ties to revolutionary Russia in March 1918 and announced its medium-term integration into the Romanian state. At that time, the state still formulated its own demands, which included extensive regional – including fiscal – autonomy for Bessarabia. The tangible annexation of Bessarabia under great military pressure in November 1918 then took place unconditionally and with only weak legitimacy.

This was the challenging situation in late 1918 – Romania had doubled its land and population in one fell swoop: the territory had grown from 138,000 km² to 295,049 km², the population from 7.9 million (1915) to 14.7 million (1919) and was to increase to 18 million by 1930. However, the different historical influences that characterized the merged regions weighed even more heavily: the main regions of the "Old Kingdom", Walachia and Moldavia, could look back on a common statehood with relative independence since 1859, as described above, but at the same time the country had a traditional social order. The Romanians of the Crown of St. Stephen, on the other hand, could point to a tradition of political participation, which was strengthened by the growing pressure to assimilate to the Magyar hegemonic culture. In Bukovina, the Romanians benefited from Vienna's relatively liberal regime. Thus, one can speak of a relatively well-functioning system of ethnic coexistence for the historical *Kronland*, even if the new electoral order of 1910, designed to balance out the groups, could not be applied due to the war. Even the Romanians in Bessarabia, which had been part of the Russian Empire since 1812, could call on their traditional regional and local representative and administrative bodies. And in any case, the case of Dobruja, which was populated by various linguistic, religious, and ethnic groups and had fallen to the Kingdom of Romania in several stages since the Congress of Berlin in 1878, must be differentiated from the 'core areas' of the "Old Kingdom" for its diverse social structure; it had served as an experimental field for the integration and Romanianization of multi-ethnic and multi-confessional areas before World War I.

In addition to the different historical traditions, the high degree of confessional and ethnic diversity is thus an essential and common feature of the territories annexed by or united in the "Old Kingdom". For in this small pre-war

Romania, minorities played only a subordinate role. Especially in Moldova's few urban settlements, there was a large proportion of 'ethnic non-Romanians' (predominantly Jewish, Aromanian, Greek, or Italian families), but they did not challenge the dominance of "the Romanian" and were merely tolerated by the (nationalizing) state. The Jews living in the country, who represented a large and culturally active group, had been systematically denied citizenship, even after they were officially granted the right of naturalization, following interventions at the Berlin Congress in 1878, and even though they had a number of obligations towards the state.

In 1918, however, this state suddenly had to incorporate about one third of 'ethnic non-Romanians', including many Orthodox, and one third of 'confessional non-Orthodox', including many Romanians.

The 1930 census provides a good basis for quantitatively tracing the demographic structure after 1918: Romanians (as an ethnic-national group) accounted for 71.9% of the total population at the time, the rest being distributed between a variety of ethnic groups, including 7.9% Hungarians, 4.1% Germans, and 4% Jews. 72.6% of the total population professed the Orthodox faith, 7.9% were Greek Catholic (united with Rome), 6.8% Roman Catholic, 6.1% Protestants of various denominations, and 4.2% considered themselves Jews.

If one analyses the figures for the areas that largely belonged to other empires before 1918, the extent to which the demographic conditions in the state of Romania changed becomes even clearer: in Transylvania, for example, there were 57.6% Romanians, in the Banat 54.4%, in the Partium 60.7%, while the large rest of the population belonged to "minorities", the most significant being Hungarian and German groups. The new regions were also uneven from a confessional point of view: in Transylvania, about half of the Romanians belonged to the Greek Catholic Church, and even in the Partium only 36.8% were Orthodox. In Bukovina, 44.5% were of Romanian ethnicity, 27.7% were Ruthenians (Ukrainians), and 10.8% Jews. In Dobruja, there were 44.2% Romanians, 22.7% Bulgarians and 8.5% Turks. In the parts of the Old Kingdom, on the other hand, there were about 90% Romanians, more or less identical with the number auf Orthodox people. The data clearly show that especially in the 'neo-Romanian' areas there was an ethnic and confessional mix.[12]

As the Habsburg historian Pieter Judson, to whom we owe an important recent book on the Danube Monarchy, its end and its aftermath, has noted, the Habsburg lifeworld continued to exist *mutatis mutandis* in the successor states: from this point of view, in the interwar period we are dealing with post-imperial small empires[13] that did not quite know how to deal with themselves: established and

---

12 Kührer-Wielach, "Siebenbürgen ohne Siebenbürger," 66.
13 Cf. Pieter Judson, *The Habsburg Empire. A New History* (Cambridge: Harvard University

proven structures were shattered, especially since the borders drawn after the war cut through and shifted regional historical-cultural contexts. Greater Romania, having emerged so suddenly, had yet to achieve its effective *translatio imperii* in the shape of comprehensive economic, social, political, cultural, institutional, and mental integration. In the years following the "Great Unification", the form this new society should take was negotiated at different levels and by different means.

So, in the first weeks after nominal and military-supported unification, a struggle between the "old" and the "new" Romania for supremacy in the country already began to emerge. In addition to regional demarcation lines, the relationship between the "majority" and the "minority" – a concept that was only nascent on the international level – was a defining factor of the transformation period after 1918.

7. Minorities in Greater Romania

Ultimately, for the various non-Romanian and non-Orthodox inhabitants of the annexed territories, there was, similarly to the national und confessional mainstream, no alternative to the new situation, for there was no realistic return to the pre-war order. Thus, as in the case of the Magyars in the west and the Russians in the northeast, the "majority people" became part of a minority. They became citizens of a state whose centralist basic structure was to gradually assert itself in the new territories too – Romanians and, from the confessional point of view, Orthodoxy were given *de facto* and increasingly also *de jure* priority.

The various minority groups reacted accordingly: they either maintained their tendency to reject the Romanian state decisively and permanently, like a larger part of the Magyar actors who took refuge in political passivity, or still withheld recognition of the annexation, as the Transylvanian Saxons did in January 1919. Or they just waited for international recognition, like the Hungarian Jews who, in contrast to the Jews in the Old Kingdom, were skeptical about the creation of Greater Romania and only officially recognized the existence of the enlarged Kingdom of Romania after the Treaty of Trianon on 4 June 1920. The Bessarabian Germans, on the other hand, tended to view the annexation positively, as they expected protection from the Bolsheviks within the framework of the Romanian state.

To understand the minority situation, it is important to note that we can by no means assume *homogeneous* ethnonational groups in this post-imperial setting. *The* German minority, *the* Jewish minority, *the* Hungarian minority existed only

Press, 2018).

on paper and in the rhetoric of politicians. For understandable reasons, they had to have a vested interest in generating solidary groups that were large, powerful, and homogeneous enough to defend specific interests and rights, and which they intended to represent and lead. Yet, like the Romanians in the different parts of the country, the so-called "nationalities" were composed of highly disparate elements and minority groups. In this regard, let us consider just three paradigmatic examples:[14]

- The two bigger German neighboring groups in western Romania – Protestant Transylvanian Saxons in Transylvania and Catholic Swabians in the Banat – differed in terms of confession, historical and regional cultural self-image, and dialect, and, since the Danube Swabians bowed more readily to Magyarization before 1918 than the Transylvanian Saxons, in part even in terms of language.
- When the Lutheran communities (*Confessio Augustana*) united on the soil of the state that had just come into being, one of the debates concerned this church's new center: should it be in Transylvanian Sibiu, where the "Saxon" bishop sat? Or should it be in the capital, Bucharest? Dogmatic differences were even noted and discussed by the Saxons and the – also Lutheran – Bessarabian Germans. Moreover, an ethnic stratification took place in 1921, when the Hungarian-speaking Lutherans founded their own ecclesial structure. There have been two Lutheran churches in Romania ever since.
- Most of the Jews living in the former Hungarian regions spoke Hungarian and were what could be called loyal to the crown or the dynasty. A similar attitude prevailed among the liberal and in many cases secular-minded Jews of Bukovina, who were inclined towards German culture. These in turn differed markedly from the very traditional Hasids, who were also a large group in Bukovina. Therefore, the emancipated Jews in Bukovina and its new western part as well as the Yiddish- and Russian-speaking, but hardly Tsarist-dynastic Bessarabian Jews naturally regarded themselves as a *national* minority in Greater Romania. Spokespersons of the Jews in the "Old Kingdom", who lived under the worst conditions until 1918, on the other hand, interpreted their community – probably also due to a lack of alternatives – as part of the Romanian culture and merely as a *religious* minority. In addition, there was the Zionist movement, the increasing acceptance of which ran across linguistic and regional-cultural differences among the Jews.

---

14 Cf. Florian Kührer-Wielach, "(Was) Minderheiten schaffen. 'Eigen-sinnige' Lebenswelten und ethnonationale Blockbildung am Beispiel 'Großrumäniens'," in *Zerfall, Trauma, Triumph. Das Epochenjahr 1918 und sein Nachleben in Zentral-, Ostmittel- und Südosteuropa*, edited by Steffen Höhne (Munich: Oldenbourg Verlag, 2020), 327–362.

Accordingly, the establishment of ethnic umbrella organizations proved difficult. It was only when the new state situation proved to be permanent that nationwide political representations of the minorities established themselves, delimited according to ethnonational criteria.

8.   A Transylvanian Episode, 1919/1920

The Paris Peace Treaties were intended to solve all these 'ground problems' from a bird's eye view, as it were, and to provide international recognition of the postwar order that had emerged so spontaneously. Geopolitics was at the center of this: the vague idea of the peoples' right to self-determination provided the basis for establishing the broadest possible and most stable buffer zone of new or enlarged states in East Central Europe; the idea was to keep at bay the greatest factor of insecurity after the collapse of the Ottoman Empire: the revolutionary and thus completely unpredictable Russian Soviet Republic, which was to expand into the Soviet Union in 1922.

The two treaties relevant to Romania – St. Germain for the former Austrian territories in 1919 and Trianon for the former Hungarian territories in 1920 – were preceded by a bilateral Minority Treaty, which the League of Nations (*Völkerbund*) made a condition for concluding the Paris Peace Treaties. It was part of a whole system of treaties for the protection of minorities, which was established as a balancing act between the claims of the nation-state and its reality.

The treaty obliged the Romanian government to guarantee full protection of life and liberty to all inhabitants, regardless of birth, nationality, language, ethnicity, and religion (Art. 2). It was also to recognize as equal citizens those persons residing on Romanian territory at the time the treaty came into force (Art. 3). Moreover, the treaty stipulated that all persons with Austrian or Hungarian citizenship who were "born on the territories annexed to Romania" were to be recognized as Romanian citizens and that the use of the mother tongue be guaranteed in the official sector. The government was to grant permission to establish self-financed schools and – as a special feature – "local autonomy" for Saxons and Szeklers in school and church matters. Only some of these conditions were later implemented.[15]

An additional obligation was to fulfill the requirement that had already existed since the Berlin Congress of 1878, namely to finally grant citizenship to the approximately 250,000 Jews living in the country. Ion I. C. Brătianu, experienced in the politics of the Kingdom of Romania and now once again prime minister

---

15 Kührer-Wielach, "Was Minderheiten schaffen," 14.

and leader of the National Liberal Party, thought this step would be so unpopular that he preferred to protest against the decision, leave the negotiating table in Paris, and resign from his post as prime minister. Further negotiations were conducted by Alexandru Vaida-Voevod, who had been in power since 5 December 1919 as the first Romanian prime minister to be legitimized by nationwide elections after 1918.

Vaida-Voevod's cabinet, which tended to be minority-friendly, only existed until March 1920, however. Then, the (partially) autonomous administration of the territories that had separated from Hungary, led by his colleagues in the Romanian National Party (*Partidul Naţional Român*) anchored politically, mentally, and culturally in the former Hungarian territories, was also finally dissolved. This was a decisive moment: with the failure of the Vaida-Voevod administration, legitimized by the electorate, a phase dominated by the politics of the Old Kingdom began, led by Brătianu's National Liberal Party and enjoying the support of the king. In other words, one could say that here the pre-war networks continued to function. For the other parties – first and foremost the old Transylvanian 'ethnic party' of Maniu and Vaida-Voevod – it was a matter of first learning the craft of political opposition under pluralistic conditions. The course was now set, however; the path that had been taken was to lead to a central state.

9.   Institutional Transformation

The institutional transformation into a functioning state, which was to be followed by the mental one, was characterized by three fundamental processes: *centralization, Romanianization*, and *socialization.*

Centralization

The question as to how Romania's administration was to be organized in the future concerned all Romanian citizens: should it be a decentralized state, as a significant number of 'New Romania's' elites demanded? Or should they continue to adhere to the French model of the central state? In the end, all further steps in shaping society depended on this (ostensibly) merely technical question, especially on those levels on which important political decisions were made. As early as 1920, with the abolition of autonomy in western Romania, the administration was centralized step by step. The final decision was made after tough political wrangling in 1923 with the adoption of the new constitution: it was largely based on the old constitution of 1866, which had been explicitly modeled on that of Belgium and was considered particularly modern at the time of its introduction. Romania was thus to remain a central state.

Even after this landmark decision, the opposition – often in cooperation with the minorities in the new territories – fought against the constitution, which was perceived as having been imposed by a small elite. One point of criticism was that the ideals formulated in the declaration of 1.12.1918 had not been taken into account: the constitution did not address the rights of the workers, the national minorities, women, and the confessions to the same extent as had been formulated in Alba Iulia. In fact, the constitution granted comprehensive rights to individual citizens, but did not stipulate any group rights for the "nationalities".

Romanianization

The governments of Greater Romania, and ultimately most of the parties in opposition too, demanded and forced the rise of the "Romanian element" in the new state. In this context, the 'national argument' can be seen above all as a vehicle for exploiting the economic and social opportunities offered by the new state and the transforming social environment. For although the Romanians were in the quantitative majority in almost all parts of Greater Romania, they still felt in a position of inferiority due to their historically determined, rather weak social and economic status.

This situation was to be changed with targeted Romanianization measures in all areas of public life – school, the economy, culture, administration, etc. This began with the denial of group rights to minorities, led to language examinations for non-native speakers in the civil service at relatively short notice, and ended with the Romanianization of public spaces in the form of renaming streets and erecting new monuments. This became particularly clear when the Romanian fraternity between Rome and Romania was emphasized by the city of Rome sending several Capitoline She-Wolves at once: while such a statue had already been on display in Bucharest since 1906, further copies were gradually erected in Cluj-Napoca (1921), Târgu Mureş (1924), and Timişoara (1926), and many more copies were made as a visible sign of the progressing enforcement of the "Romanian element".

What the Romanian government was ultimately engaged in was what in today's contexts is often referred to as *affirmative action* – "positive discrimination" to establish equality of opportunity and resources. In practice, this meant putting in place policies aiming at rapid and undifferentiated social leveling while favoring the Romanians.

Socialization

One tendency that affected minorities such as Romanians was the state's extensive absorption power: on the one hand, censorship and the state of emergency were imposed far beyond what was necessary in internationally and nationally turbulent but actually peaceful times. Additionally, the system of confessional schools, which was common especially in the territories of the former Danube Monarchy, was starved out and at the same time many state schools were established. This was certainly important in the fight against illiteracy – but of course it also led to the loss of an important institution for the promotion of collective identity beyond the national level, be it the Orthodox and Uniate Romanian-language schools or the schools of the 'non-Romanian' churches: within such communities, the confessional schools were seen as a particularly important instrument for the sustainable preservation of identity.

Thus the state's interventions were a combination of economic and ideological factors: for example, the comprehensive, albeit inconsistent, agricultural reform, which favored Romanians, brought about a certain redistribution that was supposed to lead to the self-empowerment of the socially weaker sections of the population. At the same time, however, the nationalization and redistribution of their forest property deprived the Transylvanian Saxon Protestant community of the financial basis for their schools. Yet the reforms generated discontent even beyond minority issues when the Romanians living in the regions annexed by the Old Kingdom dominated the administration, which usually appointed its supporters even in the new territories.

Thus, the hopeful, if surprising, union soon turned into a struggle for distribution of resources and political dominance. The development did not go unchallenged and the 'Habsburg Romanians' took the lead in the opposition.

10. Habsburg Revenants on Victory Road

After the abrupt end to the ephemeral coalition of 'New Romanians' and smaller opposition parties from the "Old Kingdom" in the spring of 1920 and the initiation of the change towards a central state, the opposition took quite a while to gather itself.

Essentially, the Transylvanian National Party built on its anti-centralism and on – at least pretended – empathy for the minorities. The fact that the campaigns conducted both in the newspapers and on the streets (as well as in the churches!) were increasingly popular was partly thanks to Alexandru Vaida-Voevod: in contrast to the rather thoughtful party leader Iuliu Maniu, he provided catchy slogans and provoked the anger of his opponents with his statements. Vaida-

Voevod's most famous battle cry was "Transylvania for the Transylvanians". This alluded to a statement made by Prime Minister Brătianu in the course of the Union in 1918/1919, when he was said to have expressed the wish that Romania wanted Transylvania, but preferably without the Transylvanians. "Transylvania for the Transylvanians" was soon adopted in the other united territories and, obviously, also found favor among the minorities, some of whom, probably thinking back to allegedly better times, expected decentralization to ease the pressure of Romanianization.

Vaida-Voevod, who obviously enjoyed repeatedly becoming the center of debate in this way, had copied his style of policy making from one of the first 'masters of populism': in his memoirs, written secretly under communist house arrest, Vaida-Voevod told of his admiration for the Christian Social politician Karl Lueger, who held the office of mayor of Vienna from 1897 to 1910. He had been able to climb to the top of the capital's government by implementing his long-standing demand for universal suffrage and distinguished himself as a decisive modernizer of Vienna. He was also successful with his social policy. At the same time, however, he positioned himself as anti-Semitic and anti-Magyar, which even earned him honorary citizenship of Bucharest. Thus Lueger's and Vaida-Voevod's attitudes display great parallels: modernist, reformist, anti-liberal. Hence it may come as little surprise that Vaida-Voevod, the former parliamentarian in Budapest, and his comrades-in-arms were ostentatiously reproached for their "dynastic, patriotic, and traditional sentiments" in political discussions.

Delicately, it was a Transylvanian compatriot, the politically increasingly radicalizing writer Octavian Goga, who had already turned away from Transylvanian regionalism early on and took the conflict to extremes: he saw politicians like Maniu and Vaida-Voevod as specters of the past, as "revenants of Habsburg loyalty". Like the "ghosts" from Henrik Ibsen's stage drama, they wandered around Bucharest to take revenge on the Romanians in service of the old Hungary. Goga and his fellow campaigners considered the Austro-Hungarian influence to be alien and harmful, in contrast to the Romanians' "Latin roots", and preferred to point to an affinity with French culture. He argued that the Transylvanian politicians had to finally take the "right" intellectual path, so that the "hybrid mixture" that had served as their "intellectual nourishment" would finally come to an end. For Goga, Vaida-Voevod was a "man from Budapest" and wanted to separate Transylvania from the rest of the country by bringing the idea of a Greater Austria out of the "Viennese rag store" (*Lumpenkammer*). Politicians of his ilk were now walking around uprooted on Bucharest's Victory Road (*Calea Victoriei*, one of the central boulevards in the Romanian capital), refusing food and rejecting local humor, harboring general mistrust, arguing with hotel porters and political parties alike, telling Hungarian anecdotes and invoking the

Budapest parliament's rules of procedure, getting annoyed, protesting and voting with "everyone and no one" – they were simply regionalists.

This harsh criticism, which probably also says a lot about the critics themselves, could not prevent the gradual rise of the opposition. In 1926, the Transylvanian National Party united with the Peasants' Party anchored in the "Old Kingdom" to form the National Peasants' Party (*Partidul Național-Țărănesc*). This fusion is tantamount to a double expansion of the political combat zone: on the one hand, it opened up new territories, and on the other hand it also expanded its ideological profile by taking over the agendas of the Peasants' Party, which were very much focused on social issues concerning the peasantry.

The complete loss of confidence in the governments of the Liberals and their satellite parties, which secured their power by manipulating the elections and instrumentalizing the authorities, was a favorable factor for the new constellation that was staging itself as a movement. Iuliu Maniu, the central figure of the opposition, was stylized as Romania's savior and redeemer, not least by the party 'spin doctor' Vaida-Voevod. The concept of "Transylvania" had long since ceased to stand only for the territorial keystone of a Romanian *Risorgimento*, but rather became a political program itself: "Transylvania" stood for a counter-vision that had been clearly formulated in Alba Iulia on 1.12.1918 – Transylvanian values would cure Romania.

11. Another Moment of Hope: 1928

hus, in late 1928, the National Peasants' Party was able to achieve a brilliant electoral victory, almost 78% of the electorate voting for them. Maniu became prime minister, while Vaida-Voevod held the post of minister of the interior. The party leaders had understood in the meantime how to deal with the form of mass democracy that was new to Romania, and in fact hardly needed any means of pressure. It was quite sufficient to take advantage of the real, crisis-ridden political climate and to develop a vision to which the masses of voters responded. It was therefore obvious that the issues of the electoral law and the land reform were at the center of the political discourse. In this logic, the new line of conflict ran between political cultures, regions, and generations. The thematic focal points can be reduced to pairs of opposites:
– the *ancien régime* versus democratic minds,
– arbitrariness versus rule of law,
– oligarchy versus parliamentary representation.

These developments must be seen against the background of the emergence of mass democracy, multiple transformation crises including economic and administrative dysfunctions, and the ideological aggravations related to all these factors throughout Europe. The arrival of the Maniu government itself was presented as a radical turning point, as the end of a "nightmare", as a return to the common values and goals formulated in 1918: the "fruitful and flourishing garden" seemed within reach.

12.   Escalation of Violence and the End of Hope

The Maniu administration immediately began to reform the state apparatus. The executive was reorganized, its training improved and its powers of access restricted, with the aim of reducing acts of arbitrary officialdom. A comprehensive administrative reform was to restructure the country along decentralized lines. On the level of economic policy, the protectionist system was abolished, and foreign investment was to be made possible and encouraged. The inalienability of the right to land allocated by the land reform was abrogated. This allowed the pooling of smaller agricultural areas and thus their more efficient cultivation. The government also tried to create a better legal framework for the labor force.

Only a short time after Maniu's inauguration, however, the Great Depression also began to manifest itself, so that many of the government's measures became stuck in the implementation phase and their anticipated positive effects never materialized. The prices for Romania's most important export product, grain, fell appreciably, and the advancing debt not only affected the farmers and the enterprises, but also brought the state budget to the brink of insolvency. Contrary to the announcements made during the opposition period, taxes had to be increased, which further fueled the already poor morale within the populace caused by the economic crisis. During a workers' strike in Lupeni, located in the Transylvanian mining region of Valea Jiului, 29 people were killed in 1929 by the intervention of the gendarmerie. The government immediately suspended the local decision-makers responsible for the brutal action against their own population. Ultimately, however, these violent events marked the first break with the promises made by the National Peasants' Party leaders in their election campaign. Thus Maniu's government now also resorted to restrictive measures. Censorship of the press also continued to exist, albeit via different methods. (Print runs were already confiscated instead of being censored before going to press). Trust in the government rapidly declined.

There followed an unsteady period of several National Peasant cabinets, interrupted by the equally unsuccessful experiment of an ostensibly technocratic cabinet, which, however, was primarily there to implement the authoritarian tendencies of King Carol II. This first attempt by the king to rule over the heads of party politicians, however, failed, for the time being, due to the "authoritarian government without authority". In 1933, Vaida-Voevod acted as prime minister for a few months, but he was not only confronted with increasing social tensions in the country, but also had to pursue an austerity policy enforced by foreign countries, which soon exceeded the limits of what was socially acceptable. Moreover, the old comrades Maniu and Vaida-Voevod were increasingly at odds with each other, thus splitting their party into two camps.

The economic hopelessness and the disappointed hopes that the National Peasants' Party activists had nurtured intensified the ongoing unrest among the populations. For instance, Undersecretary of State Armand Călinescu had to organize the eviction of the railway workshops in Bucharest's Grivița district in February 1933, where the workers protested particularly violently. In contrast to the bloody army operation of 1929, where those responsible were at least stripped of their posts, this time the operation, which resulted in the deaths of seven workers, was approved by parliament with a broad consensus. Only the Social Democrat Party and smaller Peasants' Parties protested against this course of action. Vaida-Voevod argued that he had stopped "a torrent" of spilled blood – namely a Bolshevik revolution. However, this repeatedly evoked enemy scenario could not prevent the Vaida-Voevod government from discrediting itself – and ultimately its entire at least to some extent democratically-oriented policy. Vaida-Voevod and his fourth cabinet resigned in November 1933. The king now reappointed a government led by the National Liberals.

13.   Starting Shots for an Authoritarian Era

In 1933, the National Peasants' movement government chapter ended violently, then – but the beginnings of the second liberal era were also bloody: at the end of this turbulent year, supporters of the fascist Legion of the Archangel Michael shot the new prime minister, Ion G. Duca. The coming years were marked by a radicalization of the political landscape, as in many parts of Europe. An anti-Semitism that could almost be described as 'traditionally endemic' in Romania became increasingly respectable not only in the various opposition movements but also in government circles. Vaida-Voevod founded a fascist movement called the "Romanian Front", and the clearly anti-Semitic slogan "Romania for the Romanians" became its new battle slogan. The Romanian parties kept their own party armies, each with their own color of shirt. The streets became a parade ground. The Legion of the Archangel Michael, also known as the Iron Guard, was the most prominent such organization. It grew into what for a time was the third-largest fascist movement in Europe.[16]

Elections no longer had a democratic meaning; the Romanian political system finally turned to parliamentarism without democracy. This was accompanied by the economic marginalization of the minorities, especially the Jews, culminating in a new citizenship law passed by the last 'democratic' government led by the radical right-wing Octavian Goga (1937/38), which expatriated around 35% (!) of the Jews living in Romania.

In the spring of 1938, King Carol II ended party democracy – which was always more party than democracy – with the introduction of a royal dictatorship. His first prime minister was Patriarch Miron Cristea – the same Orthodox regional bishop that had stood in the front row at the reading of the resolution in Alba Iulia twenty years earlier. Vaida-Voevod, however, gained a seat in the Crown Council and even became leader of the unity party Front of National Rebirth (*Frontul Renașterii Naționale*, FRN) in 1940. He withdrew the same year, however, because dictator-king Carol II had to abdicate after Northern Transylvania became Hungarian again at Hitler's behest. Vaida-Voevod died under house arrest in 1950, Maniu three years later in the notorious Sighet prison. Meanwhile, the red flags had long been flying on the Victory Road in Bucharest.

14. Selected Bibliography

Adam, Magda, *The Versailles System and Central Europa*. Aldershot: Variorum, 2004.

Beer, Klaus P., *Zur Entwicklung des Parteien- und Parlamentssystems in Rumänien, 1928–1933: Die Zeit der national-bäuerlichen Regierungen*, vol. 1. Frankfurt am Main: Peter Lang, 1983.

Hausleitner, Mariana, *Die Rumänisierung der Bukowina: Die Durchsetzung des national-staatlichen Anspruchs Großrumäniens, 1918–1944*. München: Oldenbourg, 2001.

Ivan, Marcel, *Evoluția Partidelor noastre politice în cifre și grafie. 1919–1932: Studiu comparativ al rezultatelor oficiale ale alegerilor pentru Camera Deputaților din anii 1919–1932*. Sibiu: Krafft & Drotleff, 1933.

Kührer Wielach, Florian, "(Was) Minderheiten schaffen. 'Eigen-sinnige' Lebenswelten und ethnonationale Blockbildung am Beispiel 'Großrumäniens'," in *Zerfall, Trauma, Triumph. Das Epochenjahr 1918 und sein Nachleben in Zentral-, Ostmittel- und Südost-europa*, edited by Steffen Höhne, 327–362. München: Oldenbourg Verlag, 2020.

Kührer-Wielach, Florian, "A fertile and flourishing garden. Alexandru Vaida-Voevod's Political Account Ten Years after Versailles," in *Special Issue "Romania and the Paris Peace Conference (1919). Actors, Scenarios, Circulation of Knowledge"*, Journal of Romanian Studies, Vol. 1 No. 2, edited by Svetlana Suveica, 135–52. Stuttgart: ibidem, 2019.

---

16 Cf. Oliver J. Schmitt, *Capitan Codreanu. Aufstieg und Fall des rumänischen Faschistenführers* (Wien: Paul Zsolnay Verlag, 2016).

Kührer-Wielach, Florian, *Siebenbürgen ohne Siebenbürger?: Zentralstaatliche Integration und politischer Regionalismus nach dem Ersten Weltkrieg.* Berlin: de Gruyter Oldenbourg, 2014.

Livezeanu, Irina, *Cultural Politics in Greater Romania: Regionalism, Nation Building and Ethnic Struggle, 1918–1930.* Ithaca: Cornell University Press, 1995.

Pecican, Ovidiu, *Regionalism românesc: Organizare prestatală şi stat la nordul Dunării în perioada medievală şi modern.* Bucharest: Curtea Veche, 2009.

Schmidt-Rösler, Andrea, *Rumänien nach dem Ersten Weltkrieg: Die Grenzziehung in der Dobrudscha und im Banat und die Folgeprobleme.* Frankfurt am Main: Peter Lang, 1994.

Schultz, Helga and Angelika Harre (eds.), *Bauerngesellschaften auf dem Weg in die Moderne: Agrarismus in Ostmitteleuropa 1880 bis 1960.* Wiesbaden: Harrassowitz, 2010.

Scurtu, Ioan (ed.), *România întregită. 1918–1940.* Bucharest: Editura Enciclopedică, 2003, (Istoria Românilor 8).

Suveică, Svetlana, *Basarabia în primul deceniu interbelic (1918–1928): Modernizare prin Reformă.* Chişinău: Pontos, 2010.

Vaida-Voevod, Alexandru, "Ten Years of Greater Roumania," *The Slavonic and East European Review* 7 (1929) 20: 261–67.

Katharina Ebner

Ideology Transfer of Italian Fascism. Fascist Transmission Belts in Vienna and Budapest

1.   Introduction

Fascist Italy under Benito Mussolini assumed the role of a protective power in foreign policy vis-à-vis Austria and Hungary. Italy had a great interest in shaping the power vacuum left behind by the disintegration of the Habsburg monarchy, as it saw the Danube basin as a natural space for expansion. By means of a temporary "Troika danubiana di Mussolini" (H.J. Burgwyn), Austria's "Anschluss" with Germany was to be prevented and Hungary was to serve as a buffer against the Slavs to the north and south.

Italian Fascism's "seizure of power" in 1922 had great impact as a model for many sympathizing movements in post-war Europe. But Mussolini did not officially make the export of Fascism a general directive until 1930. This decision was facilitated by the strong gain in prestige at the international level that the Fascist regime enjoyed in 1929 as a result of the 'reconciliation' between Fascism and the Catholic Church in the form of the Lateran Treaties – especially in the Catholic-influenced successor states of the Habsburg Empire.

Between 1927 and 1936, Italy aimed to create a philo-Fascist climate in the Austrian and Hungarian public spheres and, in Austria in particular, to fascistize the political system. In view of the academic research debates that the political classification of the Austrian Dollfuß/Schuschnigg regime as well as the reign of Gyula Gömbös in Horthy's Hungary still triggers, the Italian attempts at penetration, but also the reception effect of Fascist ideology in both countries are highly relevant.

The leading function of Italian Fascism, as a product of the European interwar period, serves as the starting point for this transfer-historical investigation, as it emphasizes the importance of transfers and interconnections between fascisms and fascist movements.

In the understanding of transfer research proposed by Michel Espagne/Michael Werner, the results of the reception process are not the primary object of research. It is therefore not the aim of this work to answer the question as to the fascist character of the Austrian or Hungarian regimes. The main focus of this transfer-oriented inquiry is rather the investigation of the channels of mediation, the actors, their interests, and the peaks of a reception; likewise, their reception mechanisms should be pointed out. Thus, using the examples of Vienna and Budapest as *partes pro toto* for the successor states of the Habsburg Empire, the selection mechanisms of the transfer are examined more closely and mediation instances are identified, as are the Austrian and Hungarian peculiarities that helped shape the reception process, i. e. an intensified confrontation with Fascist ideology.

2.   Fascist Transmission Belts: Ideology Transfer via Fasci, Language/Culture and the Church

In Vienna and Budapest, Italian foreign institutions and mediators in the po-litical-propaganda field (*Fasci all'estero*, the Fascist foreign party cells), in the educational and cultural field (Italian language and cultural mediation in-stitutions), and in the ecclesiastical sphere (Catholic Church with Italian and local priests) could be identified as *transmission belts* for Fascist ideology.

2.1   The Fascist Transmission Belt of Fasci all'estero

The first *Fasci all'estero* were founded even before the Fascist "seizure of power" and were soon among the central foreign propaganda institutions. They were intended to contribute to the regime's goal of fascistizing émigré compatriots, to secure their loyalty to the fatherland and to promote the spread of Fascist ideology abroad. Their activities were caught between the omnipresent formula of non-interference and their highly political goals, not only towards their own compatriots but also towards the local population. Although the regime tried to adapt the mission of the *Fasci* to the historical and political characteristics of the host countries, the latter's distrust of the sections of a political party was quite justified. But once diplomacy had been fascistized and foreign policy had taken hold of all areas, the foreign local groups lost relevance in the course of the formation of a state propaganda system and the Ethiopian war of aggression.

For strategic reasons, Mussolini had long been reluctant to declare Fascism an "export article". However, in 1930 his political position changed drastically when he proclaimed the international spread of Fascism, which can also be explained by Fascist foreign policy. In addition to the increased international prestige due to the alliance with the pope, from the early 1930s onwards it was necessary to distinguish Fascism from National Socialism, with which it was increasingly competing for ideological primacy, and to stand up for Italian hegemony.

2.2   The Fascist Transmission Belt of Language/Culture

Those institutions abroad which were concerned with the transmission of the Italian language also became places of ideological conflict. A common language was important for the Fascist transfer of ideology because it maintained the connection to the homeland and served as a cultural and political influence. Initially, the Italian schools abroad, the *Società Dante Alighieri*, the flagship institution for the dissemination of Italian culture, and later also the Italian cultural institutes were dedicated to this task.

While the schools abroad underwent a gradual fascistization of their organs, teaching staff and teaching content, the Dante Alighieri Society, as an institution of the liberal era, proved its ability to change by making itself a propaganda instrument of the regime of its own free will. However, this could not prevent its loss of importance. Ultimately, in the 1930s, the Italian cultural institutes, as originally Fascist institutions, were used to take over the existing structures.

2.3   The Fascist Transmission Belt of the Church

With the conclusion of the Lateran Treaties in 1929, the Catholic Church con-solidated Mussolini's power base and contributed to the domestic stabilization of the regime. The international prestige that the 'reconciliation' between state and Church brought to Italian Fascism necessitated a new step in the regime's foreign policy. The export of Fascism then became the general directive.

However, the partnership between the regime and the Church did not turn out to be as harmonious as expected: the area of youth education, the strengthening lay organization of Catholic Action and the introduction of the racial laws led to fierce confrontations. The Fascist–Catholic alliance was also put to the test abroad, for example in looking after the Italian emigrant communities. The congruence of the *Italianità* with Fascism had to be continually renegotiated, especially with the Catholic orders abroad. Mussolini was indeed aware of the central importance of a "Catholic connotation" of Italians abroad in the pres-ervation of Italian nationality and language. However, competition in youth education in particular was to become a flashpoint in the colonies.

With the Abyssinian War of 1935/36, Mussolini achieved the greatest con-sensus among the population and also the greatest agreement between Fascism and Catholicism. For Fascism and the Church, the ideological elements of this war of aggression against the empire of Abyssinia, today's Ethiopia, ranged from imperialism and expansionism to racism.

3. The Rise and Decline of Italian Fascism in Vienna

3.1 Austrian National Characteristics

Country-specific characteristics, but also the common history with Italy, had a clear influence on how the spread of Fascist ideology was received in Vienna, how successful the various Fascist transmission belts were, and what adaptation strategies were pursued.

The 'treacherous' entry into the First World War by its former ally had reinforced Austria's traditional, deep-rooted mistrust of Italy. The South Tyrol issue also permanently strained bilateral relations with regard to the repressive denationalization policy of the Fascists. The Italian Fascists faced particular opposition in "Red Vienna" from the dominant Social Democratic Party, but numerous opponents of Mussolini's regime whom Vienna had granted political asylum also tried to act as an anti-Fascist control authority. Another local specificity is the *Minoritenkirche* as the Italian national church, which was to develop into the spiritual centre of the Italian colony. The close relationship between Fascists and Catholics naturally led to conflicts at first, but later also to cooperation.

3.2 Phases of the Reception of Fascism in Vienna and their Impact on Fascist Transmission Belts

The reception context in Vienna initially tended to be hostile towards Italian Fascism until around 1926/27, then changed to a receptive, affirmative context (until 1936), only to change back to a hostile environment from 1936 onwards.

It is noteworthy that the phase of Fascism's positive reception began in 1927, long before the establishment of the Dollfuß/Schuschnigg regime. The Fascist ideas, institutions or values that were taken up and adopted in this phase fostered a philo-Fascist climate of opinion. All this encouraged a process of political change that led to an authoritarian regime under Chancellor Engelbert Dollfuß.

Those responsible for school propaganda described the political context of reception in Austria in the 1920s as difficult to penetrate – historical sources of conflict continued to have an impact. There were sensational school closures by "Red Vienna", while on the federal level the Christian Socialists took a pro-Italian stance. Against the background of a mutual bilateral political and cultural rapprochement that culminated in the signing of the Cultural Agreement in 1935, the adoption of school institutions in Vienna was much more successful in the following decade: the increased accommodation by the Dollfuß government helped open up the Austrian population intellectually, including to the former hereditary enemy, Fascist Italy. However, the path to becoming a cultural power of influence and a counterweight to Nazi propaganda was often impaired by the Fascist side itself; ultimately, Fascist cultural policy degenerated into a foreign policy pawn.

In the 1920s the anti-Italian sentiment in "Red Vienna" was formative for the propaganda work of the Italian Fascists. Due to political agitations, the *Fascio* secretary Attilio Tamaro was recalled under international, but also socialist pressure. But even in this phase of resistance to Fascist content (until about 1927), there were requests from bourgeois as well as Christian-Social circles for contact and funding for the Fascists. These attempts at reception were turned down, as the time was not yet ripe and failure would be damaging to Italy's reputation. Nevertheless, this led to the dispatch of a parallel diplomat to Vienna in 1927 who was directly subordinate to Mussolini – significantly, before the Palace of Justice fire in the July of the same year, which is commonly perceived as a turning point in the radicalization of Austrian domestic politics. Eugenio Morreale's goals were to be the seizure of power by the *Heimwehr* and later Nazi opposition. Improved relations with Chancellor Dollfuß and his path towards an Austrofascist regime, together with Morreale's special mission, meant that unofficial political agitation by the *Fascio* was no longer appropriate. When the political omens changed, Morreale's expendability also became apparent. His dismissal from Vienna in 1937 was a result of German pressure and can also be understood as a concession by Mussolini to its new Axis partner.

Negotiating support for Fascist propaganda from the Italian national church was not without conflict. Church political actors on various levels initially dared to resist the Fascist appropriation. The removal of the pugnacious Church rector, but also a Fascist-nationalist infiltration of the congregation at the *Minoritenkirche* ultimately contributed to the fascistization of Church personnel in 1926/ 1927. This allowed the Fascists to successively impose their demands (within the colony).

The defensive stance of the Austrian episcopate towards Fascist influences referred in the medium term to foreign influences, but not to authoritarian influences per se. Ultimately, however, the approaching end of "Red Vienna" and the increasing acceptance of authoritarian tendencies – the Catholic Church established itself as an important ideological authority for the legitimization of the Dollfuß/Schuschnigg regime – was conducive to certain advances on the path to fascistization. Similar to Italy, the closing of ranks between state and Church prevented ecclesiastical anti-Fascism. Moreover, the activities of the Fascist foreign party cell were under close observation by the Austrian authorities due to the immediate proximity of the church to Ballhausplatz, the centre of political power in Austria. The authorities reacted to Fascist demands with corresponding rejection and delay.

4.   The Rise and Decline of Italian Fascism in Budapest

4.1   Hungarian National Characteristics

The desire for a revision of the peace treaties, which imposed massive territorial losses on Hungary, left a lasting impression on the Hungarian population after the First World War. This also led to consistently good relations with the like-minded great power of Italy.

Due to the anti-Semitism in Hungary, which affected broad sections of the population and led to *numerus clausus* as early as 1920, Jewish pupils took refuge at the Italian school institutions in Budapest. As a result, the Italian regime was labeled "philo-Semitic Fascism", while the Germans were able to profit from the prevailing anti-Semitism. Catholic critics also felt empowered to raise their voices, since anti-Semitism had become acceptable in these circles too.

The traditional dominance of German culture in Hungarian society was hardly conducive to Italian Fascism: often, language skills first had to be taught and propaganda material brought into the country.

4.2   Phases of the Reception of Fascism in Budapest and their Impact on Fascist Transmission Belts

As in Austria, 1927 was a decisive turning point for the positive reception of Fascism in Budapest. Until then, Italy had fended off requests for contact from philo-Fascist movements from the opposition. However, the Friendship Treaty with Italy, which was supposed to bring Hungary out of international isolation and bring the revision of the peace treaties into play, saw a boom in the reception of Fascism and opened a phase of positive, appropriative reception in Hungary. Together with the Cultural Agreement of 1935, the Ethiopian War of 1935/36 constituted a last clear upswing in reception. Around 1936, however, the increasingly German orientation of Hungarian foreign policy became apparent. Prime Minister Gömbös, a strong advocate of Fascism, also died that year. Although the Hungarian population remained Italophile even in the Ethiopian conflict, the Fascists were ultimately to succumb to the competing and aggressive Nazi propaganda despite a change in strategy.

The long-time leader of the Budapest *Fascio*, Prince Riccardo Pignatelli di Montecalvo, barely had an impact on performance of the *Fascio*. The over-saturated market of Italophile associations in Budapest and the impoverished colony hampered the propaganda of the *Fascio*, which was also poorly funded. Moreover, the close relations with official Hungary were not to be clouded by contacts with local philo-Fascist movements. The focus on Hungarian youths led to the creation of institutions to capture them, which sidelined the *Fascio*. Pignatelli's dismissal, which came well after the shift of focus to cultural policy despite knowledge of his incompetence, confirms Hungary's subordinate position in Fascist propaganda strategy.

In the 1920s, the difficulties of Fascist school and cultural propaganda work became apparent; they were reflected in few resources, a lack of equipment, and competition with the cultural hegemony of the Germans and the French. Increased activities in the field of culture only occurred around the bilateral cultural agreement of 1935 – which was due to the improved reception context under the philo-Fascist Gyula Gömbös, who had been in power since 1932. The high point in the institutional expansion of cultural propaganda in Hungary was certainly the Italian Cultural Institute, which quickly advanced to become the extremely well-received centre of cultural propaganda in Hungary, eventually taking over the facilities of the *Dante* and the *Fascio*. This impressively demonstrates the initiated shift in importance from politics to culture for Hungary. With all the measures now created, it is evident that they were primarily directed against German propaganda, for the strong presence of German (and French) culture remained the constant frame of reference. But the attempt at intellectual penetration of Italy came too late and was not very sustainable: German influence remained paramount.

The pastoral care of the colony in Budapest was initially taken over by the Salesian Order, which was then replaced by the Servites around 1926. The cooperation with the Servite Order functioned smoothly, both for Fascist jubilees and for religious instruction in Italian secondary schools.

The Italian character made it possible for both the nuncio Angelo Rotta, established in Hungarian society and the highest-ranking diplomat in Hungary, and the Servite Order to be instrumentalized for Fascist purposes, as could be seen on the occasion of the *Crociera* of the Fascist *Avanguardisti* in 1932. As a result, the Vatican called for the nuncio to refrain from making controversial public statements, whereupon the papal emissary forfeited his public interpretative authority and had to avoid occasions with Fascist connotations. On the other hand, he did not renounce his nationalist, philo-Fascist sentiments: with regard to the philo-Semitic school policy of the Fascists, Rotta warned against Jewish infiltration in 1937. In doing so, he used the ecclesiastical argument of anti-communist anti-Semitism, but also promoted an economic anti-Semitism.

The anti-Semitic opening of Fascist propaganda in Budapest can be understood as a consequence of Rotta's intervention, but this should not be seen in isolation from anti-Semitic developments in Italy and Hungary.

Nevertheless, Nuncio Rotta was to be involved in the protection of persecuted Jews in the Second World War on a grand scale – while the resistance of the Hungarian episcopate in the face of the 1944 deportations remained too ineffective vis-à-vis the government.

5.   Concluding remarks

5.1   Mussolini's Ideological Goals in the Danube Region

A central finding of the study was that Austria undeniably occupied a special position in Fascist foreign policy in the interwar period. This position influenced the Fascist transfer of ideology in that Italy linked its policy of interests to ideological demands and aimed to fascistize the political system in Austria. A government with a Fascism-like system was expected to better serve the interests of the Italian regime.

The priority that Italy gave to Austria was reflected in the measures that were taken in Austria, in contrast to Hungary, at an earlier stage and also more intensively. If Hungary was sometimes given priority, it was mostly the Hungarians who took the initiative because of the excellent context of reception. The leading personnel and their ideological convictions also had a higher status in Vienna. Sometimes they had to be fascistized first or their dependence on the local environment prevented. While Mussolini even sent a parallel diplomat directly subordinate to him, Morreale, to Vienna, his incompetent Hungarian counterpart, Prince Pignatelli, was not deposed for a long time. The secondary importance of the Budapest *Fascio* also demonstrates the lack of interest in a fascistization of the country. Rather, the maintenance of a philo-Fascist climate of opinion in Hungary was promoted in view of the Hungarian population's keen admiration for Italy as a great power.

The analysis of the propaganda measures reveals that almost every step taken by the Italians can be interpreted as a reaction to the reception context. This emphasizes the reciprocal aspect of the transfer processes, but also domestic and foreign policy constellations that promoted peaks in reception. In Austria, Italy only initiated fascistization measures once the population showed signs of being ripe for radicalization. The goal of fascistizing Austria could thus only be developed via the increasingly opening reception context in Austria. Thus the process of political change under Dollfuß cannot be seen solely as the result of pressure exerted by Mussolini.

The expansion of Fascist propaganda to the native population, which, contrary to official statements, was soon considered a target group in Vienna as well as Budapest, also reflects a reaction to the reception in the respective recipient country. Temporal differences emphasize Mussolini's different priorities; Morreale went to Vienna in 1927 to act as a link to the *Heimwehren*, while in Budapest it was the *Avanguardisti*'s tour in 1932 that provided the impetus to focus on Hungarian youth.

As expected, the influence on the local population also had an impact in terms of content: the signing of the cultural agreements reveals a shift in strategy towards cultural propaganda. For when offensive, purely Fascist-political propaganda was no longer opportune, the focus was on linguistic-cultural propaganda and thus responded to the preferences of the Austrian and Hungarian population.

5.2   The Centrality of Language and Knowledge about the Country

Another central finding of the study was that the spread of language skills was the foundation for ideology transfer. The common language as a vehicle for ideology was evident in the language courses for compatriots and locals, but also in the fact that existing language skills of the mediators of Fascism and their previous experience in the host country were conducive to transfer. Commonalities of close cultures could also promote the transfer of ideology, as the example of Germany showed, and not only for Austria.

The centrality of language can also be seen in the field of political propaganda, beyond its use in language schools. For Austria, the majority of the mediators also had the relevant language skills and previous experience of the country. Since most of them came from the north-eastern Italian border region, they also brought with them a mentality similar to that of the Austrians, which was an advantage. In Budapest, on the other hand, local language skills were less widespread among the Fascists, but the use of intermediaries from Fiume (today's Rijeka, Croatia), where similar bilingualism prevailed, gave the common language a bridging function in the Hungarian capital too.

5.3   The Fascist Challenge in Europe

Regardless of the country-specific circumstances, it can be seen from the temporally parallel phases of reception in Austria and Hungary (with a peak phase from 1927 to 1936) that Mussolini's export of Fascism must ultimately be considered within the context of Italian foreign policy given the situation in Central

Europe. But foreign policy relations were also relevant for recipients and the context of reception, which is why bilateral agreements such as friendship treaties or cultural agreements in Austria and Hungary triggered special peaks in reception.

Accordingly, Italy also had to react to Hitler's "seizure of power" in 1933. Hitler increasingly developed into a competitor who also knew how to use the fascist charisma. The Italian regime responded to this fascist competition with numerous anti-German measures in both countries – albeit with different objectives and different speed. In Austria, a strategy of integration was pursued early on, for example with the National Socialist students. From the time of Hitler's "seizure of power", however, they tried to bind Chancellor Dollfuß more closely to them and insistently demanded fascistization. In addition, the *Heimwehren* were strengthened with special payments. In the intensification of cultural propaganda in Vienna, the anti-German function of the newly founded Cultural Institute was obvious. The thesis that the Italians did not intend to fascistize Hungary is supported by the delayed reaction to this competition in Hungary, which did not start until 1935. Only the German rivalry made it clear that in order to maintain the previous philo-Fascist climate, targeted action had to be taken against Nazi propaganda.

The Fascist strategy of demarcation towards National Socialism can also be understood as a reaction to the reception that took place in the host countries. Despite the reception impulses generated by the Fascist Ethiopian War, Italy was losing influence in Central Europe. In Vienna and Budapest, a declining reception and an increasing turn towards National Socialist Germany were evident at this time.

5.4   Outlook

Inspired by the research on the history of transfer and relations, this study did not seek strict subordination to a static fascism paradigm. Based on Gerhard Botz's fascistization periods for Austria, a processual approach seems promising. There were different high phases or peaks that ensured a particular receptivity to Fascist elements and their appropriation and adoption, but also – in accordance with the declining reception elaborated here – a "defascistization".

According to Aristotle A. Kallis, the dynamic concept of "fascistization" on the regime level has special added value. This conceptual category classifies the adoption of fascist elements in regimes without complete ideological self-sacrifice as fascistization, and refrains from speaking of a 'real' fascist regime. This seems to be a worthwhile approach in the future, because it is able to describe the incorporation of individual fascist aspects much more adequately than a static catalogue of characteristics for the definition of fascism could.

6. Selected Bibliography

Aust, Martin and Daniel Schönpflug (eds.), *Vom Gegner lernen. Feindschaften und Kulturtransfers im Europa des 19. und 20. Jahrhunderts.* Frankfurt am Main: Campus-Verlag, 2007.

Bischof, Günter J. (ed.), *The Dollfuss/Schuschnigg era in Austria. A reassessment.* New Brunswick, NJ: Transaction Publishers, 2003, (Contemporary Austrian studies 11).

Borejsza, Jerzy W., *Il fascismo e l'europa orientale. Dalla propaganda all'aggressione.* Rome – Bari: Laterza, 1981, (Biblioteca di cultura moderna 846).

Burgwyn, H. J., "La troika danubiania di Mussolini: Italia, Austria e Ungheria, 1927–1936," *Storia Contemporanea – rivista bimestrale di studi storici* 21 (1990) 4: 617–86.

D'Agostino, Peter R., "'Fascist Transmission Belts' or Episcopal Advisors? Italian Consuls and American Catholicism in the 1930's," *Cushwa Center for the Study of American Catholicism. Working Paper Series* 24 (1997) 3: 1–39.

Espagne, Michel and Michael Werner, "Deutsch-Französischer Kulturtransfer im 18. und 19. Jahrhundert. Zu einem neuen interdisziplinären Forschungsprogramm des C.N.R.S," *Francia* 13 (1985): 502–10.

Franzina, Emilio and Matteo Sanfilippo (eds.), *Il fascismo e gli emigrati. La parabola dei fasci italiani all'estero (1920–1943).* Rome – Bari: Laterza, 2003.

Gentile, Emilio, "La politica estera del partito fascista. Ideologia e organizzazione dei Fasci italiani all'estero (1920–1930)," *Storia Contemporanea* 26 (1995) 6: 897–956.

Guiotto, Maddalena and Helmut Wohnout (eds.), *Italien und Österreich im Mitteleuropa der Zwischenkriegszeit.* Wien – Köln – Weimar: Böhlau, 2018, (Schriftenreihe des Österreichischen Historischen Instituts in Rom 2).

Hoffend, Andrea, "'Verteidigung des Humanismus'? Der italienische Faschismus vor der kulturellen Herausforderung durch den Nationalsozialismus," in *Faschismus und Gesellschaft in Italien. Staat – Wirtschaft – Kultur,* edited by Jens Petersen and Wolfgang Schieder, 178–98. Köln: SH-Verlag, 1998.

Kallis, Aristotle A., "'Fascism', 'Para-Fascism' and 'Fascistization': On the Similarities of Three Conceptual Categories," in *European History Quarterly* 33 (2003) 2, 219–49.

Kerekes, Lajos, *Abenddämmerung einer Demokratie. Mussolini, Gömbös und die Heimwehr.* Vienna et al.: Europa-Verlag, 1966.

Nelis, Jan et al. (eds.), *Catholicism and Fascism in Europe 1918–1945.* Hildesheim: Georg Olms Verlag, 2015, (Historische Texte und Studien 26).

Niglia, Federico, "Mussolini, Dollfuss e i nazionalisti austriaci. La politica estera italiana in Austria nei rapporti di Morreale," *Nuova Storia Contemporanea* VII (2003) 1: 63–82.

Pinto, António Costa and Aristotle A. Kallis (eds.), *Rethinking Fascism and Dictatorship in Europe.* Basingstoke: Palgrave Macmillan, 2014.

Reichardt, Sven and Armin Nolzen (eds.), *Faschismus in Italien und Deutschland. Studien zu Transfer und Vergleich.* Göttingen: Wallstein-Verlag, 2005, (Beiträge zur Geschichte des Nationalsozialismus).

Rosoli, Gianfausto, "Santa Sede e propaganda fascista all'estero tra i figli degli emigrati italiani," *Storia Contemporanea* 17 (1986): 293–315.

Santoro, Stefano, *L'Italia e l'Europa orientale: diplomazia culturale e propaganda (1918–1943)*. Milan: F. Angeli, 2005.

Schieder, Wolfgang (ed.), *Faschistische Diktaturen. Studien zu Italien und Deutschland*. Göttingen: Wallstein-Verlag, 2008.

Schieder, Wolfgang, "Das italienische Experiment. Der Faschismus als Vorbild in der Krise der Weimarer Republik," *Historische Zeitschrift* 262 (1996): 73–125.

Scholz, Beate, *Italienischer Faschismus als 'Export'-Artikel (1927–1935). Ideologische und organisatorische Ansätze zur Verbreitung des Faschismus im Ausland*, PhD. thesis, Trier, 2001.

Spannenberger, Norbert, *Die katholische Kirche in Ungarn 1918–1939. Positionierung im politischen System und "Katholische Renaissance"*. Stuttgart: F. Steiner, 2006.

Spannenberger, Norbert and József Vonyó, "Die Gömbös-Diktatur und die katholische Kirche in Ungarn (1932–1936)," *Südost-Forschungen* 61/62 (2002/2003): 311–33.

Tálos, Emmerich, *Das austrofaschistische Herrschaftssystem. Österreich 1933–1938*. Berlin – Münster – Vienna: LIT-Verlag, 2013, (Politik und Zeitgeschichte 8).

Florian Wenninger

Social polarization and its historical analysis. The Example of the First Austrian Republic

After the First Republic and Austrofascism had taken a backseat in historical scholarship for two decades, they experienced a small historiographical renaissance in the 2000s. Since then, academic works have contributed new insights into various aspects. Macro-perspectives have however barely accounted for this; the established interpretation of the years 1918–38 has basically remained unchanged since the 1970s.[1]

Against this background, the dissertation's goal was – as prolegomena of an examination of historic identity formation – to illuminate the conditions of the dynamics of polarization that put an end to the first democratic period in Austrian history. In order to do this, the wealth of knowledge which has grown considerably was put in context with established syntheses.

For a better understanding of prevalent interpretative models, the examination initially was focused on the first historians' debate of the Second Republic: the dispute concerning the most comprehensive historical treatise on the years 1918–38, written in 1948 by US-American historian and economist Charles Adams Gulick.[2]

As a reaction to Gulick's book, a group of conservative intellectuals surrounding the Viennese publisher Karl Cornides under the leadership of historian Heinrich Benedikt and with financial support from the sphere of influence of the *Österreichische Volkspartei* (Austrian People's Party, ÖVP), the *Industriellenvereinigung* (Federation of Austrian Industry), and several bankers initiated a conservative reply.[3] The "Anti-Gulick" became the most-read work on the Aus-

---

1 Exemplarily: Anton Pelinka, *Die gescheiterte Republik. Kultur und Politik in Österreich 1918–1938* (Wien – Köln – Weimar: Böhlau, 2017); Michael Buchmann, *Insel der Unseligen. Das autoritäre Österreich 1933–1938* (Vienna – Graz: Molden, 2019).
2 Charles Adams Gulick, *Austria. From Habsburg to Hitler* (Berkeley – Los Angeles, 1948).
3 Heinrich Benedikt (ed.), *Geschichte der Republik Österreich* (Vienna: Verlag für Geschichte und Politik, 1954). See also the preserved publishing house documents: Wienbibliothek im Rathaus/Handschriftensammlung/Archiv Verlag für Geschichte und Politik/ZPH 1765, Box 1.

trian inter-war period and advanced numerous dominant interpretations both in
public and within the discipline.

My work focuses on the two interpretations of the Benedikt book which most
influenced the academic view of the years 1918–34 in the long term: the "reluctant state"[4] and the theory of the three political camps.[5] I attempt to understand both paradigms from the viewpoint of the political-functional context of
the period of their creation and examine them on their historical plausibility in
the light of research.

1.   On the Functionality of Two Master Narratives

The narrative of the "reluctant state" originally was not an invention of the
Benedikt group, but even before 1938 had been a prevalent wording in the conservative milieu and had been used by national socialist historian Reinhold
Lorenz in 1940 as the title of a book on the Austrian inter-war period.[6] Argu-
mentatively, the right-wing bourgeois viewpoint was generalized: the deciding
flaw of the First Republic was not seen to be its republican form of government,
but the national question, the sovereignty established by the victor states of the
First World War which had a priori taken away the First Republic's legitimacy in
its population's eyes. The responsibility for the removal of democracy and republic, euphemistically named "failure", in 1933/34 was thus indirectly spread
among all political orientations – if the state had been "unbeloved", ergo "no-
body had wanted it" and it had thus "failed", then conversely all sides were more
or less similarly to blame for its failure. The dispute over fundamental democratic
and social accomplishments of the republic was indirectly dismissed as a marginal detail. In this way the question of who had fought against the newly created
social security systems, improvements in workers' rights, communal welfare
services, and the legal protection of tenants, as well as the new means of democratic participation was largely ignored. The retrospective referral to the periphery of the past occurrences avoided uncomfortable discussions and obscured
that the conservatives had modified their attitudes regarding these subjects after
the Second World War. The second interpretation, which became style-defining
via the publication of *Geschichte der Republik Österreich* in 1954, was Adam

---

4 Martin Reisacher, "Die Konstruktion des 'Staats den keiner wollte'. Der Transformationsprozess des umstrittenen Gedächtnisorts 'Erste Republik' in einen negativen rhetorischen
Topos," unpublished PhD thesis, University of Vienna, 2010.
5 Adam Wandruszka, "Die drei Lager," in *Geschichte der Republik Österreich,* edited by Heinrich
Benedikt, 291–300, especially 291–293.
6 Reinhold Lorenz, *Der Staat wider Willen. Österreich 1918–1938* (Berlin: Junker und Dünn-
haupt, 1940).

Wandruszka's "trisection of Austria willed by nature or god" into three antagonistic camps. According to him, Austria had been shaped socio-culturally since the 1880s by a Christian-social, a social democratic and a German-national camp. This foundational structure in further consequence had defied all regime changes. The historic derivation of an independent national camp fell precisely into a phase in which the ÖVP leadership tried to realize what Christian-socials from Seipel to Schuschnigg had repeatedly failed at: the unification of the bourgeois milieu into a joint party structure. The theory of the "national" Adam Wandruszka, who remained closely associated with the *Freiheitliche Partei Österreichs* (Austrian Freedom Party, FPÖ) for the rest of his life, could be understood as the historical foundation of an autonomous "national" structure.[7] Although Benedikt and Cornides leaned more towards the ÖVP, they did not raise any objections to Wandruszka's representation. The reason for this may be that his interpretation also had advantages from the ÖVP's point of view: It accomplished a retroactive delimitation of the Christian-Social Party from National Socialism and directed the analytical focus from the social to the cultural-political level by alleging that not material contrasting interests and the attitude towards the republic and democracy had been at the center of the domestic political struggles between 1918 and 1938, but instead the stance towards the Austrian nation. Thus, the First Republic, which was still seen as a "red" state project by many in the conservative milieu, was retrospectively presented as an "unnatural" political experiment, forced onto the country from the outside. The anti-democratic tradition of the conservative block who resisted the welfare state, and the policy of passing on the cost of the crisis to the mass of low-income earners – in combination the actual reason behind the dissolution of the republic – were reinterpreted into an ideological contrast on the national question. Only against such a background the thesis of shared blame aired by conservatives became plausible. The function of this partially was to ease the conservative party members' accommodation with the democratic-republican system of the present – both sides had equally made mistakes, which they had only realized in the national socialist concentration camps: the left had understood the need for Austrian sovereignty, the right the need for democracy.

This camp theorem had extensive consequences for the historical analysis of the inter-war period. If there namely had been two explicitly conservative blocks that had agreed on most things in their distribution policy, then the ideological and personal trenches would have to have been similarly insurmountable as those between the right and left in social issues. Historians thus preferably dedicated

---

7 Hermann Fritzl and Martin Uitz, "Kritische Anmerkungen zur sogenannten Lagertheorie," *Österreichische Zeitschrift für Politikwissenschaft* 5 (1975) 4: 325–332.

themselves to actors and cultural differences and disregarded differences in opinion on social questions.[8]

2.   Analytical Prisms: Longue Durée and the Concept of Class

The early phase of the Austrian political landscape has been researched comparatively well.[9] The changes that occurred especially in the bourgeois milieu between the turn of the century and the first years after the First World War, however, were only considered in a few pioneering works.[10] This was the case, even though for example the decentralization of the Christian-Social Party from the federal to the state level, the conflicts between various supporting groups, and the culture struggle's loss of significance had far-reaching consequences. Similarly, the severe structural problems that had united all conservative parties since their beginnings and which they could not overcome were impactful, especially the lack of a centrally guided, hierarchical organization and a mobilized following. While the deciding upheavals within the national groups only started after the First World War, they had occurred before it within political Catholicism. The amount of personnel in the Christian-Social Party was particularly low in the federate states, which fostered the influence of low-level clergy but brought with it massive conflicts in the church hierarchy. The Viennese state organization was able to recruit their elite functionaries from a much larger personnel pool, but was embroiled in several corruption scandals after Lueger's death in 1910 and was paralyzed by wars of the Diadochi. In addition, the party was witness to the rise of the workers' movement and was all too aware of the danger that universal and equal voting rights presented for its communal position of power.

Apart from the extension of the observed period, this paper also stresses the need to not only understand the social structure of the First Republic as cultural milieus, but first and foremost as a class society. Social distribution battles were

---

8 Exceptions were for example Emmerich Tálos, "Interessensvermittlung und partikularistische Interessenspolitik in der Ersten Republik," in *Handbuch des politischen Systems Österreichs. Erste Republik 1918–1933*, edited by Emmerich Tálos et al. (Vienna: Manz, 1995); Fritz Weber, "Die Weltwirtschaftskrise und das Ende der Demokratie in Österreich," in *Der 4. März 1933. Vom Verfassungsbruch zur Diktatur. Beiträge zum wissenschaftlichen Symposion des Dr.-Karl-Renner-Instituts, abgehalten am 28. Februar und 1. März 1983*, edited by Erich Fröschl and Helge Zoitl (Vienna: Verlag der Wiener Volksbuchhandlung, 1984), 37–67; Karl Haas, "Industrielle Interessenspolitik in Österreich zur Zeit der Weltwirtschaftskrise," *Österreichische Gesellschaft für Zeitgeschichte Jahrbuch für Zeitgeschichte* 1 (1978): 97–126.

9 See the contributions with detailed references in Tálos et al. (ed.), "Handbuch des politischen Systems".

10 See among others John Boyer, *Culture and Political Crisis in Vienna. Christian Socialism in Power, 1897–1918* (Chicago – London: University of Chicago Press, 1995).

the starting point for the formation of the political landscape and are a deciding key to understanding the conflict dynamics until 1934. The influence of (sometimes competing) lobbies such as banking and industry capital as well as the agrarian sector and the apartment building owners – particularly well networked within the Viennese Christian-Social Party – strongly shaped conservative politics and severely impeded compromises. The concept of class is also essential to understanding the social character of Austro-Fascism: it was not simply a party dictatorship, but was based on a social alliance of various advocacy groups that feared for their power and saw in the dictatorship an instrument to stabilize the bourgeois order.[11]

On the basis of these findings, this paper argues eight theses:

1. Under the impression of a looming loss of significance, a lasting radicalization occurred particularly among young intellectuals that would come to power within the Christian-Social Party in the 1920s. This circle of people formed the group of aggressive anti-democrats that not only began supporting coup plans with their undisputed authority Ignaz Seipel in the second half of the 1920s, but had already been decidedly against the democratic changes in the republic's beginnings.

   These intellectuals were also strongly influenced by the predominant movements at the universities, especially National Socialism and the ever more radical anti-Semitism. Together with "anti-Marxism" these formed a unifying ideological ambient noise of the political right across all party- and organizational boundaries. At the same time, the anti-Clericalism of national groups significantly decreased during this time, religious traditions were absorbed into the national pool of symbols and rites as part of a cultivation of customs and traditions. Thus, there were no culturally or programmatically insurmountable divisions between the various conservative movements – but there was a unifying theme: the social question, the defense against socialist efforts of all kinds, and the repression of the workers' movement. It seems obvious to speak of a fragmented conservative block and a much more unified left instead of three camps.

2. The rise of social democracy did not include rural areas, neither before nor after 1918. For the agrarian-dominated parts of the Christian-Social Party they thus remained a more abstract opponent until the mid-1920s. The social democrats' strategic decision in the early years of the republic to focus their organization on urban centers was the result of considerations of their own

---

11 These diverging interests are addressed among others by Gerhard Senft, *Im Vorfeld der Katastrophe. Die Wirtschaftspolitik des Ständestaates Österreich, 1933–1938* (Vienna: Braumüller, 2002); Stefan Eminger, *Das Gewerbe in Österreich 1930–1938. Organisationsformen, Interessenspolitik und politische Mobilität* (Innsbruck – Wien – Bozen: StudienVerlag, 2005).

strengths and the attempt to forge an alliance of convenience with rural Christian-social organizations in the states of Upper and Lower Austria while avoiding the urban party. After they had exhausted their urban potential, social democracy started an agricultural program to now tackle rural Austria. The red expansion into smaller towns failed because the Christian-Social Party quickly had overcome their short phase of disorientation in 1918/19 and had focused on the development of their own rural organizations and thus countered the social democratic agitation. Even the attempt, the theoretical possibility, that their farmhands might unionize and set demands contributed to the strengthening of anti-democratic movements among farmers.

3. Not only in SPÖ party historiography, but also in academic papers, Red Vienna was characterized after 1945 as "anticipatory socialism": as a comprehensive attempt to show under a capitalist system what the blessings of a socialist society might look like. In reality it was less of a homogenous movement, but more a conglomerate of different initiatives to improve the housing and living conditions of the urban lower classes. This misinterpretation presents a distorted picture of the actual political process, which was defined by institutional openness, a readiness to compromise among different actors, and a strong dose of pragmatism. It was facilitated by the circumstance that the Viennese municipal authorities were interspersed with Christian-socials and the new social democratic city government in 1919 did not have to heed the objections of the city bureaucracy. With other words, not clerks but politicians defined the boundaries of the possible. At the same time, social democracy was exceedingly open to include external expertise and granted political newcomers unusual creative leeway.

4. Charlie Jeffery's assumption that the social democratic organizational culture at the periphery was defined by a considerable distance between the base on the one side and elected representatives and the leadership on the other, is also applied to the examination of the center. The leading groups of both the Viennese and the Empire-wide party were mostly comprised of closed circles that expanded themselves and that were culturally distant from their own constituency, who they had few points of contact with aside from party events. In contrast to the petit bourgeois leadership in the federate states, the Viennese social democratic leading circles mainly hailed from upper-class families. Situated between the leaders and the base in the social democratic hierarchy, a bureaucratic functional elite was located, which was significantly expanded in the 1920s. Despite the dominant position of the leftist wing of the party, this bureaucratization led to an opposition policy that presented itself in the public with aggressive criticism, but in the parliamentary day-to-day was marked by efforts to compromise and explicitly avoided making too forceful demands. All movements within the SDAPÖ proved themselves in-

capable of finding a strategic answer to the constantly rising pressure of the political right. After the dissolution of the party in February 1934, the break occurred that the party had essentially been able to avoid during and after the First World War. Since the leading circle around Otto Bauer had almost no direct connections to the party base aside from the youth organizations, the underground reorganization only partially succeeded.

5. In the literature the police massacre of 15 and 16 July 1927 is unanimously described as the tipping point of the republic. From this moment on, an incremental polarization had taken hold, which had not only made impossible any cooperation between the conservative parties and social democracy, but also a peaceful co-existence between the two sides. Even more recently there still have also been references to the offers of coalition by Buresch and Dollfuß, which supposedly had been thoughtlessly rejected by social democracy. In contrast, this examination holds the opinion that the tipping point did not coincide with any specific event during the republic, but instead was the foundation of the republic itself. The authoritarian consensus in the conservative block was not triggered by external events, but on the part of the Christian-Social Party was consolidated at the latest with the intra-party removal of Johann Nepomuk Hauser and Jodok Fink as the representatives of the moderate agrarian wing in the early 1920s. The party right had already early on conspired against them and intensified their efforts to dismantle the republican order. The rise of the *Heimwehr*-movement beginning in 1927 was not an independent development, but was implemented in close coordination with these powers. The strategy of tension applied by the conservative government and the *Heimwehr*-organizations did however not yield the expected results, since chancellors Seipel, Streeruwitz, Schober, Vaugoin and finally Buresch, in contrast to Dollfuß, were not prepared to accept the full consequences of a coup.

6. Historically, the establishment of the dictatorship is to this day mostly seen in the context of the personal motives of the main actors, especially Dollfuß. In light of the current state of research it seems much more plausible to speak of two core motifs, one political and the other economic. Dollfuß as a person was only relevant because he, in contrast to his predecessors was prepared to get his hands dirty to put into practice the authoritarian consensus in the conservative block.

    There were two possible political answers to the world economic crisis which hit Austria in 1930 and coincided with years of a banking crisis: passing on the cost of the crisis to the majority of the population by expenditure cuts and wage pressure, or the financing of social programs and job creation by forced redistribution. Against this backdrop, the Austrian government applied a policy of crisis management that severely disadvantaged the employed population and in particular also hit state employees. Under democratic rules this course was not tenable in the midterm, as Schuschnigg already mentioned in the cabinet in 1932. The then minister of justice presumably was thinking of the growth of social democracy from a relative to an absolute majority in the parliament. Instead of to the left, the conservative parties veered further right. With their own social descent in mind, these parties' petit bourgeois core voters became massively radicalized. The did not accept the egalitarian political offer of the left but on the contrary looked for opportunities to stabilize their social status. This not only led to stronger resentment against the republic and social democracy, but also to an upswing for the NSDAP, especially at the expense of established conservative parties in the cities. In light of this development, the CSP had three options: a large coalition with social democracy, a unification of the right party spectrum, or avoiding the loss of their majority by preventing elections. The first option was not desired by the leading circle and would probably only have been enforceable within the party if the social democrats did not make any demands whatsoever for government participation; the second option, a consolidation of all right-wing movements, Seipel had failed at for years, and the ongoing erosion of the greater German People's Party, the rise of the NSDAP, and the partial emancipation of the *Heimwehr*-organizations had made it even more difficult since then; so the decision finally fell on the third possibility: establishing a dictatorship. This afforded an opportunity to get rid of the workers' movement as well as disempower more moderate intra-party rivals, which was strongly supported by the episcopacy that wanted to reestablish its intra-clerical authority which it saw challenged by all-too assertive politically active clergymen.

7. In retrospect, the loss of the state monopoly on the use of force and the presence of paramilitary formations are seen as clear signs for the First Republic being a failed state. The research on this militant spectrum has so far been focused on the history of events and organizations but has avoided localizing the groups in regard to their political functions. What remains is the metaphor of a totalitarian horseshoe: in their militant extremism, the differences between left and right are muddied, they both supposedly were obstacles to a functioning parliamentary democracy. According to my interpretation, the historical state of facts points in another direction: the loss of the state's monopoly on force was not a shortcoming of the new republican order, but its prerequisite. The bureaucratic and military leadership of the young republic was interspersed by fierce opponents of the same. The fact that neither the military nor the dethroned emperor staged a coup was only due to the lack of means of force to do so: while the officers' corps remained loyal to the monarchy, the common soldiers had mostly switched over to the leftist camp in 1918. Since the breakup of the grand coalition in 1920 it had been the

joint goal of all conservative governments to once again turn the military into a reliable instrument of the right. While cleansing the army, two other strategies also aimed to gain the military upper hand: the armament of paramilitary organizations and the development of the federal executive into a civil war brigade. These strategies were answered by social democracy in 1923 with the reorganization of their defense formations under the umbrella of the *Republikanischer Schutzbund*. It was meant to prevent a right-wing coup by force. The expectation was that the opposing side would not be able to activate state troops in case of a confrontation because they would have to fear a solidarization of their men with the fighting left. In July 1927 a turning point in this regard occurred: it was a test case for the readiness of the executive branch and an indicator for the position of the troops. As they were told, the police shot into the crowd while the barracks remained calm. In this moment it became clear to all sides that the state organizations would not remain neutral in case of a military confrontation. Despite the completely changed framework conditions and after fierce debates, the Social Democratic Party decided not to unilaterally disarm the *Schutzbund* to not give the other side a reason for attack. At the same time, however, they also did not adapt their military strategy to the new circumstances. In Theodor Körner's tradition, historians have criticized this as a severe mistake in planning, but overlooked that the organization henceforth had less of a military and more a political function. It was trying to help prevent an "Italian scenario", forestalling a demoralization of its supporters by persuading them of a military power that had in truth become obsolete. Simultaneously, the *Schutzbund* was meant to form a refuge for the radicalized parts of the social democratic base and thus prevent an exodus. In the case of an actual coup attempt from the right, not much more would have been possible than perhaps make victory slightly more painful for the enemy. In retrospect it is astonishing how long this strategy worked: until fall of 1932. When the Dollfuß government finally followed through, however, the strategy collapsed like a house of cards.

8. The eighth and last thesis dedicates itself to the highly disputed question in historiography whether one can define the Dollfuß/Schuschnigg-regime as fascist. In a conceptual historical view, it is hard to ignore that the central actors of the dictatorship designed it according to fascist patterns. As early as the 30s, however, there were tactical reservations against the term among regime functionaries. On the one hand, the *Heimwehr*-organizations had monopolized the label "fascist" in the preceding years and especially the Christian workers' organizations that were competing with them for right-wing workers did not want to grant their rivals this symbolic victory. On the other hand, the ascription "fascist" was publicly naturally closely associated with Italy and thus it had to be avoided to be accused of betraying one's

country by getting too close to the sworn enemy – an accusation made especially by National Socialists. After 1945 these former tactical motives were reinterpreted as a principled opposition. Based on a fascist minimum, this examination argues that Austria can be seen as an example for a petty state fascism "from above", which mainly failed due to a lack of expansion options, economic and fiscal narrowmindedness, and a lack of understanding of the importance of expectation management.

3. Selected Bibliography

Boyer, John W., *Culture and Political Crisis in Vienna. Christian Socialism in Power, 1897–1918*. Chicago – London: University of Chicago Press, 1995.

Butterwegge, Christoph, *Austromarxismus und Staat. Politiktheorie und Praxis der österreichischen Sozialdemokratie zwischen den beiden Weltkriegen*. Marburg: Verlag für Arbeit und Gesellschaft, 1991.

Edmondson, Clifton Earl, *The Heimwehr and Austrian Politics, 1918–1936*. Athens – Georgia: University of Georgia Press, 1978.

Gruber, Helmut. *Red Vienna, Experiment in Working-Class Culture 1919–1934*. New York – Oxford: Oxford University Press, 1991.

Gulick, Charles A., *Austria. From Habsburg to Hitler*. Berkeley – Los Angeles, 1948.

Hautmann, Hans, *Geschichte der Rätebewegung in Österreich 1918–1924*. Wien – Zürich: Europa-Verlag, 1987.

Jeffery, Charlie, *Social Democracy in the Austrian Provinces 1918–1934. Beyond Red Vienna*. London – Madison – Teaneck: Leicester University Press, 1995.

Kirk, Tim, *Nazism and the working class in Austria*. Cambridge: Cambridge University Press, 1996.

Lauridsen, John T., *Nazism and the radical right in Austria 1918–1934*. Copenhagen: The Royal Library, 2007.

Rabinbach, Anson, *Vom Roten Wien zum Bürgerkrieg*. Wien: Löcker Verlag, 1989.

Stiefel, Dieter, *Die grosse Krise in einem kleinen Land. Österreichische Finanz- und Wirtschaftspolitik 1929–1938*. Wien – Köln – Graz: Böhlau, 1988.

Wasserman, Janek, *Black Vienna. The Radical Right in the red city, 1918–1938*. Cornell: Cornell University Press, 2014.

Linda Erker

The University of Vienna from 1933 to 1938 and the Dictatorship of Many Names. A Contribution to Fascism Studies

An installation at the 2018 exhibition *Aufbruch ins Ungewisse – Österreich seit 1918* (Into the Unknown – Austria Since 1918) held at the House of Austrian History (*Haus der Geschichte Österreichs*, HdGÖ) is entitled *Dictatorship of Many Names* and refers to the Austrian dictatorship from 1933 to 1938. According to this installation, the terms "authoritarian corporate state" (*autoritärer Ständestaat*) and "chancellor dictatorship" (*Kanzlerdiktatur*) are currently considered "terms of scholarly consensus", while "Austrofascism" (*Austrofaschismus*) is "disputed in academia" and "is now classified as politically left-wing".

What is at least true about this is that one of the major bones of contention in the discussion on the years 1933 to 1938 in Austria is indeed the historical, ideological and political classification and designation of the regime. It mostly saw itself as the "corporate state" (*Ständestaat*), while the contemporary opponents of the Dollfuss/Schuschnigg dictatorship were already characterizing it as fascist. Accordingly, the term and concept of "Austrofascism" has become established in research as an alternative to the "corporate state". In recent years, numerous other names have emerged, such as the "Dollfuss/Schuschnigg regime" or the "Dollfuss/Schuschnigg dictatorship", mainly used by those historians who wish to avoid the politically-shaped dispute and thus (supposedly) seek to neutrally circumvent taking any conceptual stance. In the context of this article, these terms are merely chosen as linguistic synonyms for the term "Austrofascism".

In my study on Austrofascism's appropriation of the University of Vienna (with comparisons with the *Universidad Central* in Madrid in Franco-Fascism), I have also used the term Austrofascism, which has to do with my research findings, which will be presented here.

83 years after the end of the Dollfuss/Schuschnigg regime, there have been numerous studies on this period and on many of its aspects. However, the developments in science and at universities between 1933 and 1938 have hitherto remained largely unexplored. In my doctoral thesis, I have sought to address this

research gap at least for the University of Vienna. I did not set myself the goal of serving the "scholarly consensus" addressed by the HdGÖ – which in my opinion is nonexistent. Rather, the aim was to investigate the developments at Austria's largest university and to make a contribution to research on fascism. The focus was on the interrelations between the political level, the University of Vienna and its officials, and teachers and students in Vienna between March 1933 and March 1938.

1.   The University of Vienna and the First Dictatorship in Austria

To better understand what happened at the University of Vienna during Austrofascism, it is first necessary to look back at the period before 1933, when politically and economically the First Republic was becoming increasingly unstable. In the early 1930s, the majority of students at the University of Vienna adhered to National Socialist ideas, supported by many anti-Semitic professors who had dominated the university since the 1920s and who had systematically thwarted the careers of Jewish and left-wing researchers. Important milestones on this road to dictatorship were the fascist Korneuburg Oath (*Korneuburger Eid*) in 1930 and the break with the civil bloc government (*Bürgerblockregierung*). Engelbert Dollfuß's decision to continue governing in the fall of 1932 on the basis of the War Economy Enabling Act (*Kriegswirtschaftliches Ermächtigungsgesetz*) then paved the way on the legislative level to the parliamentary shutdown in 1933. In March 1933, Dollfuß used the parliamentary crisis as an opportunity to put an end to constitutional democracy in Austria. The National Council was thus eliminated, and the chancellor continued to rule in authoritarian fashion from March onwards. Federal President Wilhelm Miklas remained in office. In the academic sphere, these developments and caesuras had been accompanied by the rupture in the German Student Union (*Deutsche Studentenschaft*), the Austrian students' umbrella organization: Cooperation between Catholic and National Socialist students shattered in early December 1932, after many years of collaboration and campaigning against left-wing and Jewish members of the university. It was in light of these dynamics that the dictatorship began.

A close look at the events reveals that between March 1933 and March 1938 several upheavals at the University of Vienna accompanied the transition from democracy to dictatorship and its consolidation. For the years from 1933 to 1938, three different stages of appropriation can be distinguished for the University of Vienna. The first stage was during the regime's establishment phase, which began with the elimination of parliament in March 1933, and lasted until the proclamation of the new constitution in the May and the attempted putsch in July 1934 (*Juliputsch*). During these months, the student council obtained an authoritarian structure and representatives, so-called trustees (*Sachwalter*), were appointed directly by the ministry. In addition, initial measures against both National Socialist and left-wing students were tightened. At the same time, for reasons of cost-cutting as well as political "cleansing", lasting interventions in the university's teaching staff began. In total, about 25 percent of professors' positions were eliminated, marking one of the deepest cuts in the long history of the University of Vienna: In total, of the 181 chairs that existed in the academic year of 1932/33, 43 positions (around 23 percent) had been cut without replacement during the Dollfuß/Schuschnigg regime by the academic year of 1937/38. The group of associate professors was hit hardest, their number shrinking from 74 posts to 46. Parallel to this, the number of professors emeritus rose from 36 to 69. Only the Faculty of Catholic Theology grew by two additional posts, which is not surprising considering the regime's Catholic authoritarian character. The Faculty of Medicine was the most affected, with a reduction of 21 professors (out of a total of 60), followed by the Faculty of Philosophy, with 24 (out of 86), especially between 1933 and 1936. A disproportionately high number of the professors proposed for (early) retirement by the university itself were of Jewish origin.

The second stage from the summer of 1934 onwards, up to the July Agreement (*Juliabkommen*) of 1936, represented the peak of Austrofascism at the University of Vienna. In these two years of political expansion and university restructuring, new university laws were passed that led to further curtailment of university autonomy. With the Higher Education Enabling Act (*Hochschulermächtigungsgesetz*) and the Higher Education Act (*Hochschulerziehungsgesetz*), both of which came into force on July 1, 1935, the education minister obtained the opportunity to intervene in almost all matters concerning the university. The universities were trimmed to act as educational institutions with the help of newly introduced compulsory lectures and student university camps for political training and ideological consolidation (*Hochschullager*) in the summer. Immediately after the putsch and the assassination of Engelbert Dollfuß in 1934, National Socialist students and teachers were – for the first time – pursued intensively and excluded from the university in most of the students' cases only for a limited period. Above all, the increase from 92 disciplinary proceedings at the University of Vienna in 1933 to 277 in 1934 points to an intensification of sanctions (with a total student population of 11,945 in 1934). 247 of the 277 trials were initiated for political reasons, 166 of them clearly for National Socialist activities, 39 for "leftist activity". Almost three-quarters of the university students who received disciplinary sanctions from the University of Vienna were thus National Socialists.

The third stage then began after the July Agreement of 1936 and led yet again to a noticeable softening toward National Socialist students and university staff. However, this phase lasted only about twenty months, until the Annexation

("Anschluss") and the pre-prepared *(Selbst-)Gleichschaltung* ((self-)enforced conformity) of the University of Vienna in March 1938 in line with the National Socialist regime. In summary, it can be said for the three phases that the development of the University of Vienna in some respects corresponded to that in other fascist systems (regarding political interference in university autonomy, student representation and teaching staff), but in some areas – such as the political "cleansing" of the personnel – proceedings were less rigorous in comparison with the Spanish Central University in Madrid after 1939, for instance.

2.   Between Autonomy and Adaptation

In order to form a better impression of the significance of the five-year dictatorship at the University of Vienna, it is worth comparing the findings presented here with previous research on the impact of dictatorships on higher education. Case studies presented in the book *Between Autonomy and Adaptation: Universities in the Dictatorships of the 20th Century* edited by John Connelly and Michael Grüttner (2003) on Russia, Poland, Italy, Germany and Spain show that their respective dictatorships were quick to exploit both: the traditionally important social significance and the system-stabilizing role of universities. At the same time, universities were not only appropriated top down. Rather, certain faculty and students benefited from the changes in political power or quickly learned to profit from them by adapting.

Broader analysis of these case studies reveals that the process of dictatorial takeover of the universities comprises five different measures of appropriation through which they are subjected to the new state control: First, intervening in teaching and research, but also founding new institutes and introducing new lectures establishing new ideological priorities and goals. Second, the teaching staff and the group of students are "purged" in line with ideological objectives. Third, entrance restrictions at universities guarantee selection, with the aim of producing a future student elite. Fourth, the self-government of universities is severely restricted or eliminated altogether. Fifth, the focus on national research is accompanied by a devaluation of international science and networks.

These five ideal-typical interventions and steps of appropriation can also be discerned *cum grano salis* in the development of the University of Vienna from 1933 to 1938, although the short duration of the Dollfuß/Schuschnigg regime partly limited the actual impact of individual measures. Furthermore, some of the steps were already taken before March 1933. In particular, the racist and political "cleansing" under the guise of the university's autonomy, as well as an accompanying nationalization of science and research, were significant processes that had already been a determining influence in everyday university life in the 1920s. It is also clear that these five approaches in Austria after 1933 appeared in an entangled form and built on each other. In comparison to Spain under the dictator Francisco Franco, for example, it is obvious that the political "purges" (*depuraciones*) of the group of university lecturers in Madrid were much more extensive than in Austria, not least due to the fact that in Austria in the 1930s hardly any left-wing lecturers were still teaching. Contributing factors were (academic) networks, groups and associations with great political importance and power, such as the Bear's Den (*Bärenhöhle*), the German Community (*Deutsche Gemeinschaft*) or the German Club (*Deutscher Klub*).

3. University and Fascism

All dictatorial European regimes in the first half of the twentieth century had their national characteristics. As an alternative to democracy, most of them resorted to similar elements to secure and stabilize their political power that can be described as fascist, including Austria. Fascist Studies scholars, such as António Costa Pinto and Aristotle Kallis, have refrained in their comparative analysis of the dictatorships in Greece, Austria, Portugal, Spain, and Hungary from defining the phenomena of fascism in a selective manner or from drawing up a "fascism checklist" in the sense of a "fascist minimum" (Ernst Nolte). Rather, they see fascism as a hybrid phenomenon that varies nationally, and at the same time they find common features in specific elements, such as repressive and indoctrinating practices. Indeed, the Austrian regime also pursued its own goals, which were, admittedly, comparable to those of other countries. In some spheres, Fascist Italy and Nazi Germany served as models for the Dollfuß/Schuschnigg regime, not least because of their demands for social change. Discussions in the Austrian Council of Ministers show, among other things, how important it was to emphasize the specifically Austrian character of some measures – be it the reintroduction of the death penalty in November 1933, the creation of detention camps (*Anhaltelager*) in September 1933, or the introduction of Italian as the first foreign language in schools (also in September 1933). Regarding universities, it can be added that the Dollfuß/Schuschnigg dictatorship pursued its own Austrofascist goals too – for example, in personnel policy, in the political organization of students, in the introduction of compulsory lectures at universities from July 1935 on, or in the use of violence. The term "fascism of imitation" (*Imitationsfaschismus*) does not go far enough in characterizing what happened at the universities from 1933 to 1938, because by no means was everything simply adopted like-for-like from Italy or the German Reich. Another peculiarity was that certain measures at the university, such as the anti-Semitic personnel policy, originated primarily within the institution itself and were "only" enforced by the state. In this context, therefore, a certain autonomy of the University of Vienna was still tolerated, especially since some officials and professors, such as Richard Meister, had excellent relations with the ministry and the government.

A characteristic of fascist systems is also a special form of violence, which has its own history at the University of Vienna. Even before 1933, daily academic life was strongly characterized by physical violence. The period between December 1932 and May 1933 saw the most brutal riots to date, with countless casualties. With the start of the dictatorship in March 1933, attempts were made to limit these excesses by imposing harsher disciplinary sanctions on rioting students. The spectrum ranged from the already comprehensive disciplinary measures to (threats of) dismissals or forced retirements for professors. The aim of these actions was also to force teachers who had hitherto been politically active out of the public and into the private sphere. Political repression was thus used in Austria – as in other fascist regimes – to secure state rule. The debate in the Austrian Council of Ministers about the above-mentioned establishment of detention camps (*Anhaltelager*) and the reintroduction of the death penalty in 1933 shows that in the early days of Austrofascism, the politicians tried to be particularly relentless. This was also done in distinction to the German Reich and to prove the originality of the regime: In some cases, the goal was even to 'out-Hitler' Hitler.

The Austrofascist regime exercised physical, psychological, and institutional violence, most directly through trials and subsequent in prisons and especially detention camps, where Socialists and Communists as well as National Socialists were detained. The best-known detention camp was Wöllersdorf, just under 60 kilometers from Vienna. In this and other smaller camps, quite a few students and, for a short time, even some professors were interned. Even though these camps in Austria were not genocidal and had far less drastic consequences than the Nazi concentration and extermination camps in Germany and in the later Nazi-occupied territories, they nevertheless contributed to the fascist character of the Dollfuß/Schuschnigg regime.

The staging of public appearances according to the Italian or German model was in turn supplemented in Austria by a Catholic character – for example via consecrations or field masses (*Feldmessen*). This became obvious in the fall of 1933 in the course of the General German Catholic Day (*Allgemeiner Deutscher Katholikentag*), Dollfuß's Trabrennplatz speech (*Trabrennplatzrede*), the "Türkenbefreiungsfeier" (Ceremony Commemorating the Liberation from the Ottomans in 1683), but also in the context of a rally held by the Fatherland Front (*Vaterländische Front*) in Vienna's Heldenplatz in August 1934 to mourn Dollfuß. Admittedly, these political "mass festivals" only very rarely achieved the same public impact as similar stagings in Italy, for example. On academic soil, such public appearances played an even less prominent role. The opening of the Auditorium Maximum on 14 December 1936, was one of the few large-scale events at the University of Vienna that had a bearing on the state. The regime thus did not use the university as a public platform – again in contrast to Italy, for example, where the University City (*Città Universitaria*) in Rome, built from 1932 to 1935, was very much used for fascist presentations. The same applies to the Central University in Madrid: In November 1939, the exhumed body of *Falange* founder José Primo de Rivera was transferred in a public procession across the university campus to the monumental *El Escorial* palace and monastery complex near Madrid. A few years later, the regime utilized the visit of the Argentine president's wife Eva Perón as part of her "Rainbow Tour" through Europe. Franco staged *Evita* at Madrid's university campus in June 1947, and the world public was once again confronted with Spain's Central University as a prestige project of the dictatorship. The Austrofascist government did not seek to use the University of Vienna for the purpose of self-representation. On the one hand, the university first had to be freed from the dominant (student) National Socialists. On the other hand, an international comparison also shows that Madrid, Rome, and Vienna had entirely different architectural and historical conditions for such fascist productions: In Rome, the new campus *Città Universitaria* was built from scratch, starting in 1932. Franco, in turn, symbolically demonstrated his power on the ruins of the formerly republican university, after three years of direct combat and trench warfare across the campus during the Spanish Civil War. In 1939, he laid the foundation for a new university under fascist auspices. In Vienna, however, no new campus was built. The main building of the University of Vienna has stood on the *Ring* since 1884. The greatest structural change during the five years of the Austrofascist regime remained the transformation of the sixth courtyard into the country's largest lecture hall, the *Audimax*.

Some of the most pronouncedly fascist actors were students. Especially in the first two stages of the regime up to July 1936, students loyal to the regime also took independent initiatives that they themselves understood to be fascist. The Homeland Protection (*Heimatschutz*) students, for example, stated unequivo-cally: "Fascism is not about talking the talk, one must commit one's life to it. [...]. There is no conception of the state that is not fundamentally a conception of life." ("Fascismus ist keine Redeübung, er muss ein Lebensbekenntnis sein. [...]. Es gibt keine Staatsauffassung, die nicht grundsätzlich Lebensauffassung ist.") Accordingly, their credo was: "A fascist principle: for the external enemy – the army, for the criminal – the police, for the internal political opponent – the active elite, the FASCISTS!" ("Ein fascistisches Prinzip: Für den äusseren Feind – das Heer, für den Verbrecher – die Polizei, für den inneren politischen Gegner – die aktive Elite, die FASCISTEN!"). Thus, a number of the Austrian students loyal to the regime proudly called themselves "Fascists" explicitly in the Italian spelling, which has been insufficiently addressed in the conceptual debate about the regime's character and especially in relation to self-identification in academic discourse. Many higher representatives or organizations of the regime also saw themselves as fascist or fascized. The *Vaterländische Front*, for example, interpreted the Austrian dictatorship as one "variety" of a fascist form of government and thus confirmed the image of a fascism of national character, as the term Austrofascism already emphasizes. However, according to historian Florian Wenninger, this view was suppressed by the Austrian People's Party after 1945 in order to avoid being classified as a "post-fascist group" by the Allies.

Of course, such self-definitions do not prove that this regime was fascist, because otherwise one would also have to follow its self-interpretation as the "Ständestaat". However, the references to the "fascist self-image" show, especially when dealing with the microcosm of the University of Vienna, that for certain people – such as the students who were loyal to the regime – fascist guiding ideas played an important role from 1933 to 1938. It also becomes clear that there was no fascist model of higher education that was predetermined "from above" and that there was no pre-designed prototype of a fascist university. Fascism, even in its original Italian version, was a much more heterogeneous ideological concept that also underwent a number of changes over the years. Thus no fascist model of higher education emerged for either Italy or Germany.

4. Future Research Fields: Continuities Everywhere

Women were generally among the losers of the years 1933 to 1938 compared to the First Republic, as the Austrofascist regime emphasized the importance of women primarily as mothers and housewives. Even though women were also underrepresented in the period before 1933 and after 1938 and 1945, especially at the higher levels of the hierarchy, Austrofascism tended to bring a step backwards in terms of women's advancement. In 1933/34, as in the previous decades, there was not a single woman among the 217 full and associate paid professors on the staff, and of the 780 academic employees, only 32 were women. It was only in administrative positions that the ratio was somewhat more balanced: Here, there were 110 women compared to 249 men.

Ultimately, women's scope for action at the universities – be it as students or as scholars – was mostly determined by men. Accordingly, female students barely played a role in the Austrofascist conception of the new student elite, as evidenced by the fact that the student university camps were set up solely for male students. Nor were community- and identity-building events aimed at women. In the Austrian Student Union (*Hochschülerschaft Österreichs*), the nationwide representation, women were not given any significant functions either; female student activists were more likely to be found on the left or on the National Socialist side. Examples of this were, on the one hand, the then convinced National Socialist Elisabeth Stipetić, who from 1934/35 led the university group "University of Vienna", part of the banned Nazi Student League, and from July 1935 was the leader of the illegal Working Group of National Socialist Female Students of Austria (*Arbeitsgemeinschaft nationalsozialistischer Studentinnen Österreichs*, ANSt), for which she was expelled from the university. Stipetić is an example of how women made a significant contribution, within the patriarchal structures, to National Socialist agitation against the Dollfuß/Schuschnigg regime – the *Arbeiter-Zeitung* newspaper had already declared in early 1931 that "swastika women can do it too" ("Die Hakenkreuzlerinnen können es auch"). On the other hand, one ought to mention Marie Tidl, who was the leader of the illegal United Red Student Association (*Geeinter Roten Studenten-Verband*) under Austrofascism and who also fought against National Socialism after the "Anschluss" in 1938. Future studies should consider the politically active female students at the University of Vienna and examine their political involvement in more detail. A comparison with other universities in Vienna or Austria would be just as interesting as the question as to how students approached their oppositional fight in Spain, Italy or Nazi Germany and what significance it had.

Another issue that has become clear in the discussion of the history of the University of Vienna and at the same time provides potential for further, comparative dictatorship studies: After the "Anschluss" in March 1938, many university employees who had held leadership positions under Austrofascism lost their jobs for political reasons. After the end of Nazi rule in 1945, these former supporters of the Dollfuß/Schuschnigg regime – in contrast to the teachers or students of 1938 who were expelled for racist reasons – quickly returned to leadership positions at the University of Vienna, at the Austrian Academy of Sciences (*Österreichische Akademie der Wissenschaften*, OeAW), and not least in the Ministry of Education. Former National Socialists followed them a few years later, albeit in smaller numbers. Yet women were just as scarcely represented in the group of full and associate professors in the first post-war years as they were as members of the OeAW.

After 1945, people who had successfully aligned themselves with both Austrofascism and National Socialism, but without having joined the NSDAP, played an important role as intermediaries. Such professors – for example Richard Meister or Wilhelm Czermak – contributed significantly to the re-integration of former National Socialists and to the extensive failure of the remigration of left-wing and Jewish scholars to post-war Austria. The return of several "alumni" makes it obvious that certain "black-brown" networks continued to exist in which former German nationalists, former National Socialists and former Dollfuß/Schuschnigg supporters were in contact with each other long after 1945.

These networks had an impact far beyond the boundaries of the university and thus included both the OeAW and the Ministry of Education as places of "restoration". The fact that the Austrian Cartel Association (*Österreichischer Cartellverband*, ÖCV) expelled former members of the NSDAP – such as Taras Borodajkewycz – after the Second World War cannot hide the fact that many close relationships and friendships remained (enduring all system changes). An important role in the delayed integration of former Nazis was played by the Minister of Education Heinrich Drimmel, who maintained contact with the Nazis even as a student politician under Austrofascism and, especially after 1954/55, reappointed some former members of the NSDAP to Austria's universities or helped them obtain pensions.

We can only speculate as why the effects of Austrofascism and the long shadow it cast over the universities beyond 1945 and 1955 has been received so little attention from researchers to date, in contrast to National Socialism. Personnel continuities from the period before 1938 to the period after 1945 certainly contributed to the fact that the history of the University of Vienna under the Dollfuß/ Schuschnigg regime – and thus the political repressions against members of the university, including the Austrofascist indoctrination attempts – has long remained a suppressed chapter of Austrian (university) history.

An international comparative study along the lines of the aforementioned work by Connelly and Grüttner, entitled *Universities under Dictatorship*, that would engage with "Universities after Dictatorship" would probably be worthwhile.

5.   Selected Primary Sources and Literature

Archive of the University of Vienna, Academic Senate, Special Series 185 for disciplinary proceedings.

General Archive of the Complutense University of Madrid (AGUCM), Inauguration of University City.

Connelly, John and Michael Grüttner (eds.), *Zwischen Autonomie und Anpassung. Universitäten in den Diktaturen des 20. Jahrhunderts*. Paderborn – Vienna: Schöningh, 2003.

Erker, Linda, *Die Universität Wien im Austrofaschismus. Österreichische Hochschulpolitik 1933 bis 1938, ihre Vorbedingungen und langfristigen Nachwirkungen*. Göttingen: V&R unipress, 2021.

Erker, Linda, "Fortschritt, Front und Franco-Regime: Die drei ideologischen Transformationen der Universidad Central de Madrid zwischen 1931 und 1945," in *Der Spanische Bürgerkrieg als (Anti-)Humanistisches Laboratorium. Literarische und mediale Narrative aus Spanien, Italien und Österreich, Broken Narratives Vol. 4*, edited by

Marlen Bidwell-Steiner and Birgit Wagner, 63–78. Vienna – Göttingen: V&R unipress, 2019.

Erker, Linda, "Die Rückkehr der 'Ehemaligen'. Berufliche Reintegration von früheren Nationalsozialisten im akademischen Milieu in Wien nach 1945 und 1955," *zeitgeschichte* 44 (2017) 3: 175–92.

Höflechner, Walter, *Die Baumeister des künftigen Glücks. Fragment einer Geschichte des Hochschulwesens in Österreich vom Ausgang des 19. Jahrhunderts bis in das Jahr 1938.* Graz: Akademische Druck- und Verlagsanstalt, 1988.

Huber, Andreas, *Rückkehr erwünscht. Im Nationalsozialismus aus "politischen" Gründen vertriebene Lehrende der Universität Wien.* Vienna: LIT, 2016.

Huber, Andreas et al., *Der Deutsche Klub. Austro-Nazis in der Hofburg.* Vienna: Czernin Verlag, 2020.

López, Carolina Rodríguez, *La Universidad de Madrid en el primer franquismo: ruptura y continuidad (1939–1951).* Madrid: Universidad Carlos III de Madrid, 2002.

Miranda, Jaume Claret, *El atroz desmoche. La destrucción de la Universidad española por el franquismo. 1936–1945.* Barcelona: Crítica, 2006.

Otero Carvajal, Luis Enrique et al. (eds.), *La destrucción de la ciencia en España. Depuración universitaria en el franquismo.* Madrid: Complutense, 2006.

Pinto, Costa and Aristotle Kallis (eds.), *Rethinking Fascism and Dictatorship in Europe.* Basingstoke: Palgrave Macmillian, 2014.

Ruiz Carnicer, Miguel Ángel and Juan José Carreras (eds.), *La Universidad española bajo el régimen de Franco (1939–1975).* Zaragoza: Institutión Fernando el Católico, 1991.

Taschwer, Klaus, *Hochburg des Antisemitismus. Der Niedergang der Universität Wien in der ersten Hälfte des 20. Jahrhunderts.* Vienna: Czernin Verlag, 2015.

Weinzierl, Erika, *Universität und Politik in Österreich. Antrittsvorlesung, gehalten am 11. Juni 1968 an der Universität Salzburg.* Salzburg – Munich, 1969.

Nathalie Patricia Soursos

Perceiving Fascism in Photographs of a Benign General

1. Starting Out from an Iconic Photograph

On the second of a set of marble steps stands an elderly gentleman in a suit, holding his hat in his right hand. Around fifty serious-looking people form a triangle around him, while uniformed men line the steps, holding pickaxes over their right shoulder. A Greek Orthodox priest has his back to the observer, and a rolled-up flag leans against the left pillar.

Image: Sappers and members of the Cabinet salute the PM, Ioannis Metaxas, December 26th, 1937. (Source: Hellenic Literary and Historical Archive (ELIA-MIET), 6K12.049)

The photograph shows the Greek prime minister Ioannis Metaxas while hearing the national anthem at the Labor Battalions' (*Tagmata Ergasias*) oath ceremony. The paramilitary organizations' ceremony on 26 December 1937 was hosted at the Hellenic Parliament at Syntagma Square. In a Greek newsreel, further elements of the ceremony are visible: the handover of the flag, and the Labor Battalions' parading before the high officials pushing wheelbarrows and holding pickaxes or spades. A photographer can also be spotted crossing the parade. We can recognize Ioannis Metaxas (1871–1941), prime minister of Greece, de facto dictator of the Fourth of August Regime, established on 4 August 1936. Behind Metaxas stands Kostas Kotzias, minister of the Administration of the Capital. On the right-hand side, in a dark coat, we can recognize Kostis Bastias, director of the Chamber of Letters and Fine Arts (*Geniki Diefthynsi Grammaton kai Kalon Technon*, established in July 1937). Above Bastias, in a lighter suit, stands Alexandros Kanellopoulos, head of the National Youth Organization (*Ethniki Organosis Neolaias*, EON, established in November 1936). Except for Metaxas in the centre and a group in the right-hand corner, everyone (even the priest) is raising their right arm for a Roman or Fascist Salute, or a Hitler or Aryan Salute. It is striking that on closer inspection, not all the raised hands are pointed towards the dictator, or even pointing in the same direction or lifted at the same angle.

A number of photographs documenting this scene have survived. They reveal that either the photographer moved around or several photographers were positioned next to each other. For the iconic picture, the photographer chose an angle from the bottom of the steps, looking upwards. The original glass plate, size 13 x 18 cm, is held in the archives of the photographer Petros Poulidis at the Hellenic Broadcasting Corporation (*Elliniki Radiofonia Tileorasi*, ERT). A similar photograph was printed on December 28, 1937, on the front page of the daily newspaper *I Kathimerini*. The publication does not name the photographer. Besides the daily newspaper, it is noteworthy that the picture was not published in any of the regime's publications, including the propaganda brochures published by the undersecretary for press and tourism – *Fourth of August 1936–1938*; *Fourth of August 1938–1939*; and *Four Years of Government by I. Metaxas, 1936–1940*.

The photograph became an iconic picture symbolizing the Fourth of August Regime. It has been published in many school history books, historical studies, magazines and newspapers, and on numerous websites. One can find several reasons for this selection: Principally, it can be justified by the visually unambiguous significant of the Roman Salute. The closeness of the Metaxas dictatorship to Italian Fascism and National Socialism is immediately clear. Beyond that, several other elements characterizing the regime – the leader cult, the EON, the Church, the military, censorship of the press and literature, and the anti-communism represented by the security apparatus responsible for the persecution of opponents – are depicted by the ministers and main agents of the regime's agenda. Other main elements are missing, such as King George II and the royal family. Besides the obvious fascist elements, there is no reason for the iconic status of this picture. Neither the aesthetic nor the event depicted is extraordinary. In my opinion, his picture is thus a paradigmatic example of the difficulties in classifying "small dictatorships" within fascist studies.

In my dissertation, I compared in detail the Fourth of August Regime, a 'smaller' copycat of Italian Fascism, with the 'original' on the level of photography. They might seem beyond comparison, as they barely appear to have similarities. How can one compare Metaxas' Greece, a country with a few photo studios, a handful of photo reporters and some artists working for the undersecretary for press and tourism with Fascist Italy, a much more experienced user of this new medium, a regime that specialized in staging political events, built up the Istituto LUCE after 1924 with dozens of photographers and film-makers orchestrating the regime's propaganda, worked with modernist and avant-garde artists, and was a worldwide role model in the field of visual propaganda? A comparison becomes reasonable if we focus on the pictures as genuine sources. The analysis of the photographs indicates analogies and distinctions that justify a comparative – diachronic, synchronic, and thematic – approach. Especially core visual themes – the cult of the leader, the monarchy, foreign policy, peasants, women, (mass) events, and antiquity – are fully comparable and surprisingly similar. Furthermore, I was able to illustrate that 'fascist elements' were not necessarily present in all the photographs, even in Fascist Italy. Photography in the Ventennio fascista is characterized by a broad variety of motifs, a climax building from the more conservative and less radical visual aesthetic to the perfect fascist propaganda motifs. Ultimately, visual propaganda was characterized by a boring repetition of the same motifs.

When I presented my dissertation's topic at international conferences, often my audience knew nothing about the Fourth of August Regime or the dictator, whose name many associated primarily with the famous Greek liquor *Metaxa*. The audience's lack of knowledge thus supports my argument that photographs can direct the interpretation of the Metaxas-dictatorship as fascist while simultaneously being used to downplay the regime's (and the dictator's) authoritarian and radical character. For instance, when I opened by showing the above described iconic picture, my audience immediately classified the regime as fascist. Upon closer inspection, the regime was downgraded as a second-class fascist regime due to the badly performed Roman Salute and the dictator's lack of a uniform. In this respect, the audience's reaction corresponds with the historical interpretation of the Fourth of August Regime. My argument is that visual sources allow one to relativize the authoritarian and radical character of the Greek regime. My article puts forward a careful, discursive, and comparative analysis of this iconic photograph and photography in general in order to offer further arguments for the use of visual sources in comparative analysis of authoritarian regimes.

2.   Uncertainties in the Classification of the Regime

In general historiography, and especially comparative studies of European fascism, the Fourth of August Regime is often ignored. It has long been treated as a minor example of authoritarianism, as a marginal approximation of fascism, as semi-authoritarian/semi-fascist, as an incomplete exercise in mimetic 'fascization', hybrid or radicalized conservatism, or at most a case of failed fascism. Recent studies consider the Metaxas dictatorship to have been a 'grey zone', but by no means an example of 'successful' fascism. Others, such as Aristotle Kallis, argue that the regime should be relocated firmly within the terrain of fascism studies. The uncertainties in the classification derive from the arguments: the Metaxas dictatorship did not originate in any mass movement, it was lacking a genuinely fascist revolutionary ideological core, and its non-charismatic figurehead came from a deeply conservative military background. As further allegedly non-fascist elements, authors point to the regime's pro-British foreign policy, the strong deference to the crown and king George II, the close relationship to the Greek Orthodox Church, and the lack of declared anti-Semitism. Moreover, the regime did not have any plans for territorial expansion: these had been buried in the wake of Greece's disastrous campaign in Asia Minor in 1920–22, to which Metaxas was a major opponent. Fascist elements, on the other hand, are anti-communism, anti-parliamentarism, and some elements transferred from fascism, such as the national youth organization, the EON, which resembled the Opera Nazionale Balilla and the Hitler Youth, and their symbols, the Cretan double axe and the Roman Salute. Another element was the policy of the Third Hellenic Civilization (invented by the regime), symbolizing a three-step history from classical Hellas (especially Sparta), Byzantium and Metaxas' 'new Greece' and influenced by the German Third Reich and the Italian Terza Roma. Although ideologically far less 'revolutionary' compared to Italian Fascism or German National Socialism, Metaxas was clearly attempting to transform the Greek mind towards a new order by understanding his regime as a long-term project. A radicalization and shift of power in 1938 is evident. The transformation project could thus not be completed by the dictator due to his death in January 1941, nor by his successors due to the occupation of Greece by Germany, Italy, and Bulgaria in April 1941.

The most irritating aspect for the classification of the regime is Ioannis Metaxas himself. Our iconic picture chooses a popular motif regularly used for demonstrations of power: a staging around the leader on steps. At the Nuremberg Rally in 1936, Adolf Hitler was photographed heading down a flight of steps accompanied by his ministers and surrounded by the Wehrmacht forming a strict guard. In the painting by Jurij Petrowitsch Kugatsch (1950), Josef Stalin is standing at the top of a flight of steps surrounded by applauding people. In comparison, in posture and facial expression Metaxas is the opposite of a staged leader. His position on the steps emphasizes his average height (estimated at around 1.65 meters). In the event that a ranking is of interest: Engelbert Dollfuss was 1.50 m, Franco 1.63 m, Mussolini 1.69 m, and Hitler 1.75 m. Unlike the majority of dictators of his time, Ioannis Metaxas propagated a paternal profile rather than a military-martial image. In 1936, he could look back on a fruitful career in the military until his resignation in 1920, two exiles in Italy and France, and a mostly unsuccessful political career as leader of the minor Free Opinion Party (*Eleftherofrones*). He was a prominent royalist, with close ties to kings Constantine I (1868–1923) and George II (1890–1947). During the Fourth of August Regime, propaganda concentrated on promulgating the notion of the 65-year-old dictator as the nation's father and grandfather: at once friendly and strict. This paternalistic mind-set was visually reflected in photographs. A further irritation is Metaxas' clothes. The Greek dictator refused to wear his general's uniform, even after Greece was forced to enter the war against Italy in October 1941; he instead donned a suit and a hat. While Mussolini adjusted his clothing to his roles (especially in the early 1920s, not without being sneered at), wearing a top hat as premier minister, on some occasions dressing as dandy in a white suit, on others as military icon and leader in uniform with a helmet, Metaxas was stable and did not adjust his clothes to the roles orchestrated by the regime's propaganda mechanisms as 'First Peasant' (*Protos Agrotis*) and 'First Worker' (*Protos Ergatis*). Instead, the regime's propaganda institution made a concerted effort to promote the image of Metaxas as a charismatic leader in order to compensate for his chronic weakness as a political communicator. Contrary to his modest, benign and harmless appearance, written sources such as his diary show an over-ambitious, power-hungry and vindictive man, as Gunnar Hering points out.

The depicted Labor Battalions were established under the command of Kostas Kotzias as occupation for unemployed men. Their subordination under the undersecretary of public security, Konstantinos Maniadakis, revealed their main purpose as a paramilitary organization in the service of the regime. Maniadakis reorganized the security police and launched the efficient and brutal persecution, torture, and execution of opponents, especially communists. Mismanagement and several rumors and controversies put an end to the Battalions. In November 1939, they were incorporated into the EON, which had already incorporated and replaced preexisting youth organizations; EON membership was made compulsory for children. These measures strengthened the EON's function as a broad political base for mobilizing fanatical support for the regime while largely retaining the Battalions' other use as a 'praetorian guard' and a network of informers. By 1940, the supposedly voluntary youth organization had become a true mass organization reaching 1,200,000. On the surface, the uniformed Labor Battalions and the EON mainly took part in the August 4 and May 1 parades. Images of marches and festivities are an integral part of the iconography of the Fourth of August Regime (and fascism in general). Strikingly similar images can be seen in the photo collages of the Slovak Hlinka Youth. The Roman Salute was depicted in photographs mainly in connection with the EON and the Labor Battalions. Metaxas is never seen returning the greeting. In written sources, the greeting is rarely discussed. Although the Roman Salute was supposed to be enforced in Greek schools, it was not implemented strictly. A few other photographs, interestingly in a similar setting as our iconic picture, illustrate a rather sloppy use of the greeting. This less strict performance should thus not be misunderstood as an act of resistance against the regime; the Roman Salute was a clear reference to fascism. The most interesting aspect is the fact that those pictures were avoided in the regime's brochures.

The Labor Battalions and the EON hardly cover their prototypes, the Nazi German Sturmabteilung (SA) and the Italian Fascist Milizia Volontaria, the Hitler Youth, and the Opera Nazionale Ballila – prototypes presumably well studied by the regime's main agents, especially by the Germanophile Kostas Kotzias, who often played host to German visitors. Kotzias was the only member of the Metaxas government to have met Göring, Goebbels, and Hitler personally. Photographs of Joseph Goebbels' visits to Greece in September 1936 and April 1939 connect the regime directly to National Socialism. After 1945, ties with Nazi Germany were overemphasized, with extensive use of photographs of Goebbels' visits. The mainly private nature of these visits thus remains hidden. From Goebbels' diaries, it is possible to discern his positive feelings for the Greek landscape and ancient culture, and to a lesser extent his thoughts about the regime and its representatives, whose neutral course in foreign policy was criticized by the German propaganda minister. In general, Metaxas rejected these *prima facie* connections with the fascist regimes or at least he deliberately toned down his pro-German tendencies vis-à-vis the king, the British, and the public, whereas the regime showed some interest in the constitutional and social experiments introduced by António de Oliveira Salazar in Portugal. By taking into account the published photographs (especially those in the regime's propaganda brochures), the Balkan Entente (a defensive pact between Greece, Turkey, Yugoslavia, and Romania) was of much greater importance. In fact, the meetings of the Balkan Entente and the visits to and from Turkey and Egypt are the only printed photographs addressing foreign policy. This ambivalent dealing with fascism – obvious borrowings on the one hand and the denial of any contact on the other – is characteristic of the Fourth of August Regime. A closer analysis of other published photographs can therefore help to paint a more realistic picture of the regime's foreign policy.

Absent in the iconic picture is the Greek monarch, an ambivalent figure whose role has been downplayed by historiography. King George II is said to have taken a dim view of the fascist greeting, to have avoided the August 4 events, and to have appeared on photographs mainly in the context of royal, cultural, or military occasions. King George's position thus is underplayed and limited to his pro-British connections. He had returned from his long exile in London in October 1935 after a military coup d'état reinstated the monarchy, and was poorly connected in the world of Greek politics. Nevertheless, he was an important factor for the establishment and development of the Fourth of August Regime, at least until the summer of 1938, when a shift in the balance of power towards Metaxas is noticeable, and for the continuation of the regime after Metaxas' death. What stands out in visual sources is the staged partnership with Metaxas bowing before the king. Comparative motives can be found in Italy and even Germany: Mussolini bowed before King Vittorio Emanuele III, and Hitler before Paul von Hindenburg. Another comparable element is the uniform. In Greece, George II preferred to wear military uniform, thus emphasizing his role as commander-in-chief of the Greek armed forces. The same can be said for King Vittorio Emanuele III in Fascist Italy, for whom the uniform was reserved during the regime's first decade. Beside their role as partners of the dictators, the king and the royal family had their own visual traditions. As Alexis Schwarzenbach shows, with their multi-layered visual tradition from portraits to the tabloid press, the European monarchies emphasize their continuity. During the Fourth of August regime, photographs of royal families were a major topic in the illustrated press. After marrying Friederica of Hanover in January 1938, King George's successor to the throne, Paul I (1901–64) was, often depicted on the cover of the regimes' youth magazine *I Neolaia*. He and Frederica also accepted the fascist greeting by the EON – at least in visual sources. As *general leader* of the EON (with the royal princesses leading the equivalent girls' organizations), Paul I and the royal family were presented as a part of the regime. This extends to the dictator's daughters and sons-in-law, who held core positions (especially in the EON). Although they were depicted in the press, their role as heirs is not comparable with the well-rooted royal tradition. By taking into account royal traditions, the (visual) royal protocol, the king's role in authoritarian and fascist regimes was much more important than historiography has suggested. The monarchy has to be re-introduced to comparative fascist studies.

A further missing feature in our iconic photograph is the people, the masses. The regime was not based on a mass movement and had its difficulties generating genuinely popular support. It thus showed a strong willingness to stage the presence of mass support at official events – especially those celebrating August 4 in the Panathenaic Stadium in Athens. Afterwards, the propaganda department intensively published photographs of those events. The photographs' perspective thus (unwittingly) shows the end of the crowd within (!) the frames. In Fascist Italy, festive gatherings and the state-orchestrated speeches by Mussolini were indeed mass events. The fascist regime invested significant amounts of money and organizational efforts in them, since they constituted an integral part of Fascist self-representation and were promoted as an important moment of ideological fusion between the *Duce* and his people. All of these events were photographed taking into account modern aestheticizing techniques such as lighting and camera angle. The presence of the camera influenced the festive experience, provoked certain individual and crowd behavior and added another layer of performance to the events. At the same time, institutions monitored and guided the production, distribution, and interpretation of images. Afterwards, the pictures circulated in the press influencing the retrospective understanding of the event and the narration of the viewer as part of the festive crowd. The illustrated press used several effects, especially photo-collages, photomontages and fold-outs in order to show the "never-ending" fascist mass. In addition, the mass phenomena were artistically transformed in exhibitions, as has been shown by Nanni Baltzer and Jeffrey Schnapp. In Greece, the Metaxas propaganda was inspired by these multilayered events and photographs from Fascist Italy and later National Socialist Germany, and also experimented with photography and simple photo collages. In general the multiple levels of political staging before, during, and after an event were central for erecting and stabilizing fascist regimes. On a second level, the massive reliance on visual materials provided fascist regimes around the world with a common language that helped frame a unified self-image of power. After 1945, perfectly staged photographs were used as synonyms for totalitarian leadership that still resonate today. Therefore historians must consider the unaesthetic, untidy and heterogeneous elements of the mass events as well as smaller festivities, which are easily disregarded, as Linda Conze points out in her analysis of May Day festivities in Germany and the visually less appealing photographs of these events. It is obvious that the Greek crowd was indeed much smaller and the aesthetic was not as elaborated. By comparison with Leni Riefenstahl's photographs, the staging of which was perfect (even in the context of fascist propaganda), one is led to focus on the Fourth of August Regime's pale imitation skills and to forget that for Greece, the motif of 'the masses in dialogue with the dictator' was innovative but ultimately expresses the same level of ideological intensity. The way our iconic picture was handled particularly illustrates the triumph of the mass media, especially the visual media, and the high level of success of German and Italian propaganda photographs, which guide our interpretation of fascism and its charismatic leaders to this day. The reasons for this influence of iconic photographs have notably been discussed since the rise of visual history, *Bildwissenschaft* or *Bildforschung* and the pictorial turn in the 1980s.

3.   The Photographer's Role in Dictatorships

Photographs are often willingly interpreted as an 'imprint of reality', as if the photograph is not an artifact of a human being who bought the film, chose the field of view, and pressed the release at a certain moment. In the interwar years, photographers worked in studios, as photo-reporters, and/or as artists experimenting with the capabilities of the medium. Most photographers (both male and female) worked for several clients under diverse production conditions and their products were disseminated in a variety of ways. Photographs were shown in exhibitions, printed in the (illustrated) press and re-used for postcards or photo-collages. The photographers' working situation must therefore be taken into greater consideration in visual history studies.

Our iconic picture's photographer, Petros Poulidis (1885–1967), was originally from Epirus. He learned his profession in Constantinople. In 1903 he arrived in Athens, where he became a self-taught photo reporter – and presumably "the first photo reporter in Greece", as he himself signed his work. He opened his first photographic studio in Athens in 1916, married in 1920, and became a father to eight children. In 1929, he founded the Greek Union of Photoreporters and Cinematographers together with the photo reporters Vassileios Tsakirakis, Kyriakos Kourbetis, Manolis Megalokonomou, and Dimitris Yangoglou. Poulidis is considered a talented recorder of the interwar years. He worked for Greek and foreign newspapers and for international agencies such as Keystone and Reuters. Beside political daily business, Poulidis documented fundamental changes in Greek society, such as the rise of the urban working and the middle class. Ioannis Metaxas can be found in his archive as a member of the Greek political elite since the 1920s. Under the Fourth of August Regime, Poulidis photographed Metaxas at parades and in several group pictures. It is unknown whether he also took photographs for the regime's brochures or for the richly illustrated youth magazine *I Neolaia*. One can thus generally say that Poulidis' photographic aesthetic does not imitate any of the European fascists' styles and models, of which he was surely aware. For instance, in our photograph, the photographers' position makes the steps look slightly diagonal. The triangular staging, which could have been supported by the building's architecture, the steps and pillars, and the formation of the uniformed men and their raised hands, thus fails to heighten the picture's overall impression. As John Stathatos states, it seems as if Poulidis took a business-as-usual approach as a mere recorder of events.

In contrast, the comparably well-studied photographer, Elli Seraidari (1899–1998) (whose works bore the label "Nelly's"), depicted events such as the August 4 celebrations over several days and in perfect settings, in order to guarantee well-exposed portraits of young attendees and dancing scenes from different angles. Seraidari later made albums, printed the pictures in the regime's periodicals, and created collages, which were exhibited. She also photographed the portraits of Metaxas and King George II. While older portraits by Georgios Boucas and Nikos Zografos focused on the leaders' strengths, Seraidari photographed both from the same angle, with similar lightning and facial expressions: a visual partnership of power. In particular, her "comparisons" or "parallelisms"– photographs of contemporary Greeks alongside ancient monuments that accentuate their striking resemblance – are inspired by German studies of race. The connection is obvious in an article by Michel Doris in the journal *In Griechenland* (1937) entitled "Die Griechische Rasse" ("The Greek Race") and illustrated with "Nelly's" photographs. Seraidari was educated in Dresden at the studios of Hugo Erfurth and Franz Fiedler. During the interwar years, she regularly went to Germany, and even met Joseph Goebbels. These relations made her a perfect example of Nazi-inspired photography in Greece, a Greek Leni Riefenstahl, who Seraidari also met. She herself rejected that role and emphasized in her auto-biography and in later interviews her political naivety. Furthermore, she narrates that the Gestapo stole photographs and film reels from her hotel room in Germany. Another film reel from Crete, sent to Germany to be developed, got lost. She suspected that two German spies she met earlier in Crete were responsible for the loss. Historians have yet to verify her stories. Many questions regarding her collaboration with the undersecretary for press and tourism remain unanswered. Some photographs in regime publications were presumably taken by her, but have yet to be integrated into her opus. Hence research and the Greek public are reluctant to accuse the well-known photographer of sympathizing with fascist aesthetics.

As Rolf Sachsse points out, living and working in a regime is not enough reason for a clear classification of photographers. Of central importance is the context of production, the photographer's biography, and his visually and verbally expressed opinion about a regime as well as his or her cooperation with it. In analyzing the pictures, one has to focus on the conventions, on variations on the norm, and the staging of the depicted scene. For Greek historiography, the production conditions as well as mechanisms of indoctrinations and censorship are almost unknown, largely because the archives of the undersecretary for press and tourism have been destroyed, but also because the photographers' names were seldom printed next to their image. Furthermore, there are only a few (written) ego-documents for Greek photographers that would enable researchers to analyze their cooperation with the regime and transfer from other regimes. Neither do we know much about the dissemination of illustrated press from Europe about foreign (amateur and professional) photographers visiting Greece or about the reciprocal influences between various forms of image production.

Walter Benjamin claimed that the camera produces images embedded with what the photographer intended to capture in the frame, but also with what evaded his gaze but nevertheless managed to penetrate to the picture's surface. This enables photographs to be re-examined at any time, allowing for new discoveries and changing the determination of the past in relation to them. Researchers should take a closer look at the pictures and the photographer's archive – the picture's reverse, stamps, its titling and categorization (for instance in albums), the negatives and the photographer's other (unpublished) work. The disadvantage of the destroyed archives in Greece turned out to be an advantage, as I was able to focus on smaller existing collections such as albums donated to Metaxas in the archives of the Hellenic Parliament. There are thus archives from Greek photographers – for example, the archive of the Megalokonomou brothers or the abovementioned members of the Greek Union of Photoreporters and Cinematographers – which remain unexplored. Hitherto, examinations of photography in twentieth-century dictatorships have primarily focused on state-controlled image production, but it is certainly worth taking a broader look at the full spectrum of photography, ranging from propaganda to amateur photography, published photographs, unpublished negatives, and exhibitions. By analyzing iconic images, we can re-interpret the interwar years. I would like to make a passionate plea for the careful, sensible and responsible use of photographs in historical research, including detailed picture analysis. We should question our visual memory, especially iconic pictures, by comparing and by letting other (not as easily accessible) photographs guide our interpretation. Then visual history can be more than an illustrative contribution to comparative fascist studies.

4.   Selected Bibliography

Antola, Alessandra, "Photographing Mussolini," in *The Cult of the Duce. Mussolini and the Italians,* edited by Stephen Gundle et al., 178–192. Manchester: Manchester University Press, 2013.

Baltzer, Nanni, *Die Fotomontage im faschistischen Italien. Aspekte der Propaganda unter Mussolini.* Berlin: De Gruyter, 2015, (Studies in Theory and History of Photography 3).

Chatziiosiph, Christos, "Koinovoulio kai diktatoria," in Istoria tis Elladas tou 20ou aiona. 1922–1940, vol. B2, edited by Christos Chatziiosiph, 37–124. Athens: Vivliorama Ekdoseis, 2007.

Cliadakis, Harry C., "The Political and Diplomatic Background to the Metaxas Dictatorship 1935-1936," *Journal of Contemporary History* 14 (1979): 117-138.

Close, D. H., "The Character of the Metaxas Dictatorship. An International Perspective," *Centre of Contemporary Greek Studies* 3 (1991): 1-42.

Conze, Linda, "Filling the Frame: Photography of May Day Crowds during the Early Nazi Era," *Journal of Modern European History* 16 (2018): 463-486.

Falasca-Zamponi, Simonetta, *Fascist Spectacle. The Aesthetics of Power in Mussolini's Italy.* Berkeley: Univ of California Press, 1997, (Studies on the History of Society and Culture 28).

Fleischer, Hagen (ed.), *I Ellada '36-'49. Apo ti diktatoria ston Emfylio. Tomes kai synecheies.* Athens: Kastaniotis, 2003.

Gundle, Stephen et al. (eds.), *The cult of the Duce. Mussolini and the Italians.* Manchester: Manchester University Press, 2013.

Metaxas, Ioannis, *Logoi kai skepseis. 1936-1941.* Athens: Govostis, 1969.

Metaxas, Ioannis and Siphnaios Panagiogis M. (eds.), *Ioannis Metaxas. To prosopiko tou imerologio,* vol. 4. Athens: Govostis, 2005.

Hering, Gunnar, "Rache am Vaterland? Anmerkungen zur Persönlichkeit des Ioannis Metaxas," in: *Byzantios. Festschrift für Herbert Hunger zum 70. Geburtstag,* edited by Wolfram Hörandner and Herbert Hunger, 121-136. Vienna: Fassbaender Verlag, 1984.

Higham, Robin and Thanos Veremis (eds.), *The Metaxas Dictatorship. Aspects of Greece 1936-1940.* Athens: Sunflower University Press, 1993.

Kallis, Aristotle A., "Neither Fascist nor Authoritarian. The 4th of August Regime in Greece (1936-1941) and the Dynamics of Fascistisation in 1930s Europe," *East Central Europe* 37 (2010): 303-330.

Kofas, Jon V., *Authoritarianism in Greece. The Metaxas Regime.* Boulder: East European Monographs, 1983, (East European monographs 133).

Koskina, Katherina (ed.), *Nelly's. A great Greek Photographer.* Athens 1999.

Lazzaro, Claudia (ed.), *Donatello among the Blackshirts. History and modernity in the visual culture of Fascist Italy.* Ithaca: Cornell University Press, 2005.

Machaira, Eleni, *I Neolaia tis 4is Avgoustou. Fotografies.* Athens, 1987.

Marder, Everett J., "The Second Reign of George II. His Role in Politics," *Southeastern Europe* 2 (1975) 1: 53-69.

Metton, Bertrand, "Youth Movements, Nazism, and War. Photography and the Making of a Slovak Future in World War II (1939-1944)," in *Visualizing Fascism. The Twentieth-Century Rise of the Global Right,* edited by Julia Adeney Thomas and Geoff Eley, 211-235. Durham – London: Duke University Press, 2020.

Nelly's and Kasdagles, Emmanuel, *Aftoprosopografia.* Athens 1989.

Harder, Matthias (eds.), *Nelly. Dresden – Athens – New York,* 97-103. München – London – New York: Prestel, 2001.

Nitz, Wenke, *Führer und Duce. Politische Machtinszenierungen im nationalsozialistischen Deutschland und im faschistischen Italien.* Köln: Böhlau, 2013, (Italien in der Moderne 20).

Papacosma, S. Victor, "The Metaxas Dictatorship. Aspects of Greece 1936-1940," *Journal of Modern Greek Studies* 15 (1997) 1: 143-145.

Papaioannou, Hercules (ed.), *I elliniki fotografia kai i fotografia stin Ellada. Mia anthologia keimenon.* Athens: Nefeli, 2013.

Papastratis, Procopis, "Metaxas. A dictator of compromise," *Portuguese Journal of Social Science* 4 (2005) 1: 27–37.

Pelt, Mogens, *Tobacco, arms and politics. Greece and Germany from world crisis to World War 1929–41.* Copenhagen: Museum Tusculanum Press, 1998, (Studies in 20th & 21st century European history 1).

Pelt, Mogens, "Stages in the Development of the 'Fourth of August' Regime in Greece," in *Rethinking Fascism and Dictatorship in Europe,* edited by António Costa Pinto and Aristotle Kallis, 198–218. New York: Palgrave, 2014.

Petrakis, Marina, *The Metaxas myth. Dictatorship and propaganda in Greece.* London: Bloomsbury Academic, 2006.

Petrides, Paulos, *E.O.N. I fasistiki neolaia tou Metaxa.* Thessaloniki: University Studio Press, 2000.

Schieder, Wolfgang, *Faschistische Diktaturen. Studien zu Italien und Deutschland.* Göttingen: Wallstein, 2008.

Schnapp, Jeffrey T., "The Mass Panorama," *Modernism/Modernity* 9 (2002) 2: 243–281.

Schwarzenbach, Alexis, "Royal Photographs. Emotions for the people," *Contemporary European History* 13 (2004) 3: 255–280.

Soursos, Nathalie Patricia, *Fotografie und Diktatur. Eine Untersuchung anhand der Diktaturen von Ioannis Metaxas in Griechenland und Benito Mussolini in Italien,* unpublished PhD. Thesis, Universität Wien 2015.

Soursos, Nathalie Patricia, "The Dictator's Photo Albums. Photography under the Metaxas Dictatorship," *Journal of Modern European History* 16 (2018): 509–526.

Spiliotis, Susanne-Sophia, "Die Metaxas-Diktatur in Griechenland 1936–1941. Ein faschistoides Regime," in *Autoritäre Regime in Ostmittel- und Südosteuropa 1919–1944,* edited by Erwin Oberländer and Rolf Ahmann, 403–430. Paderborn: Schöningh, 2001.

Vatikiotis, Panayiotis J., *Popular autocracy in Greece 1936–41. A political biography of General Ioannis Metaxas.* London: Routledge, 1998.

Veremis, Thanos (ed.), *O Metaxas kai i epochi tou.* Athens: Eurasia, 2009.

Xanthakis, Alkis, , *Istoria tis Ellinikis Fotografias 1839–1970.* Athens: Papyros, 2008.

Zacharia, Katerina, "Postcards from Metaxas' Greece. The Use of Classical Antiquity in Tourism Photography," in *Re-imagining the past. Antiquity and modern Greek culture,* edited by Demetres Tziovas, 186–208. Oxford: Oxford University Press, 2014.

Zacharia Katerina, "Nelly's Iconography of Greece," in *Camera graeca. Photographs, narratives, materialities,* edited by Philip Carabott, Yannis Hamilakis and Eleni Papargyriou, 233–256. Farnham: Routledge, 2015, (Centre for Hellenic Studies King's College London Publications 16).

Kathrin Raminger

Visuelle Repräsentationen von (Ohn-)Macht. Kunstausstellungen als politisches Instrument. Die iberischen Diktaturen Francos und Salazars im Vergleich

1.   Thema, Erkenntnisinteresse, Theorie

Mit ihrer Machtergreifung 1933 bzw. 1939 und ihrem Zusammenbruch 1974 bzw. 1975 bildeten der portugiesische Estado Novo unter António de Oliveira Salazar und seinem Nachfolger Marcello Caetano sowie die Franco-Diktatur in Spanien die beiden langlebigsten rechtsgerichteten Diktaturen Europas im 20. Jahrhundert. Die Dissertation trägt dem Rechnung und analysiert den Beitrag offizieller Ausstellungen bildender Kunst, die als politisches Instrument zur Vermittlung, Durchsetzung, Verteidigung und Stabilisierung von Machtansprüchen nach innen und nach außen begriffen werden, zum Machterhalt der iberischen Diktaturen. Anhand ihrer Ausstellungspolitik werden zudem Brüche und Kontinuitäten innerhalb der ideologischen Positionierung der beiden Regime und ihrer internationalen Politik entlang geopolitisch determinierter Perioden vergleichend nachvollzogen.

Im Zentrum des Erkenntnisinteresses der Arbeit steht die Rolle von Kunstausstellungen im Rahmen der Herrschaftslegitimation und -stabilisierung durch die Herstellung kultureller Hegemonie[1] (Antonio Gramsci) bzw.

---

1 Antonio Gramscis Theorie der kulturellen Hegemonie entstand in den 1920er- und 1930er-Jahren unter dem Eindruck der faschistischen Machtergreifung in Italien. Ihr zufolge bildet kulturelle Hegemonie die Grundlage indirekter, auf gesellschaftlichen Konsens abzielender Machtausübung. An ihrer Herstellung sind meinungsbildende Institutionen, sog. „Hegemonieapparate", wie etwa Kirchen, Schulen und Hochschulen, Bibliotheken oder Zeitungen, zentral beteiligt. Ihre Funktion besteht darin, Normen und Werte der jeweiligen beherrschten Gesellschaft im Sinne der Machthaber zu definieren und zu organisieren, diese als dem Interesse aller dienend zu präsentieren und damit zur Herausbildung eines gesellschaftlichen Konsenses beizutragen, der wiederum die Macht der herrschenden Elite stabilisiert. Besonders der Umstand, dass kultureller Hegemonie gegenüber der Durchsetzung des Machterhalts mit Mitteln des Zwangs und der Gewalt eine größere Priorität eingeräumt wird, macht Gramscis Ansatz im Kontext der vorliegenden Fragestellung bedeutsam. Auch die Betonung des prozessualen Charakters der Herstellung von kultureller Hegemonie, welche auf der Ausverhandlung von Kompromissen zugunsten der Herrschenden innerhalb eines sich durch Konsens und Dissens ständig in Bewegung befindlichen Kräftegleichgewichts beruht, ist besonders

Dominanz[2] (Birgit Rommelspacher) gegenüber der eigenen Bevölkerung und in internationalen Beziehungen, aber auch innerhalb einer kolonialen Ordnung und im Rahmen imperialistischer Machtverhältnisse. Kunstausstellungen werden dabei nach Gramsci als „Hegemonieapparate" aufgefasst. Dem prozessualen Charakter kultureller Hegemonie im Sinne Gramscis Rechnung tragend, werden die iberischen Diktaturen dabei nicht ausschließlich als Senderinnen, sondern im Rahmen eines international operierenden Ausstellungswesens gleichermaßen als Empfängerinnen von Artikulationen kultureller Hegemonie verstanden. Das bilaterale Gefüge, innerhalb dessen die auswärtige Kulturpolitik operierte, wird als dynamisch und wechselseitig und keinesfalls als starr und einseitig – in Form einer *one way*-Beziehung – aufgefasst. So wird auch untersucht, in welcher Weise die iberischen Diktaturen in bilateralen Beziehungen bzw. im Rahmen imperialer Machtverhältnisse kulturelle Hegemonie aktiv herzustellen vermochten oder ihrerseits lediglich als Bühne hegemonialer Kulturpolitik dienten.

Als Analysegegenstand fungierten repräsentative Kunstausstellungen in Form offizieller, temporärer Wechsel- und Wanderausstellungen. Diese werden als visualisierte Artikulation politischer Interessen verstanden und in ihrer Eigenschaft als mehrdimensionale Medien der visuellen Repräsentation untersucht. Kunstausstellungen werden dabei als aktuelle Äußerung der AusstellungsmacherInnen gegenüber einem bestimmten Publikum, als repräsentative Momentaufnahme und Ort der Realitätsproduktion aufgefasst. Neben der politischen und historischen Kontextualisierung der Ausstellungen wurden diese in ihrer Eigenschaft als vielschichtiges Kommunikationsmedium analysiert, welches den AusstellungsmacherInnen mit den ihm eigenen medialen Qualitäten erlaubte, in einem prestigeträchtigen und öffentlichkeitswirksamen Rahmen eine ästhetisch inszenierte Botschaft zu vermitteln. Dabei wurden die Ausstellungen jedoch nicht aus einem kunsthistorischen Blickwinkel untersucht. Vielmehr soll die Arbeit aus kulturwissenschaftlicher Perspektive einen Beitrag zur vergleichenden historischen Diktaturforschung leisten, indem bei der Analyse der Ausstellungen ihr ideologischer Gehalt und ihre politischen Ziele im Zentrum stehen.

---

hervorzuheben. Siehe: Antonio Gramsci, *Gefängnishefte. Kritische Gesamtausgabe*, 10 Bände (Hamburg: Argument, 2012).

2 Einen mit Gramscis Konzept der kulturellen Hegemonie vergleichbaren Ansatz verfolgt Birgit Rommelspachers Theorie der Dominanz: Diese basiert, im Unterschied zur Herrschaft, welche sich in erster Linie auf Repression, Gebote und Verbote stützt, „auf weitgehende[r] Zustimmung […], indem sie sich über die sozialen Strukturen und die internalisierten Normen vermittelt, weshalb sie in eher unauffälliger Weise politische, soziale und ökonomische Hierarchien reproduziert". Vgl. Birgit Rommelspacher, *Dominanzkultur. Texte zu Fremdheit und Macht* (Berlin: Orlanda Frauenverlag, 1998), 26.

Indem Kunstausstellungen als Instrumente der offiziellen Politik gefasst werden, erfolgt auch ihre Analyse aus der Perspektive der jeweiligen AusstellungsmacherInnen. Die individuelle Rezeption einer Ausstellung durch die BesucherInnen ist objektiv kaum nachvollziehbar, ebenso wenig ist der „Erfolg" von Ausstellungspolitik objektiv messbar.[3] Obwohl also die AusstellungsmacherInnen letztlich keine endgültige Kontrolle über die Deutung des Gesehenen durch die RezipientInnen ausüben können, sind die Machtposition der AkteurInnen und ihr Vermögen, die Wahrnehmung und Interpretation des Gesehenen durch das Publikum entsprechend ihren Vorstellungen zu lenken, keinesfalls zu unterschätzen.[4] So sind Ausstellungen etwa im Sinne Mieke Bals als Statements zu verstehen: Wie jedes andere Ausstellungsobjekt ist auch das Kunstwerk mehrdeutig in seinen Bindungsmöglichkeiten. Durch die Präsentation eines Objekts unter einem vorgegebenen Thema und dem damit einhergehenden Akt der Rekontextualisierung nehmen AusstellungsmacherInnen Umdeutungen und Neuinterpretationen vor, die eine implizite Botschaft transportieren.[5] Mieke Bal bezeichnet daher die Zusammenstellung einer Ausstellung – die Auswahl und das Arrangement der Objekte – als „Geste des Zeigens" und multimedialen diskursiven Akt, der Sinn herstellt und vermittelt. Ausstellungen stellen demzufolge Behauptungen auf und sind Sprechakten gleichzusetzen, die sich an die BesucherInnen wenden. Die präsentierten Objekte fungieren als Konkretisierungen dieser Behauptungen und dienen zugleich als visueller Beleg für deren Richtigkeit. Der Blick der BetrachterInnen wird in die gewünschte Richtung gelenkt, während sich die Autorität, die spricht, nicht zu erkennen gibt und hinter den Objekten, die ihre Behauptungen belegen sollen, verbirgt. Die ausgestellten Objekte stehen demnach niemals nur für sich selbst, sondern weisen über sich hinaus auf einen übergeordneten Zusammenhang, den es zu erfassen gilt.[6] Als Spezifikum temporärer Ausstellungen ist schließlich hervorzuheben, dass diese in der Lage sind, auch kurzfristig auf besondere Anlässe und Umstände einzugehen. Temporäre Ausstellungen stellen im Vergleich zu Dauerausstellungen damit immer eine aktuelle Äußerung dar und suchen „die Interaktion aus der Zeitgenossenschaft heraus".[7]

---

3 Vgl. Roswitha Muttenthaler/Regina Wonisch, Gesten des Zeigens. Zur Repräsentation von Gender und Race in Ausstellungen, Bielefeld 2006, 40; Lisa Spanka, Zugänge zur Zeitgeschichte mit dem Museum. Methodologie einer Ausstellungsanalyse, in: Lisa Spanka/Julia Lorenzen/ Meike Haunschild (Hg.), Zugänge zur Zeitgeschichte: Bild – Raum – Text, Marburg 2016, 183– 222, 215.
4 Muttenthaler/Wonisch, Gesten des Zeigens, 40.
5 Vgl. Mieke Bal, Double Exposures. The Subject of Cultural Analysis, London/New York 1996, 2.
6 Vgl. ebd., 2–3.
7 Peter J. Schneemann, Wenn Kunst stattfindet! Über die Ausstellung als Ort und Ereignis der Kunst, in: Kai-Uwe Hemken (Hg.), Kritische Szenografie. Die Kunstausstellung im 21. Jahrhundert, Bielefeld 2015, 63–86, 68.

Wie Museen sind auch Ausstellungen Orte der (nationalen) Selbstdarstellung, Machtdemonstration und Legitimation einer neuen (politischen) Ordnung.[8] Gottfried Korff verweist auf die identitätsstiftende Leistung von Museen aufgrund ihrer Funktion als Gedächtnisspeicher und Erinnerungsort, aber auch indem sie Objekte aus der Vergangenheit zu Informationsträgern erheben; erst durch deren Präsentation in einer Ausstellung, in der sie in eine interpretierend-aktualisierende Beziehung zur Vergangenheit gesetzt werden, entfalten diese Objekte jedoch ihre zukunftsgerichtete Wirkung. Museen bzw. deren Ausstellungen fungieren damit auch als Generator einer zukunftsorientierten, identitätsstiftenden Vergegenwärtigung.[9] Sie sind demzufolge weder neutral noch objektiv, sondern Institutionen politischer Macht. Ihre Sammlungen und Präsentationen gelten nicht nur als Spiegel hegemonialer Machtverhältnisse, sondern auch als Orte ihrer Produktion und Reproduktion.[10] Der Museumsbesuch selbst wird als Ausnahmesituation und rituelle Distanz zum Alltag erfahren, die die BesucherInnen einerseits feierlich stimmt und andererseits einschüchtert.[11] Carol Duncan verweist auf den Effekt von Museums- und Ausstellungsbesuchen als Ritual der bürgerlichen Teilhabe und Kompensation für politische Passivität, im Rahmen dessen sich der Staat als wohlwollender und um Bildung und Wohlergehen seiner BürgerInnen besorgter Souverän präsentieren kann, ohne tatsächlich Macht abgeben zu müssen.[12]

Das spanische Franco-Regime und der portugiesische Estado Novo nutzten das Medium der Kunstausstellung und die damit sich ihnen eröffnende Bühne auf sehr verschiedene Weise und verfolgten dabei unterschiedliche, mehr oder weniger erfolgreiche Strategien. Diese mussten in den jeweiligen, oftmals durch geopolitische Konjunkturen und Dynamiken stark beeinflussten Regimephasen den sich verändernden Rahmenbedingungen und Problemstellungen immer wieder angepasst werden – von ihrer Institutionalisierung in der Zwischenkriegszeit über die Phase des Zweiten Weltkriegs, jene des Kalten Kriegs und jene des jeweiligen Regimeniedergangs. Entlang dieser geo- wie innenpolitisch wirk-

---

8 Vgl. Aikaterini Dori, Museum und nationale Identität. Überlegungen zur Geschichte und Gegenwart von Nationalmuseen, in: Joachim Baur (Hg.), Museumsanalyse. Methoden und Konturen eines neuen Forschungsfeldes, Bielefeld 2010, 209–222, 211–212.

9 Vgl. Gottfried Korff, Zur Eigenart der Museumsdinge, in: Gottfried Korff, Museumsdinge. Deponieren – Exponieren, Köln/Weimar/Wien 2002, 140–45, 141–142.

10 Vgl. Joachim Baur, Was ist ein Museum?, in: Joachim Baur (Hg.), Museumsanalyse. Methoden und Konturen eines neuen Forschungsfeldes, Bielefeld 2010, 15–48, 38.

11 Vgl. Walter Grasskamp, Museumsgründer und Museumsstürmer. Zur Sozialgeschichte des Kunstmuseums, München 1981, 39–40; Krzysztof Pomian, Der Ursprung des Museums. Vom Sammeln, Berlin 1998, 69–70.

12 Vgl. Carol Duncan, Art Museums and the Ritual of Citizenship, in: Ivan Karp/Steven D. Lavine (Hg.), Exhibiting Cultures. The Poetics and Politics of Museum Display, Washington/London 1991, 88–103, 94.

samen Bruchlinien und historischen Perioden werden die ausstellungspoliti-
schen Strategien der beiden Diktaturen einander gegenübergestellt und vergleichend analysiert. Der Rolle von Kunstausstellungen im Rahmen kolonialer
bzw. imperialistischer Ausstellungspolitik der iberischen Diktaturen wurde ein
chronologisch übergreifendes Kapitel gewidmet.[13]

2.   Methode

Die bei der Ausstellungsanalyse angewandte Methode beruht auf dem Modell
Thomas Thiemeyers. Dieser versteht Ausstellungen als historische Traditions-
quellen, „die mit der Absicht erstellt wurden, ausgewählte Erkenntnisse zu vermitteln", und schlussfolgert daraus, dass auch eine Ausstellung als Analysegegenstand zu einem Fall für die historische Quellenkritik werden kann.[14] Im
Rahmen der von Thiemeyer erarbeiteten hermeneutischen Methodik können
sowohl aktuelle als auch vergangene Ausstellungen untersucht werden, wobei
letztere den Untersuchungsgegenstand der historischen Museumsanalyse bilden
– ein Forschungsfeld, in das sich auch die vorliegende Arbeit einordnet: Im
Anschluss an die Auswahl der Analysegruppe[15] erfolgte die Untersuchung der

---

13 Die beiden Begriffe werden gemäß der Definition von Jürgen Osterhammel und Jan C.
  Jansen verwendet. Sie definieren Kolonialismus als „eine Herrschaftsbeziehung zwischen
  Kollektiven, bei welcher die fundamentalen Entscheidungen über die Lebensführung der
  Kolonisierten durch eine kulturell andersartige und kaum anpassungswillige Minderheit
  von Kolonialherren unter vorrangiger Berücksichtigung externer Interessen getroffen und
  tatsächlich durchgesetzt werden. Damit verbinden sich in der Neuzeit in der Regel sen-
  dungsideologische Rechtfertigungsdoktrinen, die auf der Überzeugung der Kolonialherren
  von ihrer eigenen kulturellen Höherwertigkeit beruhen." Imperialismus hat demgegenüber
  eine umfassendere Bedeutung: „Zum Imperialismus gehören auch der Wille und das
  Vermögen eines imperialen Zentrums, die eigenen nationalstaatlichen Interessen immer
  wieder als imperiale zu definieren und sie in der Anarchie des internationalen Systems
  weltweit geltend zu machen. Imperialismus impliziert also nicht bloß Kolonialpolitik,
  sondern ‚Weltpolitik' […]". Jürgen Osterhammel/Jan C. Jansen, Kolonialismus. Geschichte,
  Formen, Folgen, München 2010, 20 und 27–28.
14 Thomas Thiemeyer, Geschichtswissenschaft: Das Museum als Quelle, in: Joachim Baur (Hg.),
  Museumsanalyse. Methoden und Konturen eines neuen Forschungsfeldes, Bielefeld 2010,
  73–94, 84.
15 Diese erfolgte nach den folgenden Kriterien: Die Kunstausstellungen wurden von einer offiziellen oder offiziösen staatlichen Stelle organisiert und ausgeführt und sind repräsentativ
  für die jeweilige Regimephase und die sie definierende innere und äußere Politik. Aus
  Gründen der Repräsentativität wurden vorrangig Gruppen- bzw. Sammelausstellungen einer
  detaillierten Analyse unterzogen, Einzelausstellungen wurden nur in Ausnahmefällen berücksichtigt. Auch zyklisch abgehaltene Ausstellungen wie Biennalen, Triennalen, Akade-
  mieausstellungen bzw. Salons etc. wurden nicht analysiert. Dasselbe gilt für nationale Repräsentationen auf Weltausstellungen. Untersucht wurden des Weiteren lediglich temporäre
  Ausstellungen, die in Groß- und Hauptstädten zu sehen waren.

Ausstellungen entlang der von Thiemeyer formulierten Leitfragen[16] daher primär anhand bisher unpublizierter Archivquellen[17] und publizierter Primärquellen wie der Ausstellungskataloge, zeitgenössischer Presseberichte, zeitgenössischer kunsttheoretischer und (kultur-)politischer Schriften sowie auf Basis von Sekundärliteratur. Die Vorgehensweise bei der historischen Ausstellungsanalyse kommt dadurch, so Thiemeyer, dem „klassischen Forschungsfeld des Historikers besonders nahe".[18] Sie ist jedoch abhängig von der Überlieferungslage. Der eigentliche Untersuchungsgegenstand, die Ausstellung selbst, kann anhand von Fotografien und anderen Abbildungen höchstens ausschnitthaft betrachtet und rekonstruiert werden: „Die noch vorhandenen fragmentarischen Spuren aufzufinden und zu deuten, ist das Metier der historischen Ausstellungsanalyse."[19]

3.   Franquismus und Salazarismus: Machtergreifung, Machtapparat und Ideologie

Sowohl die franquistische als auch die salazaristische Diktatur haben ihren Ursprung in einem Militärputsch gegen die liberale Republik, welche in Spanien 1931 auf die siebenjährige Militärdiktatur unter General Miguel Primo de Rivera (1870–1930) folgte und in Portugal am 5. Oktober 1910 nach dem Sturz der konstitutionellen Monarchie ausgerufen wurde. Weder die Machtergreifung Francisco Francos (1892–1975) noch jene António de Oliveira Salazars (1889–1970) basierte demnach auf einer Massenbewegung mit breiter Unterstützung in der Bevölkerung. Im Gegensatz zu Spanien, wo der Putsch des Militärs gegen die Republik am 18. Juli 1936 in einen rund dreijährigen Bürgerkrieg mündete, verliefen der als *Revolução Nacional* (Nationale Revolution) bezeichnete Putsch

---

16 Neben der AutorIn der Quelle und dessen/deren Handlungsposition werden die AdressatInnen der Quelle, Entstehungsdatum und -ort sowie Entstehungssituation und Wirkungsort der Quelle identifiziert; darüber hinaus der Zweck der Quelle – die der Ausstellung zugrundeliegende Motivation – und zentrale Begriffe der Quelle – Themen, die im Zentrum der Ausstellung stehen. Zuletzt gilt es, die Form der Quelle – deren sinnlich-visuelle Inszenierung sowie formalen Aufbau – zu analysieren.

17 Folgende Archive wurden konsultiert: Madrid: Archivo General de la Administración Española (AGA), Archivo del Ministerio para Asuntos Exteriores (AMAE); Lissabon: Arquivo Histórico Ultramarino (AHU), Arquivo do Museu Nacional de Arte Antiga (MNAA), Arquivo Nacional da Torre do Tombo (ANTT); Berlin: Historisches Archiv der Preußischen Akademie der Künste (PrAdK), Ibero-Amerikanisches Institut (IAI), Politisches Archiv des Auswärtigen Amtes (PAAA); Wien: Kunsthistorisches Museum (KHM); London: Royal Academy of Arts (RAA).

18 Thiemeyer, Geschichtswissenschaft, 80.

19 Vgl. ebd., 81.

gegen die Portugiesische Republik am 28. Mai 1926 unter General Gomes da Costa und die ihm folgende Errichtung einer Militärdiktatur jedoch unblutig. Während sich General Franco rasch an die Spitze der putschenden Generäle setzte und am 1. Oktober 1936 zum *Caudillo* des nationalen Spanien, Staatschef und *Generalísimo* der national-spanischen Streitkräfte in Personalunion proklamiert wurde, arbeitete sich Salazar ausgehend von seinem Amt als Finanzminister, das er seit April 1928 in der Militärregierung innehatte, an die Spitze des Regimes. Salazar, Jurist und Wirtschaftsprofessor an der Universität Coimbra, wurde im Juli 1932 zum *Presidente do Conselho de Ministros* (Ministerratspräsident) ernannt und nutzte diese Position, um seine Macht weiter auszudehnen und seine politische Vision Portugals, den *Estado Novo* (Neuer Staat), sukzessive in die Tat umzusetzen. Die ehemalige Militärdiktatur wurde unter seiner Führung in ein ziviles Regime umgewandelt, das Salazar selbst als *ditadura da razão* (Diktatur der Vernunft) bzw. *ditadura de direito* (Diktatur des Rechts) bezeichnete.[20] Im Unterschied zu Franco, dessen Macht auf dem militärischen Sieg über die spanische Republik fußte, legitimierte Salazar seine Diktatur durch eine Verfassung, über die er 1933 per Referendum abstimmen ließ und die die Grundlage für die Institutionalisierung des Estado Novo bildete. Auch seine persönliche Machtstellung sicherte Salazar in der Verfassung ab, indem darin festgeschrieben wurde, dass er als Ministerratspräsident keinen Wahlen unterlag, sondern lediglich vom Staatspräsidenten abgesetzt werden konnte. Seine Position an der Spitze des politischen Systems des Estado Novo konnte Salazar so bis 1968 halten, als er aufgrund seiner Regierungsunfähigkeit infolge eines Unfalls durch Marcello Caetano (1906–1980) abgelöst werden musste. Sowohl im Franquismus als auch im Salazarismus waren politische Parteien und Gewerkschaften verboten; beide Regime stützten sich auf eine Einheitspartei, während die Arbeiterschaft in national-syndikalistischen Korporativen zusammengefasst und kontrolliert wurde. Das auf der katholischen Soziallehre und der Romantisierung mittelalterlicher ständischer Strukturen basierende Element des Korporativismus als „organisch-traditionelle" Form der politischen und sozialen Repräsentation und Alternative zur modernen, liberal-demokratischen Gesellschaftsordnung bildete einen zentralen Baustein sowohl der franquistischen als auch der salazaristischen Ideologie, die sich dabei am Vorbild des italienischen Faschismus orientierten.[21] Die praktische Umsetzung des Korporativismus blieb

---

20 Vgl. Manuel Braga da Cruz, Notas para uma caracterização política do Salazarismo, in: Análise Social XVIII (1982) 72–74, 773–794, 776 und 781.
21 Siehe: António Costa Pinto, Corporatism and Dictatorships in Portugal and Spain. Comparative perspectives, in: Lucile Dreidemy et al. (Hg.), Bananen, Cola, Zeitgeschichte: Oliver Rathkolb und das lange 20. Jahrhundert, Band 1, Wien/Köln/Weimar 2015, 489–504.

jedoch sowohl im Franquismus als auch im Salazarismus nur schwach ausge-
prägt.[22]

Weder Franquismus noch Salazarismus konnten eine ausgearbeitete und in
sich kohärente Ideologie im Sinne einer geschlossenen Weltanschauung aus-
bilden.[23] Vielmehr bestand die ideologische Grundlage der beiden Regime aus
einzelnen Versatzstücken und politischen Überzeugungen. Gemeinsam war
beiden Diktaturen dabei u. a. ihr überhöhter Nationalismus, der katholische
Glaube als Fundament der nationalen Identität, eine imperialistische Grundhaltung und die korporative Verfasstheit des Staats entlang „natürlicher" Organisationseinheiten. Sowohl Franco als auch Salazar stilisierten sich zu Vertei-
digern des christlichen Abendlands und präsentierten ihr Regime als Mittel zur
jeweiligen nationalen Wiederauferstehung. Zudem waren beide Verfechter eines
unumstößlichen Antikommunismus.[24]

Die faschismustheoretische Kategorisierung von Franquismus und Salazarismus wird durch ihre lange Dauer erheblich verkompliziert, die den Diktaturen
mehrfach ideologische Anpassungen, politische Richtungswechsel sowie gesellschaftliche Zugeständnisse abverlangte. Obwohl beide Regime vor allem in der
Phase ihrer Institutionalisierung und Konsolidierung Elemente aufweisen, die
als faschistisch bzw. totalitär zu klassifizieren sind[25], werden sowohl Franquismus als auch Salazarismus in der vergleichenden Faschismusforschung weitgehend konsensual als autoritäre Regime eingeordnet.[26] Die Mehrheit der Wis-

---

22 Vgl. ebd., 504.
23 Vgl. Javier Tusell, Introducción al franquismo, in: Javier Tusell/E. Gentile/Giuliana di Febo
    (Hg.), Fascismo y franquismo cara a cara, Madrid 2004, 28; Cristina Gómez Cuesta, La
    construcción de la memoria franquista (1939–1959): Mártires, mitos y conmemoraciones, in:
    Studia historica, Historia Contemporánea 25 (2007), 87–123, 88 f.; Filipe Ribeiro de Meneses,
    Salazar. Uma biografia política, Alfragide 2010, 107.
24 Vgl. José Ignacio Lacasta-Zabalza, El Estado Novo portugués y el régimen franquista: dos
    dictaduras disímiles, in: Federico Fernández-Crehuet López (Hg.), Franquismus und Sala-
    zarismus: Legitimation durch Diktatur?, Frankfurt am Main 2008, 529–558, 530.
25 Dazu zählen neben dem Führerprinzip, auf dem beide Regime beruhten, und ideologischen
    Komponenten wie Antimarxismus, Antiparlamentarismus und Antiliberalismus auch
    Strukturen im Aufbau des Staatsapparats, die sich deutlich an faschistischen bzw. natio-
    nalsozialistischen Vorbildern orientierten: Neben der Gründung einer Einheitspartei und
    einer repressiven politischen Polizei sind das die Gründung paramilitärischer Verbände und
    Jugendorganisationen sowie der damit verbundene Versuch, die Gesellschaft im Rahmen von
    Massenorganisationen und korporativen Vereinigungen in ihrer Gesamtheit zu erfassen, zu
    kontrollieren und zu indoktrinieren. Vgl. Wolfgang Merkel, Totalitäre Regimes, in: Totali-
    tarismus und Demokratie 1 (2004) 2, 183–201, URL: http://nbn-resolving.de/urn:nbn:de:01
    68-ssoar-311968 (abgerufen 5. 10. 2021).
26 Vgl. Pinto, Corporatism and Dictatorships in Portugal and Spain, 500. Stanley Payne be-
    zeichnet den salazaristischen Estado Novo als „autoritären Korporativismus", während er das
    Franco-Regime erst nach 1943 als „autoritär" einstuft. Vgl. Stanley Payne, Geschichte des
    Faschismus. Aufstieg und Fall einer europäischen Bewegung, München/Berlin 2001, 386 und
    326. Linz ordnet ebenfalls beide Regime dem autoritären Typus zu, innerhalb dessen er

senschaftlerInnen stützt sich bei dieser Typologisierung auf die 1964 von Juan José Linz am Beispielfall des franquistischen Spaniens erarbeitete Definition, mit der er autoritäre Regime als dritten idealen Systemtypus neben Demokratien und totalitären Systemen in die politikwissenschaftliche und soziologische Totalitarismus-Diskussion einführte.[27]

4. Ergebnisse

Franco, der nicht zuletzt mithilfe militärischer Unterstützung durch das faschistische Italien und das nationalsozialistische „Dritte Reich" an die Macht gelangt war, trug seine Allianz mit den Achsenmächten auch während des Zweiten Weltkriegs stolz zur Schau. Davon zeugt exemplarisch die Abhaltung der Ausstellung „Spanische Kunst der Gegenwart" in Berlin, welche 1942 auf Initiative des Ibero-Amerikanischen Instituts zustande gekommen war. Die Ausstellung wurde vom NS-Regime wie auch vom Franco-Regime gleichermaßen euphorisch als wichtiger visueller Beleg der Freundschaft und Kooperation propagandistisch vermarktet. Demgegenüber hielt sich Salazar mit einer derartigen, weithin sichtbaren Freundschaftsbekundung gegenüber dem Deutschen Reich zurück, was auch seiner generellen Skepsis gegenüber dem nationalsozialistischen Regime Hitlers entspricht.

Francos offen achsenfreundliche Haltung, aber auch seine gewaltsame Machtergreifung im Zuge des Spanischen Bürgerkriegs (1936–1939) hatten nach 1945 zur Konsequenz, dass Spanien zunächst international boykottiert wurde und isoliert blieb. Dies wiederum beantwortete Franco mit einer kulturpolitischen Offensive; auswärtige Kulturdiplomatie fungierte für das Franco-Regime dabei notgedrungen als Ersatz-Außenpolitik. Mit der im Außenministerium angesiedelten *Dirección General de Relaciones Culturales* und der ihr unterstehen Abteilung *Sección de Exposiciones y Congresos* schuf die Diktatur einen bürokratischen Apparat, dessen primäre Aufgabe in der Organisation und

---

wiederum zwischen weiteren Regimetypen differenziert. Demnach ist das Franco-Regime eher den „Bureaucratic-Military Authoritarian Regimes" zuzuordnen, der portugiesische Estado Novo eher dem Typus „Organic Statism". Vgl. Juan José Linz, Totalitarian and Authoritarian Regimes, Boulder et al. 2000, 292 und 311.

27 Als zentrale Merkmale autoritärer Systeme gelten demnach ein begrenzter Pluralismus, keine ausgearbeitete Ideologie und keine durchgehend aufrechterhaltene intensive und extensive politische Mobilisierung. Auch müssen die Führer autoritärer Regime keine charismatischen Eigenschaften aufweisen. Vgl. Juan José Linz, Ein autoritäres Regime. Der Fall Spanien, Potsdam 2011, 19–20. Autoritäre Regime unterscheiden sich von totalitären Systemen auch durch kaum vorhandene Möglichkeiten politischer Massenpartizipation. Das geringe Mobilisierungspotenzial führt zur Depolitisierung der jeweiligen Gesellschaft und politischer Apathie. Vgl. Linz, Totalitarian and Authoritarian Regimes, 278–279.

Durchführung der kulturellen Repräsentation des Regimes nach außen bestand. Die wirtschaftlich geschwächte Diktatur bediente sich der Kunstausstellungen dabei als scheinbar apolitisches Instrument der diplomatischen Annäherung, um ihre politische und wirtschaftliche Isolation zu überwinden und dadurch in weiterer Folge ihre Machtergreifung intern zu legitimieren und das Regime zu stabilisieren. Als AdressatInnen seiner kulturellen Botschaft dienten dem Franco-Regime zunächst die wenigen ihm wohlgesonnenen Nationen – vornehmlich im arabischen und lateinamerikanischen Kulturkreis angesiedelt –, in der Hoffnung, den Kreis seiner Fürsprecher sukzessive zu erweitern und mit ihrer Hilfe den internationalen Boykott des Regimes zu durchbrechen. Dabei ging die Diktatur äußerst konsequent vor und überließ den Erfolg ihrer Kunstausstellungen, der als stellvertretend für jenen des Regimes selbst präsentiert wurde, nicht dem Zufall. Die Sondierung des Geschmacks des Zielpublikums und die Anpassung der Ausstellungsobjekte an ebendiesen zählten gerade in den Jahren seiner Isolation zur standardisierten Vorgehensweise der franquistischen AusstellungsmacherInnen. Ideologisch wurde die auswärtige Kulturpolitik des Franco-Regimes in den Jahren seiner internationalen Isolation nach 1945 durch das imperialistische Konzept der *hispanidad* untermauert, im Zuge dessen es seine historisch und kulturell begründete imperiale Vormachtstellung innerhalb eines hispanisch geprägten Kulturkreises in erster Linie gegenüber den nordafrikanischen arabischen Nationen und den ehemaligen spanischen Kolonien in Lateinamerika für sich zu reklamieren suchte.[28] Exemplarisch stehen dafür die Ausstellungen spanischer Kunst in Buenos Aires (1947) und Kairo (1950).

Nach der Überwindung seiner internationalen Isolation durch die Fürsprache der USA in internationalen Organisationen als Folge des Kalten Kriegs zögerte Franco nicht, sich an der Seite des ehemaligen Gegners zu positionieren – nunmehr geeint im Kampf gegen den Kommunismus. Dieser neuen, für beide Seiten profitablen Allianz wurde durch die wechselseitige Abhaltung von Kunstausstellungen rasch Sichtbarkeit verliehen. Zwei 1955 und 1958 in Spanien abgehaltene Ausstellungen US-amerikanischer Kunst[29] visualisieren dabei den Beitrag der USA zur innenpolitischen Stabilität des Franco-Regimes aufgrund eigener machtpolitischer Interessen und sind ein Beispiel für den erfolgreichen Einsatz auswärtiger Kulturdiplomatie bei der Durchsetzung der mit dem US-

---

28 Siehe: David Marcilhacy, La Hispanidad bajo el Franquismo. El Americanismo al servicio de un proyecto nacionalista, in: Stéphane Michonneau/Xosé M. Núñez Seixas (Hg.), Imaginarios y representaciones de España durante el franquismo, Madrid 2014, 73–102.
29 El arte moderno en los Estados Unidos. Pintura, Escultura, Grabado, Arquitectura, hg. vom Museum of Modern Art (New York), Barcelona 1955; La Nueva Pintura Americana, Madrid, Museo Nacional de Arte Moderno, 1958.

amerikanischen *Cultural Cold War* verbundenen Ziele.[30] Das Franco-Regime wiederum organisierte nach seiner erfolgreichen Rehabilitierung parallel zu gezielt konzipierten Kunstausstellungen auf bilateraler Ebene eine Reihe von Wanderausstellungen, mit denen es im Gießkannenprinzip eine weltweite Charme-Offensive der auswärtigen Kulturdiplomatie innerhalb des westlichen Blocks durchführte. Der *Informalismo*, das spanische Pendant des US-amerikanischen Abstrakten Expressionismus, mit dem das Regime unter dem Kommissariat von Luis González Robles auf den Biennalen von São Paulo 1957 und Venedig 1958 große internationale Erfolge feiern konnte, bildete das künstlerische Herzstück dieser franquistischen Kulturoffensive: Das Regime orientierte sich dabei an der Strategie der USA und deren Propagandaoffensive im Rahmen des sogenannten *Cultural Cold War*, im Zuge derer abstrakte Kunst als Gegenpol zum sozialistischen Realismus inszeniert und zum Aushängeschild demokratischer und pluralistischer Gesellschaften westlicher Prägung gekürt wurde.[31] Die franquistische Diktatur profitierte von dieser wirkungsmächtigen Zuschreibung und präsentierte den spanischen *Informalismo* ebenfalls als Visualisierung ihrer vermeintlich pluralistischen und toleranten – kurz: den Werten der westlichen demokratischen Gemeinschaft verbundenen – Politik.[32] Auch in Großbritannien, dem wichtigsten europäischen Verbündeten der USA, zeigte das Franco-Regime trotz kontinuierlicher Differenzen über Gibraltar im Rahmen einer Kunstausstellung in der renommierten Londoner Tate Gallery Präsenz, während umgekehrt auch der British Council eine beachtenswerte Aktivität in der franquistischen Diktatur entfaltete, die jener im traditionell verbündeten *oldest ally*, Portugal, durchaus ebenbürtig war. Auch das zeigt die strategische Bedeutung, die dem stramm antikommunistischen Spanien im Zuge des Kalten Krieges von den westlichen Bündnispartnern beigemessen wurde.

Der Zugehörigkeit des Salazar-Regimes zum westlichen Block wurde in Portugal demgegenüber verhältnismäßig wenig Sichtbarkeit verliehen. Zwar entwickelte der British Council eine rege Ausstellungstätigkeit in Portugal, doch der kulturdiplomatische Austausch des Regimes mit den USA beschränkte sich auf

---

30 Der Begriff *Cultural Cold War* spiegelt den *cultural turn* in den *Cold War Studies* wider und beschreibt sowohl das Phänomen der politischen Indienstnahme von Kunst und Populärkultur als Propagandainstrumente des Westens im Kalten Krieg als auch deren Einfluss auf gegnerische Gesellschaften. Vgl. Kathleen Starck, Between Fear and Freedom. Cultural Representations of the Cold War, Newcastle 2010, 2–3.

31 Siehe: Eva Cockroft, Abstract Expressionism, Weapon of the Cold War, in: Francis Frascina (Hg.), Pollock and After. The Critical Debate, New York 1985, 125–133; Max Kozloff, American Painting During the Cold War, in: Artforum 11 (1973) 9, 43–54.

32 Vgl. Kathrin Raminger, Fortschritt in abstrakter Form. Eine US-amerikanisch-spanische Annäherung in Bildern (1951–1964), in: Ilcea. Revue de l'Institut des langues et des cultures d'Europe et d'Amérique, 16 (2012) 7, URL: http://ilcea.revues.org/1327 (abgerufen 19.8. 2021).

ein Minimum. Das Druckmittel der Militärbasen auf den Azoren sowie sein traditionelles Bündnis mit Großbritannien bewahrten das salazaristische Portugal auf internationaler Ebene vor zahlreichen Herausforderungen politischer und wirtschaftlicher Natur, mit denen sich das Franco-Regime nach dem Zweiten Weltkrieg zunächst konfrontiert sah. So erhielt Portugal etwa Wirtschaftshilfe im Zuge des Marshall-Plans und zählte 1948 zu den Gründungsmitgliedern der OEEC. Gleichzeitig machte seine verteidigungspolitische Integration in die NATO kulturdiplomatische Maßnahmen zur Stabilisierung der salazaristischen Diktatur obsolet. Auch hinsichtlich seiner europäischen Integration profitierte das salazaristische Regime von seiner engen Bindung an das Vereinigte Königreich: Ihr verdankte es 1960 seine Gründungsmitgliedschaft in der EFTA, während das franquistische Spanien in Europa zwar inzwischen als politische Realität anerkannt wurde, seine Versuche, sich der 1958 gegründeten EWG anzunähern, jedoch mit Verweis auf seine undemokratische Verfasstheit zurückgewiesen wurden. Einzig die BRD vertrat die Position, durch eine Aufnahme in die Gemeinschaft könne die Demokratisierung Spaniens gefördert werden, und setzte sich für einen Beitritt des Franco-Regimes ein. Auch diese wohlwollende Haltung fand 1974, kurz vor dem Zusammenbruch des Regimes, Ausdruck im Rahmen einer Ausstellung unter dem Titel „Spanische Kunst heute" in München.

Lag der Tenor der auswärtigen Kulturpolitik Spaniens in den Jahren seiner internationalen Isolation nach dem Zweiten Weltkrieg noch auf der beinahe verzweifelt anmutenden Beschwörung der im Franco-Regime herrschenden politischen und gesellschaftlichen Normalität, um sich als Opfer einer ungerechtfertigten Bestrafung durch die Vereinten Nationen zu positionieren, ging die Diktatur nach ihrer internationalen Anerkennung in ihrer vom *Informalismo* getragenen Image-Kampagne zur Propagierung eines selbstbewussteren *„España es diferente"* (*„Spain is different"*) über. Bereits vor der Etablierung dieses werbewirksamen Tourismus-Slogans wurde die Abhaltung von Kunstausstellungen ab 1950 und damit parallel zur Einrichtung des *Ministerio de Información y Turismo* unter Gabriel Arias Salgado auch in den Dienst der touristischen Werbung gestellt. Ab Mitte der 1960er-Jahre, als sich die innen- und außenpolitische Situation des Franco-Regimes weitgehend konsolidiert hatte, die wirtschaftliche Situation saniert war und der Spanien-Tourismus boomte, sodass eine permanente Charme-Offensive durch auswärtige Kulturdiplomatie keine politische Priorität mehr darstellte, ist im Hinblick auf die Abhaltung internationaler Kunstausstellungen – sowohl im Rahmen bilateraler Beziehungen als auch im Bereich der Wanderausstellungen – ein drastischer Rückgang zu erkennen. Dies macht deutlich, dass das Franco-Regime internationale Präsenz und Sichtbarkeit durch Kunstausstellungen bewusst als Mittel zur Durchsetzung seiner zentralen Ziele, der Stabilisierung seiner politischen und wirtschaftlichen Situation, die zugleich seinen Machtanspruch legitimieren und die Zustimmung zu seinem Machterhalt fördern sollte, einsetzte. Paradoxerweise wurde jedoch gerade die mit der wirtschaftlichen Öffnung des Regimes einhergehende gesellschaftliche Modernisierung und Prosperität zum Motor für die System- und Identitätskrise des Regimes. Versuche der Herstellung und Aufrechterhaltung kultureller Hegemonie nach innen durch die Abhaltung monumentaler Kunstausstellungen in Spanien selbst sind insbesondere in Krisenzeiten wie der Phase des Regimeniedergangs ab 1969 zu beobachten. Die an die eigene Bevölkerung als Publikum adressierten Ausstellungen verfolgten primär das Ziel, eine kollektive franquistische Identität zu kreieren bzw. zu verfestigen.[33] Wie bei internationalen Ausstellungen wurde Kunst auch im Rahmen nationaler Schauen als Ergebnis des vom Franco-Regime geschaffenen gesellschaftlichen Friedens und der kulturellen Blüte Spaniens und damit wiederum als Beleg für die Legitimität der franquistischen Machtergreifung inszeniert. So präsentierte die Ausstellung „XXV Años de Arte Español" anlässlich des 25-jährigen Regimejubiläums, das 1964 unter dem Titel „XXV Años de Paz" („25 Jahre des Friedens") begangen wurde, die Ergebnisse, welche das Franco-Regime auf dem Gebiet der bildenden Kunst seit seiner Machtergreifung für sich beanspruchte, und stellte dabei eine Art Bildprogramm und künstlerische Identität des Regimes zur Schau, das den konservativen Kunstvorstellungen des Franquismus wesentlich mehr entsprach als sein fortschrittliches Erscheinungsbild im Ausland. Die im Juni 1975 eröffnete Ausstellung „La Época de la Restauración" hingegen sollte die spanische Gesellschaft auf eine franquistische Zukunft ohne die Person Francos vorbereiten. Bereits 1947 war die Diktatur im Zuge der *Ley de la Sucesión* formal in eine Monarchie umgewandelt und Mitte der 1960er-Jahre Prinz Juan Carlos als Nachfolger Francos präsentiert worden. 1975 wurde die Einleitung der sogenannten Restauration angesichts Francos schwindender Gesundheit schließlich unumgänglich. Ausstellungspolitische Initiativen wie diese waren jedoch nicht in der Lage, den gesellschaftlichen Konsens über Hegemonie und Dominanz des Franquismus konstant aufrechtzuerhalten und konnten schließlich auch den Zusammenbruch des Regimes nicht verhindern.

Den Spanien nach dem spanisch-amerikanischen Krieg von 1898 verbliebenen Kolonien und Protektoraten in Afrika widmete die Diktatur im Rahmen ihrer Ausstellungspolitik keine Aufmerksamkeit: Sie spielten für das wirtschaftliche und politische Überleben des Regimes nur eine untergeordnete Rolle. Auch innerhalb des vergangenheitsbezogenen, transzendental begründeten Konzeptes der *hispanidad* wird ihnen nur erstaunlich geringe Bedeutung beigemessen.

---

33 Siehe: Kathrin Raminger, Politik der Bilder. Offizielle Ausstellungen im Franquismus und ihre politischen Funktionen (1936–1951) (Schriften der Guernica-Gesellschaft 18), Weimar 2011.

Während das Franco-Regime also kulturelle Hegemonie primär im Zuge einer als imperialistisch einzuordnenden Ausstellungspolitik zu errichten trachtete, die seine Macht gleichermaßen nach innen wie nach außen festigen sollte, fokussierte das Salazar-Regime bei der Konstruktion kultureller Hegemonie im Rahmen seiner Ausstellungspolitik auf die kolonial verfasste eigene Nation mit dem Hauptaugenmerk auf seine Kolonien in Afrika. Dies spiegelt die enorme Bedeutung wider, die das Regime seinem Kolonialreich für sein wirtschaftliches Überleben und die ideologische Legitimation seiner Machtergreifung wie seines Machterhalts zuschrieb.[34] Außerhalb Portugals selbst und seiner Kolonien engagierte sich die salazaristische Diktatur ausstellungspolitisch dagegen kaum. Im Gegensatz zu Spanien gab es für das seit seiner Entstehung international anerkannte Salazar-Regime zunächst keinen Anlass für eine global angelegte Charme-Offensive im Zuge auswärtiger Kulturdiplomatie. Dies manifestiert sich auch in dem Umstand, dass für die Organisation von Ausstellungen entweder das der *Presidência do Conselho* und damit direkt Salazar unterstehende *Secretariado da Propaganda Nacional* (SPN)[35] oder die dem Kolonial-Ministerium untergeordnete *Agência-Geral das Colónias* (AGC, ab 1951 *Agência-Geral do Ultramar*, AGU) verantwortlich zeichneten. Ihre Ressourcen bündelte die salazaristische Diktatur daher in der Etablierung einer kolonialen Ausstellungspolitik, die sich an die portugiesische Bevölkerung sowohl in Portugal selbst als auch in den Kolonien wandte und der kolonialen Identitätskonstruktion nach innen sowie der Kohäsion des portugiesischen Imperiums unter dem kulturell determinierten Überbegriff *portugalidade*[36] dienen sollte. Die visuellen Repräsentationen des

---

34 Siehe: Fernando Rosas, Estado Novo, Império e Ideologia Imperial, in: Revista de História das Ideias 17 (1995), 19–32; Paulo S. Polanah, „The Zenith of our National History!" National identity, colonial empire, and the promotion of the Portuguese Discoveries: Portugal 1930s, in: e-Journal of Portuguese History 9 (2011) 1, 39–62, URL: http://www.brown.edu/Depart ments/Portuguese_Brazilian_Studies/ejph/html/issue17/pdf/v9n1a03.pdf (abgerufen 5.10. 2021); Valentim Alexandre, Ideologia, economia e política: A questão colonial na implantação do Estado Novo, in: Análise Social XXVIII (1993) 123–124, 1117–1136.

35 Der SPN wurde am 25. September 1933 gegründet und im November 1944 in Secretariado Nacional da Informação, Cultura Popular e Turismo (SNI) umbenannt. Unter Marcello Caetano erhielt er 1969 den Namen Secretariado de Estado da Informação e Turismo (SEIT).

36 Der Begriff Portugalidade bezieht sich auf ein nationales Identitätskonzept, das in den letzten Jahrzehnten des 19. Jahrhunderts, insbesondere rund um die Feierlichkeiten zum 300. Todestag des portugiesischen Nationaldichters Luís de Camões 1880, entstand. Die von Camões in seinen Lusíadas besungenen portugiesischen „Entdeckungen" – das portugiesische Kolonialreich – standen im Zentrum der Diskussion um eine nationale Identität. Als Mittel zur nationalen Regeneration wurde nach dem Verlust Brasiliens Portugals zukünftige Rolle als Kolonialmacht in Afrika betont. Damit war das Projekt der nationalen Identität und ihrer Erfüllung bereits als zukunftsorientiertes Projekt definiert, das eng mit dem Schicksal Portugals als Kolonialmacht verknüpft war – eine Lesart, die auch der Estado Novo weiterführen sollte. Siehe: Abdool Karim A. Vakil, Nationalising Cultural Politics: Representations of the Portuguese ‚Discoveries' and the Rhetoric of Identitarianism, 1880–1926, in: Clare Mar-

portugiesischen Imperiums und der kolonialen Hierarchien waren dabei Veränderungen unterworfen, welche der zunehmend kritischen Haltung der internationalen Gemeinschaft gegenüber der portugiesischen Kolonialpolitik Rechnung trugen: Während in den 1930er- und 1940er-Jahren die Betonung des als besonders fremd und exotisch inszenierten „Anderen" im Vordergrund stand, um die Notwendigkeit der portugiesischen Kolonialherrschaft über die „rückständigen" Völker zu illustrieren und die durch das *Indigenato*-Regime[37] etablierte Hierarchisierung der kolonialen Bevölkerung in „zivilisierte" und „unzivilisierte" BewohnerInnen visuell zu fixieren, lag der Fokus ab Mitte der 1950er-Jahre nicht mehr auf der Präsentation des Trennenden, sondern nunmehr stand, als Reaktion auf wachsende Souveränitätsbestrebungen und den internationalen Trend zur Dekolonisierung, die Zurschaustellung verbindender Elemente im Vordergrund, um die kulturelle Einheit des als „plurikontinentale" Nation imaginierten portugiesischen Imperiums zu demonstrieren.[38] Erneut bestand das Ziel jedoch in der Legitimation des portugiesischen Kolonialismus, der als modern, effizient und vor allem tolerant präsentiert wurde. Nach dem

---

Molinero/Angel Smith (Hg.), Nationalism and the Nation in the Iberian Peninsula. Competing and Conflicting Identities, Oxford/Washington 1996, 33–52; Sérgio Campos Matos, Portugal: The Nineteenth-century Debate on the Formation of the Nation, in: Portuguese Studies 13 (1997), 66–94; Nuno G. Monteiro/António Costa Pinto, Cultural Myths and Portuguese National Identity, in: António Costa Pinto (Hg.), Contemporary Portugal. Politics, Society and Culture, Boulder 2011, 55–72.

37 Durch den 1929 von der portugiesischen Militärdiktatur erlassenen Estatuto político, civil e criminial dos indígenas de Angola e Moçambique (kurz: Indigenato-Statut) wurde die indigene Bevölkerung Guineas (heute: Guinea-Bissau), Mosambiks und Angolas unter einer anderen Gesetzgebung regiert als die „assimilierte" bzw. „zivilisierte" Bevölkerung dieser Kolonien, die dem portugiesischen Gesetz unterstanden. Die Kolonien S. Tomé e Príncipe in Afrika und Timor in Asien wurden nach dem Zweiten Weltkrieg ebenfalls dem Indigenato-Regime unterstellt, während die BewohnerInnen des restlichen portugiesischen Kolonialreichs – Macau, Portugiesisch-Indien und Cabo Verde – als „zivilisiert" anerkannt wurden. Der als „indigen" kategorisierten Bevölkerung wurden die portugiesische Staatszugehörigkeit und damit verbundene Bürgerrechte verwehrt. Das segregationistische Indigenato-Statut förderte einen institutionellen und gesellschaftlichen Rassismus und diente der systematischen Unterdrückung sowie der strukturellen Diskriminierung und Ausbeutung der Bevölkerung zum Vorteil der „zivilisierten" kolonialen Elite. Vgl. Omar Ribeiro Thomaz, „The Good-Hearted Portuguese People": Anthropology of Nation, Anthropology of Empire, in: Benoit de L'Estoile/Federico G. Neiburg/Lygia Sigaud (Hg.), Empires, nations, and natives. Anthropology and state-making, Durham 2005, 58–87; Cristina Nogueira da Silva, A dimensão imperial do espaço jurídico português. Formas de imaginar a pluralidade nos espaços ultramarinos, séculos XIX e XX, in: Rechtsgeschichte 23 (2015), 187–205.

38 Vgl. Cláudia Castelo, Developing „Portuguese Africa" in late colonialism. Confronting discourses, in: Joseph M. Hodge/Gerald Hödl/Martina Kopf (Hg.), Developing Africa. Concepts and practices in twentieth-century colonialism, Manchester/New York 2014, 63–86.

Ausbruch der Kolonialkriege in Afrika[39] wurde die bereits erfolgte Assimilation der indigenen Bevölkerung insbesondere der afrikanischen Kolonien noch stärker ins Zentrum der in den Kunstaustellungen vermittelten Aussage gerückt. Sie sollte die portugiesische Öffentlichkeit vom Erfolg der schon geleisteten „zivilisatorischen" Arbeit, welcher etwa durch verwestlichte afrikanische Kunst visuell „belegt" wurde, überzeugen. Dadurch sollte das koloniale Bewusstsein geschärft und die portugiesische Öffentlichkeit für die weitere Unterstützung der Kolonialkriege gewonnen werden, denn nur dadurch ließe sich die erfolgreiche Arbeit in den Kolonien zu einem endgültigen Abschluss bringen, so das Argument der Regimepropaganda.[40] Gemäß der salazaristischen Ideologie, der zufolge die Identität des Estado Novo untrennbar mit dem Fortbestand des portugiesischen Imperiums verwoben war, bedeutete der militärische und propagandistische Kampf um sein Kolonialreich nichts weniger als den Überlebenskampf des Salazarismus selbst.

Ausstellungen portugiesischer Kunst im internationalen Ausland waren angesichts des rund 40-jährigen Bestehens des Estado Novo rar und fanden überwiegend in Portugal traditionell nahestehenden Ländern wie Großbritannien, Frankreich oder auch Spanien statt. Initiativen, diese altbewährten Muster zu überwinden und im Rahmen der auswärtigen Kulturdiplomatie neue Allianzen zu suchen und zu etablieren, sind nicht erkennbar. Symptomatisch für die Passivität des salazaristischen Ausstellungsbetriebs ist auch, dass die überwiegende Mehrheit der salazaristischen Kunstausstellungen sowohl im internationalen Ausland wie auch in den Kolonien und im kontinentalen Portugal rund um historische Jubiläen oder Anlässe wie pompös inszenierte Staatsbesuche organisiert wurden. Erst ein äußerer Anstoß war also notwendig, damit der salazaristische Propagandaapparat die Organisation einer Kunstausstellung in Betracht zog. Auch in der bilateralen Ausstellungspolitik zwischen Franco- und Salazar-Regime bildete Ersteres den deutlich aktiveren Part – allerdings abhängig von den eigenen Bedürfnissen: Obwohl geografisch aneinandergrenzend und ideologisch affin, blieb das Verhältnis der beiden letzten im Nachkriegseuropa noch bestehenden rechtsgerichteten Diktaturen, die sich im sogenannten autoritären Zeitalter der Zwischenkriegszeit etabliert hatten, über den langen Zeitraum ihrer Koexistenz mit wenigen punktuellen Ausnahmen unterkühlt. Zwar kooperierten die beiden Regime, wenn äußere Umstände es erforderten, doch

---

39 Am 4. Februar 1961 brach in Angola der bewaffnete Widerstand gegen die portugiesische Kolonialherrschaft aus, im Januar 1963 der Krieg gegen die portugiesische Kolonialmacht in Guinea (heute: Guinea-Bissau) und im September 1964 schließlich jener in Mosambik.

40 Siehe: Exposição de Arte Portuguesa, Luanda und Lourenço Marques [heute: Maputo, Anm.], 1948; Exposição da Vida e da Arte Portuguesas, Lourenço Marques [heute: Maputo, Anm.], 1956; Uma Acção de Estímulo aos Artistas Portugueses de Temática Ultramarina, Lissabon, 1974.

gingen die bilateralen Beziehungen nie über diese Form einer Zweckbeziehung hinaus. Die bilaterale Ausstellungspolitik spiegelt sowohl das gegenseitige Desinteresse, aber auch das inneriberische, mitunter von Rivalität geprägte Machtverhältnis wider, welches sich im Zuge der endgültigen Überwindung seiner internationalen Isolation ab Mitte der 1950er-Jahre deutlich zugunsten Spaniens verschob: Während Spanien in den 1940er- und frühen 1950er-Jahren noch um Portugals Aufmerksamkeit warb,[41] verlor es mit seiner Aufnahme in die Vereinten Nationen 1955 das Interesse an seinem iberischen Nachbarn und konzentrierte seine kulturdiplomatischen Avancen auf geopolitisch vielversprechendere Allianzen. Dieses Verhalten sorgte in Portugal für eifersüchtige Verstimmung, auf die Spanien 1959 nur widerwillig mit der von Portugal gewünschten Entsendung einer Kunstausstellung reagierte, die unter dem Titel „20 Años de Pintura Española Contemporánea" in Lissabon und Porto gastierte. Erst nach der Machtergreifung des spanienaffinen Technokraten Marcello Caetano ist verstärkt das Bemühen Portugals zu erkennen, sich umgekehrt im benachbarten Franco-Regime Sichtbarkeit und Präsenz zu verschaffen, wofür ihm dieses zu einem Zeitpunkt, als zahlreiche Nationen wegen seiner unerbittlich geführten Kolonialkriege nicht offen mit dem Estado Novo kooperieren wollten, bereitwillig eine Bühne bot.

1955 organisierte Portugal auf Einladung Großbritanniens eine Ausstellung portugiesischer Kunst in London.[42] Dass dieser spektakuläre Auftritt Portugals in der Londoner Royal Academy of Arts nicht auf eigene, sondern auf englische Initiative zurückging, ist bezeichnend, wenngleich das Salazar-Regime die sich ihm bietende Gelegenheit kompromisslos und ohne finanzielle Ausgaben zu scheuen ergriff. Das portugiesische Engagement versandete jedoch rasch wieder: Mehr als zehn Jahre vergingen bis zur nächsten portugiesischen Kunstausstellung im Ausland, einer in Kooperation mit der privaten *Fundação Calouste Gulbenkian* (FCG) organisierten Wanderausstellung, die 1967/68 in Brüssel, Paris und Madrid gastierte.[43] Bezeichnend ist, dass diese schüchterne Ausstellungsoffensive mit Belgien, Frankreich und Spanien in drei (ehemaligen) Kolonialmächten stattfand, die das Salazar-Regime bei seinen Anstrengungen, sich der Dekolonisierung seiner afrikanischen Kolonien zu widersetzen, diplomatisch und militärisch unterstützten und ihm nun in einem positiv besetzten Rahmen eine internationale Bühne boten.

Abseits seiner kolonialen Agenden nutzte das Salazar-Regime Ausstellungen in Portugal selbst als hegemoniale Instrumente vor allem im Rahmen von Re-

---

41 Exposição de Pintura e Escultura Espanholas (1900–1943), hg. v. Museu Nacional de Soares dos Reis, Lissabon und Porto 1943/44.
42 Portuguese Art, 800–1800, hg. v. Royal Academy of Arts, London 1955.
43 Arte Portugués. Pintura y Escultura del Naturalismo a nuestros Dias, Brüssel, 1967 – Paris, 1967 – Madrid, 1968.

gimejubiläen, die traditionell von enzyklopädisch überladenen Leistungsschauen gerahmt wurden. Ihren Höhepunkt erreichte diese Praxis in der 1966 abgehaltenen Ausstellung „As Artes ao Serviço da Nação" anlässlich des 40. Jubiläums der sogenannten Nationalen Revolution, in der das Regime ein letztes Mal seine hegemoniale Vorstellung der salazaristischen Kultur im großen Stil visuell kommunizierte.[44] Wie auch die franquistische Diktatur blieb das Salazar-Regime seinem traditionellen Erscheinungsbild dabei weitgehend treu und verzichtete auf erneuerte Elemente zur Visualisierung des für sich reklamierten revolutionären Geistes. Durch die Beschwörung der Vergangenheit im Stil der *Política do Espírito* António Ferros mit ihrem Fokus auf domestizierte klassische Moderne einerseits und nationale Volkskunst andererseits versuchte das Regime vielmehr, sich auf seine frühen konstituierenden und profilierenden kunstpolitischen Erfolgsmomente zu beziehen.[45] Die mithilfe der Schau erhoffte Mobilisierung und Indoktrinierung der als wichtigste Zielgruppe definierten Jugend misslang: Sie, die für die Weiterführung der portugiesischen Kolonialkriege in Afrika eine zentrale Rolle spielte, musste aufgrund mangelnder Eigenmotivation zum Besuch der Ausstellung verpflichtet werden.[46]

Die geringe Innovationsfreude im Salazarismus manifestiert sich auch auf der Ebene der in den offiziellen Kunstausstellungen präsentierten Kunst: Anders als im Franco-Regime fanden international reüssierende Kunststile in der salazaristischen Diktatur keine offizielle Förderung und nur schwache Rezeption. Beides entspricht dem konservativen, vergangenheitsorientierten und sowohl im kontinentalen Portugal als auch in seinen Kolonien lediglich auf die Bewahrung des Status quo fokussierten Charakters des Salazar-Regimes. Auch die aggressive franquistische Strategie der Aneignung und Umdeutung oppositioneller Künstler und ihrer Werke, wie etwa am Beispiel der katalanischen Künstler Tàpies und Picasso zu sehen, verweist auf ein im Franco-Regime deutlich ausgeprägteres Bewusstsein in Bezug auf Bedeutung und Herstellung von kultureller Hegemonie. Zugleich lässt sie den Rückschluss zu, dass auch bildender Kunst im Allgemeinen in der franquistischen Diktatur größere Macht zugesprochen wurde als im portugiesischen Estado Novo. Auch dort erkannte man zwar das bildrhetorische Potenzial abstrakter Kunst, die im kolonialen Diskurs als visueller Beleg für die Fortschrittlichkeit Portugals und, davon abgeleitet, für seine Befähigung als modernisierende und „zivilisierende" Kolonialmacht eingesetzt wurde – eine gezielte Kunstpolitik mit einem nachdrücklich geförderten und

---

44 As Artes ao Serviço da Nação, hg. v. Museu de Arte Popular, Lissabon 1966/67.
45 Sh. Jorge Ramos do Ó, Os Anos de Ferro. O dispositivo cultural durante a „Política do Espírito", 1933–1949, Lisboa 1999; Nuno Rosmaninho, António Ferro e a propaganda nacional antimoderna, in: Luís Reis Torgal/Heloisa Paulo (Hg.), Estados autoritários e totalitários e suas representações, Coimbra 2008, 289–299.
46 Vgl. ANTT, SNI, cx. 2396.

stringent propagierten Bildprogramm, vergleichbar der franquistischen Instrumentalisierung des *Informalismo*, hatte dies jedoch nicht zur Folge.

Für einen vorsichtigen, aber nichtsdestotrotz nachhaltigen Paradigmenwechsel in den salazaristischen Ausstellungskonzepten steht die oben bereits erwähnte, unter César Moreira Baptista (von 1958 bis 1973 an der Spitze des SNI/SEIT) sorgfältig kuratierte Wanderausstellung „Arte Portugés. Pintura y Escultura del Naturalismo a nuestros Dias" von 1967/68. Sie bricht mit althergebrachten kuratorischen Konzepten, die bis dahin eher dem etwas willkürlichen Prinzip „Mehr ist mehr" folgten. Zudem ist diese Schau die erste des Regimes, die nicht Werke längst vergangener Epochen ins Zentrum rückte, sondern den Fokus auf Kunst des 20. Jahrhunderts legte. Zwar waren in der Ausstellung auch zahlreiche Künstler des portugiesischen Modernismus wie Mário Eloy, Eduardo Viana oder Carlos Botelho vertreten, die das Regime schon in den 1930er- und 1940er-Jahren repräsentiert hatten, doch stellt sie nichtsdestotrotz ein klares Aufbruchssignal dar. Neu ist auch die Integration und politische Instrumentalisierung einer jungen, oppositionellen Künstlergeneration. So ermöglichte die Organisation der Ausstellung in Partnerschaft mit der FCG die Präsentation einiger portugiesischer KünstlerInnen, die dem Regime den Rücken gekehrt hatten und im Ausland lebten und arbeiteten. Unter Caetano blieb der Estado Novo diesem reformierten Auftreten nicht nur treu, sondern konnte Schritt für Schritt an die internationale Kunstszene anschließen, wie die Ausstellung „Pintura Portuguesa de Hoy. Abstractos y Neofigurativos" in Barcelona 1973 belegt.

5. Fazit

Das Franco-Regime nutzte Kunstausstellungen mit großer Regelmäßigkeit und Konsequenz, um hegemoniale Machtansprüche visuell zu kommunizieren. Bereits im Zuge ihrer Machtkonsolidierung etablierte die franquistische Diktatur einen regen Kunstausstellungsbetrieb, der mit professionellen Mitteln routiniert und auf internationalem Niveau global agierte. Gelegenheiten, Kunstausstellungen im Ausland zu realisieren, nutzte die Diktatur selbstbewusst und mit großer Entschlossenheit. Die auswärtige Ausstellungspolitik des Franco-Regimes spiegelt damit dessen ausgeprägten Willen wider, sich international Reputation und Anerkennung als ernstzunehmender und gleichberechtigter politischer Akteur auf der Weltbühne zu verschaffen. Die franquistische Strategie zielte dabei auf internationalen Prestigegewinn, welcher konsolidierend nach innen zurückwirken sollte.

Demgegenüber zeigte sich im Salazar-Regime zunächst kaum die Notwendigkeit einer internationalen Sympathie-Kampagne. Die Diktatur konzentrierte

ihre kultur- und ausstellungspolitische Tätigkeit nach innen und auf ihr Kolonialreich. Erst im letzten Jahrzehnt ihrer im Wesentlichen durch die Ablösung
Salazars durch Marcello Caetano und die anhaltenden Kolonialkriege in Afrika
definierten Existenz ergriff die portugiesische Diktatur Maßnahmen zum ver-
stärkten Einsatz von Kunstausstellungen im Dienst der auswärtigen Repräsentation und damit einhergehend auch zur Modernisierung des Ausstellungsbetriebs. Während der Estado Novo also erst in den letzten Jahren seines rund 40-
jährigen Bestehens wie aus einem Dornröschenschlaf langsam erwachte und
begann, Initiative auf dem Gebiet der auswärtigen Kulturdiplomatie zu ergreifen,
ebbte umgekehrt das rege Engagement des Franco-Regimes in ebendiesem Bereich im letzten Jahrzehnt seines Bestehens deutlich ab. International rehabili-
tiert und anerkannter Partner des westlichen Blocks im Kalten Krieg, wandte die
franquistische Diktatur ihre Aufmerksamkeit, bedingt durch innenpolitische
Krisen, nun verstärkt nach innen. Umgekehrt ist aber auch die vermehrt nach
außen zielende Ausstellungstätigkeit des Salazar-Regimes als Zeichen der Krise
zu werten: Angesichts seines langsam zerbröckelnden und nur noch mithilfe von
bewaffneter Gewalt aufrechtzuerhaltenden Imperiums sowie der damit verbundenen internationalen Kritik sah sich die Diktatur zu einer internationalen
Sympathie-Kampagne gezwungen.

Gegenüber der vergleichsweise agilen franquistischen Ausstellungspolitik bot
die salazaristische insgesamt ein dem Puls der Zeit kaum entsprechendes Bild.
Während Erstere rasch an die internationalen Standards eines modernen Ausstellungsbetriebs anknüpfen konnte und über Spaniens Kunst in der Lage war,
international ein selbstbewusstes, aktives und fortschrittliches Bild des Franco-
Regimes zu vermitteln, entwickelte das Salazar-Regime kein nachhaltiges Bewusstsein für die Bedeutung eines zeitgemäßen Kunstbetriebes und einer professionellen Ausstellungspolitik als wesentlicher Teilbereich der auswärtigen
Kulturdiplomatie.

6.   Auswahlbibliografie

Valentim Alexandre, Ideologia, economia e política: A questão colonial na implantação do
       Estado Novo, in: Análise Social XXVIII (1993) 123–124, 1117–1136.
Mieke Bal, Double Exposures. The Subject of Cultural Analysis, London/New York 1996.
Walther L. Bernecker, „Spaniens ‚verspäteter' Faschismus und der autoritäre ‚Neue' Staat
       Francos", in: Geschichte und Gesellschaft 12 (1986), 183–211.
Horst Bredekamp, Bildakte als Zeugnis und Urteil, in: Monika Flacke (Hg), Mythen der
       Nationen. 1945 – Arena der Erinnerungen, Mainz am Rhein 2004, 29–66.
Peter Burke, Augenzeugenschaft. Bilder als historische Quellen, Berlin 2010.
Manuel Braga da Cruz, Notas para uma caracterização política do Salazarismo, in: Análise
       Social XVIII (1982) 72–73–74, 773–794.

Alex Demirovic, Löwe und Fuchs – Antonio Gramscis Beitrag zu einer kritischen Theorie bürgerlicher Herrschaft, in: Peter Imbusch (Hg.), Macht und Herrschaft. Sozialwissenschaftliche Theorien und Konzeptionen, Wiesbaden 2012, 137–150.

Carol Duncan, Civilizing Rituals. Inside Public Art Museums, London/New York 1995.

Stuart Hall, Ideologie, Identität, Repräsentation, Hamburg 2004.

Ivan Karp/Steven D. Lavine (Hg.), Exhibiting Cultures. The Poetics and Politics of Museum Display, Washington/London 1991.

Juan José Linz, Totalitarian and Authoritarian Regimes, Boulder et al. 2000.

Roswitha Muttenthaler/Regina Wonisch, Gesten des Zeigens. Zur Repräsentation von Gender und Race in Ausstellungen, Bielefeld 2006.

António Costa Pinto, O salazarismo e o fascismo europeu. Problemas de interpretação nas ciências sociais, Lisboa 1992.

Birgit Rommelspacher, Dominanzkultur. Texte zu Fremdheit und Macht, Berlin 1998.

Fernando Rosas, Estado Novo, Império e Ideologia Imperial, in: Revista de História das Ideias 17 (1995), 19–32.

Fernando Rosas, O salazarismo e o homem novo: ensaio sobre o Estado Novo e a questão do totalitarismo, in: Análise Social XXXV (2001) 157, 1031–1054.

Ismael Sanz, El primer franquismo, in: Ayer 36 (1999), 201–221.

Viktoria Schmidt-Linsenhoff (Hg.), Ethnizität und Geschlecht. (Post-)koloniale Verhandlungen in Geschichte, Kunst und Medien, Wien/Köln/Weimar 2005.

Jana Scholze, Medium Ausstellung. Lektüren musealer Gestaltung in Oxford, Leipzig, Amsterdam und Berlin, Bielefeld 2004.

Lisa Spanka, Zugänge zur Zeitgeschichte mit dem Museum. Methodologie einer Ausstellungsanalyse, in: Lisa Spanka/Julia Lorenzen/Meike Haunschild (Hg.), Zugänge zur Zeitgeschichte: Bild – Raum – Text, Marburg 2016, 183–219.

Thomas Thiemeyer, Geschichtswissenschaft: Das Museum als Quelle, in: Joachim Baur (Hg.), Museumsanalyse. Methoden und Konturen eines neuen Forschungsfeldes, Bielefeld 2010, 73–94.

Javier Tusell/Emilio Gentile/Giuliana di Febo/Susana Sueiro Seone (Hg.), Fascismo y franquismo cara a cara, Madrid 2004.

Brian Wallis, Selling Nations. International Exhibitions and Cultural Diplomacy, in: Daniel J. Sherman (Hg.), Museum culture. Histories, discourses, spectacles, Minneapolis 1994, 265–281.

Robert J. C. Young, Postcolonialism. An Historical Introduction, Malden, MA/Oxford/Carlton, Victoria 2001.

Inga Paslavičiūtė

Petitions to the Regime. (Rhetorical) Strategies in Communication with the Communist Bureaucracy in the Lithuanian Soviet Socialist Republic 1953–89

1. Introduction

The emergence, duration, and collapse of totalitarian regimes have been ex-
tensively analyzed by historians since the opening of the Soviet archives. Thirty
years after the collapse of the regime in the Lithuanian Soviet Socialist Republic
(LSSR), it is time to turn the historical gaze "downward" to several thousands
of letters documenting the "voice of the people" at a time when glasnost and
transparency were not possible.[1]

If one observes the developments in Lithuania's history, they have always been
accompanied by existential questions. The extent to which these have shaped and
continue to shape Lithuania is particularly evident in its efforts to achieve independence. For life itself, the basic functions of living, working, and education
were of particular importance. The Lithuanian people in the Soviet Socialist
Republic of Lithuania wrote letters demanding fulfillment of these basic functions. From 1953 to 1989, hundreds of thousands of letters, written personally or
collectively, were sent to state and party institutions, but above all to the most
important body of the communist party – the Central Committee (CC).[2]

Petitioning is not seen as a phenomenon in itself, but as increasing communication with the state, encompassing all social spheres and affecting all private,
social, and societal matters, it can provide a basis for understanding it as such for
socialist Lithuania. The extent of this communication, together with the issues,
strategies, and claims of participation – the central starting point – developed a
mutual interaction with the political system, in this case a totalitarian one. Petitions as appeals to the political leadership thus served as a substitute for the

---

1 Thomas Bohn called for a perspective on reactions "from below" when studying nonconformist behavior under real socialism. Cf. Thomas Bohn, "'Resistenz' und 'Eigensinn'.
Kategorien für widerständiges Verhalten in der Sowjetunion nach Stalin," *Osteuropa* 12 (2007)
57, 1.

2 All sources are from fonds 1771 (Central Committee of the Lithuanian Communist Party) of
the Lithuanian Special Archive (Lietuvos ypatingasis Archyvas) in Vilnius.

increasing non-functioning of institutions, understood here as a fundamental systemic flaw in the totalitarian regime and the reason for the proliferation of this type of letters to the elites. How, then, is the interrelationship between two powers, namely the state (the party) and the people, to be interpreted and this ambivalent interaction, indeed communication, to be clarified from the perspective of the two "powers"?

2.   A Localization of Petition Writing

The overwhelming practice of petition writing in socialist Lithuania is located in the context of rule. The legalization of the Lithuanian Communist Party (LKP) in 1940 brought rapid structural changes and the Central Committee became the center of all political and administrative institutions.[3] Under this condition, the LSSR immediately implemented the "new" policy. The quantity and quality of the petitions addressed to the CC of the LKP between 1945 and 1989 reveal the strategies as well as the shortcomings of the Sovietization policy.

There are no petitions in the archives of the CC of the LKP for the period from the mid-1960s to the mid-1980s, because they were destroyed due to a lack of space. Thus two temporal blocks of investigation emerged. The first temporal break was the "thaw" period (1953–64) under Nikita Sergeyevich Khrushchev until his ouster by Leonid Ilyich Brezhnev. In the spirit of settling accounts with Stalin, Khrushchev did not criticize the socialist state, but distanced himself from political repression and its recurrence. However, it was precisely the functioning of the socialist state that most opportunistic writers to Khrushchev's Lithuanian party comrades were concerned with; through complaints and suggestions for improvement, they tried to draw the party leadership's attention to the reality in the deficit economy and to persuade it to solve explosive problems. The voice of the people, preserved in many thousands of letters in archives, used the symbolic terms "Khrushchevka" and "corn paranoia" as a *pars pro toto* for the deficit economy in the Khrushchev era.[4] The second temporal caesura was the phase of transformation from 1988 to 1989, because it served as a foil for the contrast between the petitions in the post-Stalinist era, which were mostly motivated by economic mismanagement, and the petitions that indicated the emergence of

---

3 Cf. Arvydas Anušauskas et al. (eds.), *Lietuva 1940–1990: Okupuotos Lietuvos istorija. Lietuvos gyventojų genocido ir rezistencijos tyrimo centras* (Vilnius, 2005), 92.
4 The term Khrushchevka was a metaphor for the housing problem, which was given significant attention among the priority issues of Soviet policy under Khrushchev's leadership in 1954, as well as for the construction of low-value three- to five-story houses that emerged during and are considered typical of the Khrushchev era; corn paranoia describes the widespread cultivation of corn in the Kazakh steppe countryside in 1955 and the subsequent harvest fiasco.

civil society initiatives and movements through glasnost, perestroika, and transparency.

The petitions, complaints, and other statements represented a special form of public expression or private communication with the rulers in the Soviet Union. The aim of these letters was to assert private interests or to draw attention to social deficiencies. In this way, petitions communicated to the state problems in all areas of public and private life (for example, work, consumption, housing, etc.).

The Lithuanian petition system was characterized by Sovietization. Over time, the practice of writing petitions increased to such an extent that some of the letters were no longer archived due to lack of space. Nevertheless, the "people's voice" is thus documented for this period in Lithuania in bizarre fashion. The Soviet state considered it its responsibility to communicate with citizens, on the one hand in order to gain insights into their concerns and needs (control function), and on the other hand to maintain control of power in the socialist democracy (valve function). The state thus felt responsible for promoting petitioning, be it by establishing complaints offices or placing complaint boxes in state or public institutions. Under these conditions, citizens attempted to write petitions individually, collectively, or anonymously in order to free themselves from the constraints of the economy of scarcity.

Petition, request, or complaint? The separation results from the historical development of the right of petition, because the right of request and the right of complaint were to some extent treated separately. In the case of a complaint, there is a component of reprimand; in the case of a request, there is a wish for a concrete change.[5] In any case, the three terms have in common the desire for change. The right to complain was used when citizens were not heard anywhere else. A number of mass complaints, anonymous or with several signatures from the Central Committee, known as collective letters, were intended to provoke public discussion, especially in the late 1980s.

In the following, the term "right of complaint" will be used synonymously with right of petition and right of input. The Central Committee dubbed the phenomenon "letters of the working people." Thus the citizens (the working people) tried to use the letters (their claims to civil rights) to enforce their concerns (complaints) against the state. As source material, the petition provides insight into how elementary changes in economic, governmental, and social contexts are understood and interpreted by the individual.[6] After the representative evalua-

---

5 Cf. Rupert Schick, *Petitionen. Von der Untertanenbitte zum Bürgerrecht* (Heidelberg: Hüthig, 1996), 61.

6 Winfried Schulze defines sources in which "[...] Aussagen oder Aussagenpartikel vorliegen, die — wenn auch in rudimentärer und verdeckter Form — über die freiwillige oder erzwungene

tion of the first-person nature and individuality of the sources, it was determined that petitions belong to the source corpus of "ego-documents."

3.   The (Un)dominated Public Sphere

In Soviet Lithuania, the public sphere was constituted as a "party-state event": an appellate body was created – the Central Committee – which attempted to generate participatory public opinion.[7]

Making visible and staging the practice (by placing complaint boxes in stores) was a project of the Soviet elite that took on such scope that it could not be controlled (from the mid-1960s to the late 1980s). So what was the regime's interest and motivation, and why did the system encourage this kind of petitioning?

The dominated participatory sub-public sought to discipline the party-state as a discursive figure. The limits of domination were revealed by the fact that the "writing public" dominated the issues, no matter how the paternalistic party-state sought to control them. The bureaucracy dealt with itself (correspondence and disciplinary writings to officials) because the practice was to control "its own" bureaucracy. This also explains the phenomenon of secrecy – the recipients of the disciplinary letters had no interest in their content becoming public; the opposite was public denunciations by the petition writers or authors of letters to the editor that were propagated by the Soviet press.

It is important to note that the authors influenced the existing system insofar as they learned from the "writing public" that their concerns ended up with the same institution to which the concern related, although they were addressed to the highest organ of the Communist Party. In this context, it is noteworthy that the writing public had a regulative or disciplinary function. The letters to the Central Committee often ended up back at the local organs; nevertheless, as a "signal from above," they had more influence on disciplining the institutions. Petitioning thus represented a sphere of communication between the state and

---

Selbstwahrnehmung eines Menschen in seiner Familie, seiner Gemeinde, seinem Land oder seiner sozialen Schicht Auskunft geben oder sein Verhältnis zu diesen Systemen und deren Veränderungen reflektieren [...]" as "Ego-Dokumente". Winfried Schulze, "Ego-Dokumente: Annäherung an den Menschen in der Geschichte? Vorüberlegungen für die Tagung 'Ego-Dokumente'. Schlussbemerkungen zur Konferenz über 'Ego-Dokumente'," in *Ego-Dokumente. Annäherung an den Menschen in der Geschichte*, edited by Winfried Schulze (Berlin: Akademie-Verlag, 1996), 28.

7   Cf. Gábor Rittersporn et al., "Öffentliche Räume und Öffentlichkeit in Gesellschaften sowjetischen Typs: Ein erster Blick aus komparativer Sicht," in *Sphären von Öffentlichkeit in Gesellschaften sowjetischen Typs. Zwischen partei-staatlicher Selbstinszenierung und kirchlichen Gegenwelten*, edited by Gábor Rittersporn et al. (Frankfurt am Main: Lang, 2003), 7–22.

society and led to a practice of petitioning and complaint culture on the part of the population and social disciplining on the part of the state.

In terms of its claim to legitimacy, the party leadership gave the highest priority to coordinating "work with letters from working people." For the party, the complaints system functioned as a litmus test, on the one hand, for satisfaction with socialist democracy and, on the other, for the claim to control implicit in the relations of rule. In addition to the written sphere of "letters from working people," complaint boxes and complaint books were set up to cultivate the "legitimate culture of public expression," people's universities were founded with the goal of better reporting, and "open letter days" were introduced by the press. The party organized rural meetings, days of the enterprises or the brigade, "political days," and radio and television forums. "Above" was regulated, "below" reacted. The growth of this communication between the two "powers" played a central role in the later process of transformation and democratization.

4. Transformation of the Public and the Private

The intertwining of the public and the private took on a significant role in the petitions. The letters carried the private sphere to the greater public. To the authors, the central organs of the party appeared to be competent addressees – here the boundary between private and public was blurred. It was almost paradoxical that the citizen made use of this instrument, believing that the authorities would listen to his voice. In the same way, the state saw petitioning as an instrument of governance, because nowhere else was the regime so "close" to the citizens than through letters. Feedback was constantly given to the totalitarian system, because it was much easier to pick up a pen than to go to an authority or to present one's rights in court. Quite different in their behavior, the citizens also sought attention and care, among other things, because it was metaphorically suggested to the citizens that the state and the party were their parents. The authors' messages were dictated by the economy of scarcity, and the themes emerged in interaction with the regime: the public wrote and the regime reacted.

The dichotomization of the public and the private was blurred precisely in the petition system in socialist systems.[8] Individuals hoped to achieve success through the representative representation of the private sphere. Due to the participation demands of the socialist state, the private sphere was also politicized in reverse. The private sphere of the individual merged with the public sphere of a collective and virtually formed a unity of work relations and private

---

8 Cf. Kurt Imhof and Peter Schulz (eds.), *Die Veröffentlichung des Privaten – Die Privatisierung des Öffentlichen* (Wiesbaden: Springer, 1998), 11.

life. *De facto*, an inverted reality emerged: according to the party, the individual shaped the socialist ideal, while the petition writers themselves were often making a last cry for help with which they hoped to free themselves from the constraints of this ideal.

The boundary between private and public was transparent; it was precisely with the disclosure of private or intimate life that the letters attempted to convince their recipients. The authors assumed that after a letter was sent or posted, the complaint was read by officials and discussed at meetings; accordingly, it remains open to debate whether there was an intention to "persuade" in this argumentative, emotional, and private structure.

5.   Criticism of the Insinuations/Suggestions

As early as the 1920s, faced with the danger of social polarization and the fragmentation of class cohesion, the communist party had been confronted with the essential question of "criticism" and "self-criticism." The party taught that criticism and self-criticism were the most powerful driving forces in society; the principle of "self-criticism" and "criticism" established a discursive form of intercourse among party members.[9] The principle of "good" criticism was welcome within the party, but it was supposed to tie in with the euphorically propagated "socially useful criticism." Berthold Unfried addressed the issue that self-criticism was always accompanied by criticism of others involved, because the communist principle of responsibility for one's environment was based on this.[10] "Criticism and self-criticism" was a form of intercourse, a form of communication among comrades, and a framework for party events of all kinds in which one "criticized one another." It was also a form of manners on the kolkhoz, at whose meetings one "expressed oneself self-critically" or "testified self-critically" – but only *pro forma*.[11] In denunciation-like petitions, the Central Committee received, among other things, anonymous letters denouncing communists who did not face up to proper criticism, did not draw any consequences from it, and at worst spread resentment of those who criticized them.

"Criticism and self-criticism" was applied as a contrasting foil to eliminate corrupt officials in various party institutions. It seems to have been a sophisti-

---

9 Cf. Lorenz Erren, "'Kritik und Selbstkritik' in der sowjetischen Parteiöffentlichkeit der dreißiger Jahre. Ein missverstandenes Schlagwort und seine Wirkung," *Jahrbücher für Geschichte Osteuropas 50* (2002), 157.

10 Cf. Berthold Unfried, "Kritik und Selbstkritik," in *Der stalinistische Parteikader. Identitätsstiftende Praktiken und Diskurse in der Sowjetunion der dreißiger Jahre*, edited by Brigitte Studer and Berthold Unfried (Wien – Köln – Weimar: Böhlau 2001), 149–91.

11 Fond 1771, fonds 210, file 66, 42–62.

cated approach to act under the pretext of "criticism and self-criticism." The two-word combination underwent a metamorphosis into a single phrase, because the formulations in various letters were almost identical and served, on the one hand, to eliminate the grievances and arbitrariness caused by the regime's representatives, but also, when employed by the functionaries, to eliminate persons disloyal to the regime.

For the regime-compliant writers, "criticism and self-criticism" were a yardstick for the success of the regime and the construction of the socialist state. Socialism, in their eyes, was based on the work of its communist activists, who were to make "criticism and self-criticism" a guiding principle of the work ethic. "Criticism and self-criticism" were used in a discourse with criticism of "suppression of criticism". Expression of criticism and "suppression of criticism" found a strategic place in the petitions. They were integrated into a framework of expression of desire and denunciation and were rhetorically underpinned. If the desired situation did not occur as a result of the criticism ("criticism and self-criticism") of the person in question (denunciation), the question was asked whether it was a communist mode of communication to "suppress criticism".[12]

Criticism featured as positive criticism, self-criticism, criticism of institutions, system or economic criticism, and regime criticism. If the regime was criticized, one must by no means assume that the criticism was compromising, since the writers signed their names and "harsh" criticism of the regime was voiced only in exceptional cases. Writing a letter to the party's institutions meant subjecting oneself to complete scrutiny, because the facts were usually checked and under certain circumstances a false statement was equated with "libel" and could have severe consequences for the writer. Hence critical statements were very moderate, very cautious approaches to statements that were intended to convey to the party that real life under socialism did not reflect its promises.

Contrary to the widespread party rallying cry of "work for all," the strong preference for Russian-speaking cadres, often resulting in the replacement of Lithuanian speakers, meant that the topic of work was addressed and criticized in the complaints system mainly from 1953 to 1962. In the course of industrialization and the urbanization of the Lithuanian Soviet Republic, the writing masses demanded more and more living space in the cities from the 1970s onward; this does not mean that the rural population represented an exception, because they sometimes lived in cellars.[13] The discursive framework in the grievance system was characterized by corruption and abuse of service and the relationships of necessity that arose from them.

---

12 Fond 1771, fonds 210, file 61, 34.
13 Fond 1771, fonds 169, file 85, 47–53; Fond 1771, fonds 205, file 46, 138–140.

With proposals, workers tried to criticize the economy of scarcity and draw attention to the informal sides of trade (*blatas*) in the shadow economy. Within the discursive framework of "self-criticism," "criticism from below" was carefully pursued (as economic criticism and criticism of institutions). Relevant systemic criticism was voiced anonymously, if at all. Criticism of the abuse of service extended into 1989.

6. Drastic Communication

Alf Lüdtke called denunciation a central means of securing rule.[14] Part of Soviet policy was the detection and elimination of hostile "elements," be it in secret (petitions) or public actions (letters to the editor)[15] that made equal use of rhetorical propaganda. While it was common practice within the Communist Party to search through texts for denunciatory content, the practice of denunciation by authors was already apparent in the earliest phase of the petition system in the LSSR and was implicit in a considerable number of the petitions.[16] The instrumentalization of the petition system for denunciation can be interpreted as an expression of the manipulative power of the totalitarian system. As a point of reference, Jörg Baberowski's categorization of the motivation for denunciation as a Stalinist practice stood in this context.[17] Examination of the petitions from this perspective showed that there were Stalinist continuities in this practice and that citizens implied a denunciatory statement with a petition or complaint.

The writers who denounced people in the years 1953 to 1962 were, on the one hand, primarily addressing local officials and, on the other hand, wanted to deal with their everyday problems. Denunciations of local officials were primarily about people from the bureaucratic apparatus: superiors or former superiors, colleagues, or former colleagues. The reasons for denunciation were arbitrariness

14 Cf. Alf Lüdtke, "Sprache und Herrschaft in der DDR. Einleitende Überlegungen," in *Akten. Eingaben. Schaufenster. Die DDR und ihre Texte. Erkundungen zu Herrschaft und Alltag,* edited by Alf Lüdtke and Peter Becker (Berlin: Akademie-Verlag, 1997), 14.

15 Cf. Katarzyna Korzeniewska, *Vykdomasis kabinetas praneša… Sovietų valdininkai skundžia katalikų kunigus (1962–1965) Kas? Kam? Ką? Naujasis Židinys-Aidai* (2006), 157.

16 The pursuit of denunciatory content can be identified by a mark in the petitions.

17 Jörg Baberowski establishes the following categorization of denunciation in Stalinism: denunciation out of ideological conviction, denunciation to cope with everyday problems, denunciation for ethnic reasons, denunciation as an archaic conflict on the periphery, and denunciation as a weapon against the despotism of local officials. Cf. Jörg Baberowski, "'Die Verfasser von Erklärungen jagen den Parteiführern einen Schrecken ein': Denunziation und Terror in der stalinistischen Sowjetunion 1928–1941," in *Denunziation und Justiz. Historische Dimensionen eines sozialen Phänomens,* edited by Friso Ross and Achim Landwehr (Tübingen: Edition Diskord, 2000), 165–197.

in the administration, corruption, and ideology. Leaders – be they teachers or kolkhoz chairmen – who were "foreign" to the Soviet system, who had a bourgeois background, who owned land, or whose family had been deported were not in a position to carry out ideological work and were therefore denounced.[18] Convinced communists who believed in the functioning of the system and gave the impression in their letters that it was a public matter that directly contributed to the success of building socialism and whose solution would, for example, raise labor standards, denounced people who were corrupt. Such indications were taken seriously by the party and followed up.[19] The representatives from the Central Committee went to the site to hold talks and to interview other people.[20]

Denunciation was carried out either for a private purpose, such as coping with everyday problems, or for a public purpose, such as opposing local officials or center-periphery conflict. On the one hand, the center-periphery conflict was about the city-rayon conflict and the rayon-center-village conflict; on the other hand, it was about the power center of Moscow and the Lithuanian Soviet Republic. For example, writers quoted Khrushchev's speech at the XXIth Congress of the CPSU, in which he claimed that it was vital to maintain political vigilance. The letters followed this up with remarks on differences in the policy of the Soviet Republic of Lithuania. Many denounced persons were Soviet public figures from the bureaucratic apparatus; they were either superiors or former superiors, or colleagues or former colleagues. On the other hand, there were also private denunciations, for example, neighbors or spouses.[21]

The Central Committee investigated the denunciation reports and issued notices, both positive and negative; it is difficult to assess the truthfulness in this combination of personal relationships, protection, randomness, and goodwill. In cases of pure denunciation, the party responded by listing what measures it took against whom.

Denunciation was a significant component of many letters. It was either implemented in the letters or the letters were pure denunciations. Denunciation was politically or privately motivated and aimed at material or ideal rewards. Attempts were made to achieve a kind of disciplining through denunciation. The regime nevertheless promoted it as a means of obtaining information. Denunciation was omnipresent in everyday life in the Lithuanian Soviet Republic; even public denunciation was propagated by order of the Central Committee and

---

18 Fond 1771, fonds 146, file 117, 60–5.
19 Fond 1771, fonds 146, file 117, 60–5.
20 Fond 1771, fonds 188, file 90, 62–4, 73–8.
21 Cf. Sheila Fitzpatrick, "Denunciation and Problems of Loyalty and Citizenship," in *Der Staatsbürger als Spitzel. Denunziation während des 18. und 19. Jahrhunderts aus europäischer Perspektive*, edited by Michaela Hohkamp and Claudia Ulbrich (Leipzig: Leipziger Universitätsverlag, 2001), 383–95.

realized through the press. A large number of denunciations were guided by negative emotions such as envy and jealousy.

These denunciations also concerned acts of violence. In the sociological debate of the last three decades, two concepts of violence exist: the concept of "structural" violence advanced by Johan Galtung and the understanding of violence as an action of power to intentionally hurt others by Heinrich Popitz.[22] The first approach to violence sees itself as a social construction of reality, the second as an instrument, a power of action to determine the situation. The fact that violence can be instrumentalized for both the destruction and the production of social order, depending on specific historical and social backgrounds, applies to both authoritarian and democratic developments.

In the historical examination of the topic of violence, the gaze tends to fall on the experiences of manifest extreme visible violence in the National Socialist and Stalinist dictatorships. This mainly concerns violence in periods of "set" power-political change during the "thaw" period and everyday violence in so-called quiet periods, when latent violence prevailed that was not yet present but could easily come to the fore in this unstable situation.[23]

On the macro level, concerning the totalitarian system, we speak of a violence in which the perpetrators are invisible, because it is built into the system, for one thing, and manifests itself through unequal power relations and unequal opportunities.[24] It is precisely here that one can locate the petitions that included reports of violence, which arrived in such large numbers at the CC of the LKP due to the feeling of inequality and powerlessness. On the other hand, for example in the glorification of violence in the petitions, one can speak of an effect of the psychological use of violence, in which such a perfidious attitude toward violence arose through lies, brainwashing, and indoctrination.[25] On the micro level, the petitions address concrete, direct, personal, actor-related, visible violence, which can be traced back to specific persons and is to be understood as a threat.[26]

The petitions to the highest body of the LKP that reported violence in all areas of public and private life must be differentiated according to their provenance. On the one hand, the descriptions of violence were embedded in a request, complaint, or statement. Personal attitudes toward the violence described conveyed the addressee's positioning toward the state. On the other hand, there were reports of physical violence whose boundaries to denunciations were fluid.

---

22 Cf. Manuela Boatcă and Siegfried Lamnek, "Gewalt als Phänomen unserer Zeit," in *Sozialwissenschaften und Berufspraxis (SuB)*, 26 (2003) 2, 123.
23 Cf. Johan Galtung, *Strukturelle Gewalt. Beiträge zur Friedens- und Konfliktforschung* (Reinbek bei Hamburg: Rowohlt, 1975), 14.
24 Ibid., 12.
25 Ibid., 11.
26 Ibid.

7.   Petitions in 1988 and 1989

For Lithuania, these were two years of conflict, full of violence and threatening gestures. In 1988, petitions were dominated by the hunger strike and the ensuing police violence, and the year 1989 was marked by the "Baltic Way", the critical response in the party newspaper *Pravda*, and the public response to it in the form of collective letters. Thematically, the years 1988 and 1989 represented departures from the norm, since the "usual" subject matter of shortage was absent.

In view of glasnost and perestroika, popular discontent increased and the slogan "demand more sovereignty" played an increasingly important role. Public criticism still used the line of argument based on socialist principles; people tended to think that the reforms were feasible within perestroika.[27] The LKP reacted to the reform path in accordance with a principle originating in the physics of the so-called inertial system.[28] When there were no external forces moving the LKP, the party remained in a state of *nihil novo* – a familiar state for the communist apparatus. Due to the consciousness typical of stagnation, neither the local actives, the nomenklatura, nor the KGB accepted the new situation.[29]

The public discourse was reflected in two sets of issues: first, in 1988, in the rally and hunger strike demanding the release of political prisoners, and second, in reprisals by the police (Baltic Way 1989).

Lithuanian society underwent significant political changes in 1988 and 1989. Along with glasnost and perestroika, letters were an instrument of democratization. The collective letters addressed to the Central Committee of the LKP were testimony to the fact that violence perpetrated by the police was discussed in public, thus preventing censorship. Through collective letters, the Lithuanian public now demanded political changes, first and foremost Lithuanian sovereignty. In this context, the letters had a system-changing function.

8.   Language of Criticism

The historical and linguistic study of communication strategies in the petition system of the LSSR was virtually predestined for tracing the boundaries of loyalty and exploring in which situations and with what goals certain communication behaviors were used. The petitions provided answers to the question as to the extent to which nonconformist and system-resistant or system-

---

27 Cf. Arthur Hermann, *Die Phasen des baltischen Unabhängigkeitskampfes 1985–1991*, <http://annaberger-annalen.de/jahrbuch/1994/Annaberg%20Nr.2%20Kap5.pdf> (22.2.2018), 116.
28 From the Latin "inertia" for "inertia".
29 Cf. Danutė Blažytė, *Lietuvos elito įtaka komunistinės struktūros transformacijai į politinę partiją. Lietuvos istorijos metraštis* (Vilnius 2001), 277–98.

conformist thought and action existed, remained constant, or changed within communication with the communist elite, and to what extent an absolute claim to rule pushed "the voice of the people" into (non)conformity.

Criticism was expressed using the propagandistic party language of the ruling system. Quotations from the party and state leadership were taken up and sometimes even rhetorically implemented in an adept manner and repeated relentlessly. To draw attention to the prevailing abuses of service and to corruption, Khrushchev's criticism of Stalin's cult of personality was repeated longer after the former's ouster. By using party-generated word association, the writers sent signals of conformity and hedged their bets. Many letters alluded in one way or another to the idea of "the education of Soviet man", either countering the narrative or asserting it as a goal.

The structure of the letters was influenced by propaganda or propaganda language. As Thymian Bussemer observes, propaganda works with and through language, among other things.[30] Communication was manipulated through new linguistic links, propaganda language being used to support representation and to generate sympathy on the part of the ruler. Because of the absolute claim to validity between the system and the lifeworld, the party and the government were assigned a familial position; they were personified as universal wills. Functional expression was achieved by de-differentiating and mixing the levels of language; a sphere of language was institutionalized.

The authors of petitions consciously or unconsciously used a set of instruments to influence practice. They attempted either to describe the concern in a rational line of argument (urgency of the situation, denunciation, or open conformity to the party, description of the objective evidence with the help of codes, paragraphs, facts, and witnesses) or to emotionally persuade the addressee (role of victim and subject, complaints, the party as a superior, denunciation out of envy, comparisons, expressions with religious connotations). Apart from greetings and farewells, each letter resorted to different "rhetorical," "communicative," and "argumentative" strategies. In this respect, no common strategy could be determined.

---

30 Cf. Thymian Bussemer, *Propaganda. Konzepte und Theorien. Mit einem einführenden Vorwort von Peter Glotz*, 2. Überarbeitete Auflage (Wiesbaden: VS Verlag für Sozialwissenschaften, 2008), 34.

9. Conclusion

The complaints system played a major role for both parties, citizens and the state. Soviet society in Lithuania accepted the claim to participation ascribed to it and articulated its requests in this formalized framework. In this way, citizens actively communicated their private needs or raised public issues in hundreds of thousands of letters. The state enacted grievance regulations to regulate this communication. The Central Committee communicated by means of established order(s). The bureaucracy tried to control the flood of letters, and thus continued to deal with the preparation and collection of reports. For its part, the party and state leadership tried to ensure an "operational response" and to analyze conflict situations and their prophylaxis.[31] In fact, there was no longer any private, let alone public, sphere that did not come into contact with letters. The "ceaseless flow" of letters challenged the political elite,[32] which took control of its own bureaucracy in the state apparatus. From 1953 on, citizens voiced their complaints about economic shortcomings.

In contrast, in 1988 and 1989 the main concern was to stop violence and to demand democratization and transparency as part of the reform policy. The failure of the socialist economic system could be seen and precisely understood in the complaints system. Certainly, because of their political character, the collective letters to the Central Committee were a signal of the failure of the socialist regime in Lithuania.

10. Selected Bibliography

Baberowski, Jörg, "'Die Verfasser von Erklärungen jagen den Parteiführern einen Schrecken ein': Denunziation und Terror in der stalinistischen Sowjetunion 1928–1941," in *Denunziation und Justiz. Historische Dimensionen eines sozialen Phänomens*, edited by Friso Ross and Achim Landwehr. Tübingen: Edition Diskord, 2000.

Bilinsky, Andreas, "Rechtsmittel im sowjetischen Verwaltungsverfahren. Das Beschwerderecht der Bürger als Ersatz der Verwaltungsgerichtsbarkeit?," *Jahrbücher für Ostrecht* 13 (1972).

Boatcă, Manuela and Siegfried Lamnek, "Gewalt als Phänomen unserer Zeit," *Sozialwissenschaften und Berufspraxis (SuB)* 26 (2003) 2.

Bohn, Thomas M., *Das "Phänomen Minsk". Stadtplanung und Urbanisierung in Weißrussland nach dem Zweiten Weltkrieg*. Habilitationsschrift, Friedrich-Schiller-Universität Jena, 2004 (erschien 2008 unter dem Titel "Die sozialistische Stadt in der Sowjetunion nach 1945. Studien zum Minsker Phänomen").

---

31 Fond 1771, fonds 259, file 241, 50.
32 Fond 1771, fonds 260, file 250, 60.

Bussemer, Thymian, *Propaganda. Konzepte und Theorien. Mit einem einführenden Vorwort von Peter Glotz*, 2. Überarbeitete Auflage. Wiesbaden: VS Verlag für Sozialwissenschaften, 2008.

Celikates, Robin, *Kritik als soziale Praxis. Gesellschaftliche Selbstverständigung und kritische Theorie*. Frankfurt – New York: Campus-Verlag, 2009.

Christophe, Barbara, "Kohäsion und Differenz. Nation und Nationalismus in Litauen," in: *Nationalismus im spät- und postkommunistischen Europa*. Bd. 2, edited by Egbert Jahn. Baden-Baden: Nomos, 2009.

Erren, Lorenz, "'Kritik und Selbstkritik' in der sowjetischen Parteiöffentlichkeit der dreißiger Jahre. Ein missverstandenes Schlagwort und seine Wirkung," *Jahrbücher für Geschichte Osteuropas* 50 (2002).

Erren, Lorenz, *Selbstkritik und Schuldbekenntnis. Kommunikation und Herrschaft unter Stalin (1917–1953)*. München: Oldenbourg, 2008.

Filtzer, Donald, *Die Chruschtschow-Ära: Entstalinisierung und die Grenzen der Reform in der UdSSR 1953–1964. Internationale Einführungsreihe*, Bd. 2. Mainz: Decaton-Verlag, 1995.

Fincke, Martin, "Die Kontrolle der sowjetischen Verwaltung. Ursprünge, Entwicklung, Gegenwart," *Jahrbuch für Ostrecht* 6 (1965).

Fitzpatrick, Sheila and Robert Gellately (eds.), *Accusatory Practices: Denunciation in Modern European History*. Chicago – London: The University of Chicago Press, 1997 [Original: *The Journal of Modern History* 68 (1996) 4.].

Fitzpatrick, Sheila, "Denunciation and Problems of Loyalty and Citizenship," in *Der Staatsbürger als Spitzel: Denunziation während des 18. und 19. Jahrhunderts aus europäischer Perspektive*, edited by Michaela Hohkamp and Claudia Ulbrich. Leipzig: Leipziger Universitätsverlag, 2001.

Foitzik, Jan, "Ostmitteleuropa zwischen 1953 und 1956. Sozialer Hintergrund und politischer Kontext der Entstalinisierungskrise," in *Entstalinisierungskrise in Ostmitteleuropa 1953–1956: vom 17. Juni bis zum ungarischen Volksaufstand; politische, militärische, soziale und nationale Dimensionen*, edited by Jan Foitzik. Paderborn: Schöningh, 2001.

Frings, Andreas, *Sowjetische Schriftpolitik zwischen 1917 und 1941. Eine handlungstheoretische Analyse. Quellen und Studien zur Geschichte des östlichen Europa*. Bd. 73. Stuttgart: Steiner, 2007.

Galtung, Johan, *Strukturelle Gewalt. Beiträge zur Friedens- und Konfliktforschung*. Reinbek bei Hamburg: Rowohlt, 1975.

Garcelon, Marc, "The Shadow of the Leviathan: Public and Private in Communist and Post-Communist Society," in *Public and Private in Thought and Practice. Perspectives on a Grand Dichotomy*, edited by Jeff Weintraub and Krishan Kumar. Chicago – London: University of Chicago Press, 1997.

Habermas, Jürgen, *Strukturwandel der Öffentlichkeit. Untersuchungen zu einer Kategorie der bürgerlichen Gesellschaft*, 1962, Neuauflage mit einem Vorwort von 1990. Frankfurt am Main: Suhrkamp, 1999.

Hausmann, Guido, "Öffentlichkeit," in *Studienhandbuch Östliches Europa. Bd. 2. Geschichte des Russischen Reiches und der Sowjetunion*, edited by Thomas M. Bohn and Dietmar Neutatz. Köln – Weimar – Wien: Böhlau, 2002.

Hennig, Heinz, "Ohnmacht, Macht und Rivalität – Zur Psychodynamik der Denunziation," in *Denunziation. Historische, juristische und psychologische Aspekte*, edited by Günter Jeroushek et al. Tübingen: Edition Diskord, 1997.

Hildermeier, Manfred, *Geschichte der Sowjetunion 1917–1991*. München: Beck, 1998.

Horstmann, Thomas, *Logik der Willkür. Die Zentrale Kommission für staatliche Kontrolle in der SBZ/DDR von 1948 bis 1958*. Köln – Weimar – Wien: Böhlau, 2002.

Imhof, Kurt and Peter Schulz (eds.), *Die Veröffentlichung des Privaten – Die Privatisierung des Öffentlichen*. Wiesbaden: Springer, 1998.

Inkeles, Alex and Kent Geiger, "Critical Letters to the Editors of the Soviet Press. Areas and Modes of Complaint," *American Sociological Review* 17 (1952).

Inkeles, Alex and Kent Geiger, "Critical Letters to the Editors of the Soviet Press. Social Characteristics and Interrelations of Critics and Criticized," *American Sociological Review* 18 (1953).

Ivanauskas, Vilius, *Work ethics of sowiet bureaucrats, informal routines and shortages oft the planning system: the case of soviet Lithuania. Filosofija*, Sociologija Nr. 4. Vilnius 2006.

Jessen, Ralph, "Diktatorische Herrschaft als kommunikative Praxis. Überlegungen zum Zusammenhang von 'Bürokratie' und Sprachnormierung in der DDR," in *Akten. Eingaben. Schaufenster. Die DDR und ihre Texte. Erkundungen zu Herrschaft und Alltag*, edited by Alf Lüdtke and Peter Becker. Berlin: Akademie-Verlag, 1997.

Jessen, Ralph, "Akten, Eingaben, Schaufenster: Die DDR und ihre Texte: Erkundungen zu Herrschaft und Alltag," in *Akten. Eingaben. Schaufenster. Die DDR und ihre Texte. Erkundungen zu Herrschaft und Alltag*, edited by Alf Lüdtke and Peter Becker. Berlin: Akademie-Verlag, 1997.

Kohte-Meyer, Irmhild, "Denunzierung – eine psychoanalytische Sicht auf individuelle und kollektive psychische Geschehnisse," in *Denunziation. Historische, juristische und psychologische Aspekte*, edited by Günter Jeroushek et al. Tübingen: Diskord, 1997.

Korzeniewska, Katarzyna, *Vykdomasis kabinetas praneša… Sovietų valdininkai skundžia katalikų kunigus (1962–1965) Kas? Kam? Ką? Naujasis Židinys-Aidai*. 2006.

Kowalczuk, Ilko-Sascha, "Von der Freiheit, Ich zu sagen. Widerständiges Verhalten in der DDR," in *Zwischen Selbstbehauptung und Anpassung. Formen des Widerstandes und der Opposition in der DDR*, edited by Ulrike Poppe et al. Berlin: Ch. Links, 1995.

Kuss, Klaus-Jürgen, "Das Beschwerde- und Antragsrecht in der sowjetischen Verwaltungspraxis. Unter rechtsvergleichender Berücksichtigung der anderen sozialistischen Staaten," *Recht in Ost und West* 29 (1985) 3.

Lindenberger, Thomas, "Die Diktatur der Grenzen. Zur Einleitung," in *Herrschaft und Eigen-Sinn in der Diktatur. Studien zur Gesellschaftsgeschichte der DDR*. Köln – Weimar – Wien: Böhlau, 1999.

Lüdtke, Alf, "Denunziationen – Politik aus Liebe?," in *Der Staatsbürger als Spitzel. Denunziation während des 18. und 19. Jahrhunderts aus europäischer Perspektive*, edited by Michaela Hohkamp and Claudia Ulbrich. Leipzig: Leipziger Universitätsverlag, 2001.

Lüdtke, Alf and Peter Becker (eds.), *Akten, Eingaben, Schaufenster. Die DDR und ihre Texte. Erkundungen zu Herrschaft und Alltag*. Berlin: Akademie-Verlag, 1997

Lüdtke, Alf, "Geschichte und Eigensinn," in *Alltagskultur, Subjektivität und Geschichte. Zur Theorie und Praxis von Alltagsgeschichte*, edited by Berliner Geschichtswerkstatt. Münster: Westfälisches Dampfboot, 1994.

Markovits, Inga, "Der Handel mit der sozialistischen Gerechtigkeit. Zum Verhältnis zwischen Bürger und Gericht in der DDR," in *Herrschaft und Eigen-Sinn in der Diktatur. Studien zur Gesellschaftsgeschichte der DDR*. Köln – Weimar – Wien: Böhlau, 1999.

Markovits, Inga, "Rechtsstaat oder Beschwerdestaat. Verwaltungsrechtsschutz in der DDR," *Recht in Ost und West. Zeitschrift für Rechtsvergleichung und innerdeutsche Rechtsprobleme* 31 (1987).

Merkel, Ina (ed.), *"Wir sind doch nicht die Mecker-Ecke der Nation." Briefe an das DDR-Fernsehen*. Köln – Weimar – Wien: Böhlau, 1998. Stark erweiterte Neuausgabe. Berlin: Schwarzkopf & Schwarzkopf, 2000.

Mommsen, Margareta, *Hilf mir, mein Recht zu finden. Russische Bittschriften. Von Iwan dem Schrecklichen bis Gorbatschow*. Frankfurt am Main – Berlin: Propyläen-Verlag, 1987.

Mühlberg, Felix, *Bürger, Bitten und Behörden. Geschichte der Eingabe in der DDR*. Berlin: Dietz, 2004.

Neumaier, Eduard, *Petitionen. Das Eingaben-Recht – des Bürgers Notrufsäule*. Bonn: AZ-Studio, 1982 (Bundestag von A–Z 16).

Nunner-Winkler, Gertrud "Überlegungen zum Gewaltbegriff," in *Gewalt. Entwicklungen, Strukturen, Analyseprobleme*, edited by Wilhelm Heitmeyer and Hans-Georg Soeffner. Frankfurt am Main: Suhrkamp, 1994.

Plett, Heinrich F, *Einführung in die rhetorische Textanalyse*. Hamburg: Buske, 1975.

Requate, Jörg and Martin Schulze-Wessel, "Europäische Öffentlichkeit: Realität und Imagination einer appellativen Instanz," in *Europäische Öffentlichkeit. Transnationale Kommunikation seit dem 18. Jahrhundert*, edited by Jörg Requate and Martin Schulze-Wessel. Frankfurt – New York: Campus-Verlag, 2002.

Rittersporn, Gábor et al., "Öffentliche Räume und Öffentlichkeit in Gesellschaften sowjetischen Typs: Ein erster Blick aus komparativer Sicht," in *Sphären von Öffentlichkeit in Gesellschaften sowjetischen Typs. Zwischen partei-staatlicher Selbstinszenierung und kirchlichen Gegenwelten*, edited by Gábor Rittersporn et al. Frankfurt am Main: Lang, 2003.

Rothmann, Stanley and Goerge W. Breslauer, *Soviet Politics and Society*. St. Paul: West Publishing Company, 1978.

Schick, Rupert, *Petitionen. Von der Untertanenbitte zum Bürgerrecht*. Heidelberg: Hüthig, 1996.

Schulze, Winfried, Ego-Dokumente "Annäherung an den Menschen in der Geschichte? Vorüberlegungen für die Tagung 'Ego-Dokumente'/Schlussbemerkungen zur Konferenz über 'Ego-Dokumente'," in. *Ego-Dokumente. Annäherung an den Menschen in der Geschichte*, edited by Winfried Schulze. Berlin: Akademie-Verlag, 1996.

Unfried, Berthold, *Ich bekenne. Katholische Beichte und sowjetische Selbstkritik*. Frankfurt am Main: Campus-Verlag, 2004.

Zatlin, Jonathan, "Ausgaben und Eingaben. Das Petitionsrecht und der Untergang der DDR," *Zeitschrift für Geschichtswissenschaft* 45 (1997) 10.

Eleni Kouki

What Can the Study of Monuments and Ceremonies Tell Us About a Dictatorship? The Case of the Dictatorship of April 21 in Greece. 1967–74

The Dictatorship of April 21 was the last military intervention in Greece. It was imposed in 1967 and lasted seven years, longer than any previous dictatorship. Nevertheless, its fall ended a vicious cycle of military interference in political life that tormented Greek society during the twentieth century.

The coup was the result of a complex political dynamic shaped by the polarization of the Greek political system in the context of the Cold War. In 1946, a bloody civil war erupted between the communists and the so-called national government. When in 1949 it ended with the victory of the latter, an austere anticommunist regime was implemented to ensure that a new communist insurgency would not be possible. To that end, the army, the crown, and the right cemented a political alliance to control the state effectively.

In post-civil-war Greece, the Army was praised as the healthiest part of society (that is, the institution less 'infected' by communism) and gained significant autonomy and political power as the guardian of the nation. This autonomy allowed a fraction of middle-ranking officers, mostly colonels, to carry out a successful coup on the April 21, 1967, against the will of the upper echelons of the army, the generals, who were then working out their own coup with the authorization of the crown. The coup was an abrupt intervention in the Greek political system, and during the first night alone, some 6,000 people were arrested. At the same time, it was a turning point for the post-civil-war anticommunist alliance.

Initially, the king decided to collaborate with the new strongmen, giving them the much-needed legitimacy to secure their position. However, a few months later, the severe internal controversies of the coalition led to an aborted royal coup that shattered the collaboration. The king was obliged to self-exile and left the country. Accordingly, few politicians on the right actively supported the new situation, while many others, including the last legitimate prime minister, openly denounced the dictatorship as a dangerous deviation.

On the international level, the Dictatorship of 21 April also had to deal with its own precariousness. The fierce anticommunist spirit of the new regime was aligned with the imperatives of the "Free World" and its ultimate fight against communism, but the prospect of a new dictatorship within Europe was not easily tolerated. As a result, Greece was forced to leave the Council of Europe, while even within the North Atlantic Treaty Organization (NATO), where it enjoyed the support of the USA, its position was constantly endangered.

It is thus apparent why throughout its seven years the dictatorship was a real work in progress in a constant state of change, trying to strike a balance between the hard factions of the regime and the international demand for democratization. Every year, a new political crisis would erupt within the so-called Revolutionary Council that acted as the unofficial directorate of the state. Ironically enough, only a year after 1972, when Western observers concluded that the leader of the dictatorship, Georgios Papadopoulos, had finally secured his position in the army and his grip on society, the internal controversies of the system had reached such a breaking point that a mass student movement exploded, proving that Greek society would not passively accept the situation. Meanwhile, secret movements by the hard factions within the army successfully mobilized and overthrew Papadopoulos, thereby initiating the last phase of the dictatorship, which ended with the catastrophic war in Cyprus and the fall of the military state in 1974.

The Dictatorship of April 21 is a crucial period in the chain of Greek post-Second-World-War history. Those seven years were a major political crisis whose resolution laid the foundation of the Third Hellenic Republic. Moreover, its fall signaled the end of a broader, post-civil-war period (1950–74). Thus, we can treat it as a laboratory in which conflicting ideas about freedom, democracy, the nation, or personal life choices collided.

However, the period remains understudied. To some extent, this is due to the weak position of contemporary history in Greek academia. After the fall of the Junta, historical studies experienced a real boom. A new generation of historians revolutionized the field, posing new critical questions about, for example, the creation of the Greek state (1830) or the social and cultural conditions of Hellenism before the 1821 Revolution. The recent dictatorial experience provoked new historical questions about topics such as the position of the army, especially during the first half of the twentieth century, when it acquired significant political power. However, the new academic interest did not extend beyond the 1940s. The Dictatorship of April 21, as a recent past, was left to public history and political scientists. The latter, mostly under the influence of neo-Marxist theories, treated the dictatorship as a failure that could reveal broader structural deficiencies in the Greek state, creating abstract models about the historical course of the Greek state from 1830 up to the present day. Thus for decades, the dictatorship was not an object of research per se. Although during the dictatorship many social scientists dealt with many facets of the regime, its ideology, its political personnel, etc., after the fall of the dictatorship such inquiries were abandoned, except by journalists, some of whom produced high-quality public history on the above themes.

After 2000, interest in the subject was revitalized as important archival material was released, new questions about the period puzzled Greek society, and new historical trends fertilized Greek academia. In the last twenty years, we have seen many important studies about the dictatorship's relations with the USA (a hot political topic that had long been left to the public debate, producing a range of conspiracy theories) and the anti-dictatorial movement. Recently, we have seen some important works on the memory of the dictatorship, but overall, however, the dictatorial regime has received little attention. It seems scholars feel that nothing more is left to be said about it, while even its most crucial aspects, such as the internal conflicts that mostly destabilized it, remain unexplored. Obviously, if there is an academic reluctance towards studying the regime, it is not because everything has been said, but, on the contrary, because new questions have yet to be spelled out. From such a perspective, I suggest that the study of monuments and ceremonies can be a new path via which to revisit the "foreign country" of the Dictatorship of April 21. Thus, before I expose the way monuments and ceremonies can help us find new outlooks, I will briefly present how the monuments and the ceremonies of the dictatorship have preoccupied both academia and public debate.

During the dictatorship, the national anniversaries celebrated by the regime became the target of criticism at home and abroad focusing on the authoritarian character of such ceremonies and emphasizing that they had become tools of mass manipulation and propaganda. The earliest mention on the subject detected to date was made by Max Van der Stoel who, as the rapporteur on the situation in Greece to the Council of Europe, mentioned in January 1969 that the dictatorship had criminalized the absence of civil servants and pupils from national anniversaries, compelling them to mass participation. He noted this in order to explain that the newsreels showing multitudes hailing the leaders of the dictatorship on such occasions were not spontaneous manifestations of support, but carefully orchestrated propagandistic images.

In 1971, an intellectual insinuated that the ceremonial culture of the dictatorship was reminiscent of the "gatherings in the stadium of Nuremberg", an obvious comparison of the dictatorship's festivals to those of the Nazi party. Meanwhile, the public appearances and speeches of the dictatorship's leaders were criticized as ridiculous and pompous, in other words as kitsch. The latter was part of a broader critique suggesting that the regime had no "real ideology" and that it exploited several ideological trends, such as nationalism, only as far as they could provide some sort of legitimation. Thus the dictatorship was discredited as fake and its manifestations as meaningless pageantry staged only to cover its opportunism. Another trend of criticism was to correlate the dictatorship's aesthetics with a petty bourgeois culture that had supposedly conquered society during the seven years of the regime as the country's economic conditions steadily improved. All the above views created a lasting framework for the academic approaches too. The few articles on the subject focus on the dictatorship's public ceremonies mainly as reflections of authoritarianism.

However, I suggest a different approach with which to analyze the ceremonies and the monuments of the 1967 dictatorship. I choose to process them as fields of real political activity, and not just as a manipulated reflection thereof. My view is inspired by the work of anthropologists such as David Graeber and A. M. Hocart, who argue that the primary jurisdiction of governance is actually the field of ritual. Graeber, especially, points out that the world of *realpolitik* and that of ceremony are entangled in multiple ways.

Having said that, I do not argue against those who maintained that the dictatorship used ceremonies and monuments for propaganda purposes. On the contrary, I acknowledge that ceremonies were of special propagandistic value to the regime from the very outset. A prime example is the way the newly founded regime treated the religious celebrations of Easter of 1967. The coup took place a few days before the Holy Week. As a strict curfew was implemented, rumors circulated that the religious processions would be cancelled. However, Stylianos Pattakos, a high-ranking member of the revolutionary council and the newly appointed minister of interior, rushed to announce that the religious ceremonies would take place as every year, as the "revolution of April 21" had prevailed and "order and security was implemented throughout the country." On this occasion, the regime projected its decision to let people gather for Easter as proof of its strength and the lack of opposition to it. Moreover, it organized the Holy Saturday ceremony in the Cathedral of Athens with grandiosity, and the ostensibly honored guest was the king, in order to emphasize the good relations between the putschists and the crown.

In the subsequent months, the high-ranking members of the dictatorship made a series of appearances all over Greece, attending local historical celebrations to spread the message of the new "national government." As they insisted, the very fact that high-ranking officials joined local historical celebrations, supposedly neglected by authorities hitherto, was clear proof that they sincerely cared for the people of the provinces, unlike the corrupt old politicians. As the dictatorship did not create mass bodies, such as a political party or youth organization, it treated national and local holidays as political rallies to establish the image of a popular government. To that end, in addition to the pre-existing ceremonies, they initiated a range of new celebrations all over Greece, including the annual anniversary of April 21 in memory of the "great historical event of the revolution of 1967."

However, I suggest that if we analyze those ceremonial practices only as propaganda, we construct a static analytical framework in which the roles are given and the results are predictable. In such a view, there is a mighty solid dictatorship that acts as the transmitter and a passive audience that receives or rejects its messages. However, ceremonial practices are contestable fields of government that any authority that wants to be acknowledged as such must control. Thus, I stress the emphasis to the ceremonial practices, including the preparation that such events demand. Consequently, I try to understand what those events meant for the regime in its effort to present itself as a lawful government and as an important link in the nation's historical chain. Instead of insisting on the falsifications that the dictatorship performed through ceremony, I focus on the real effort that the regime had to make to maintain the symbolic capital that traditionally belongs to those who govern.

In my approach, I treat monuments as ceremonial practices too. Firstly, because national monuments are often built to serve as the theaters of ceremony, and are hence part of it. Secondly, because the process of erecting a national monument is per se a kind of ceremony, that is, an instance that authority communicates with people in a theatrical manner to invest the monumental place-to-be with the supernatural allure that transforms it into a sacred space of national pilgrimage.

However, there is a question of how to apply an anthropological theory constructed to explain the way society was at first organized, in historical research regarding a political phenomenon of the late twentieth century. I believe that Hocart offers us a key to reevaluate ceremonies in a wide range of societies with the concept of the ownership of the ritual: "Rituals tend to be owned, whether it be an individual's personal ritual that they inherited from, and will pass on to a relative, or a social rite or ceremony belonging to a cult, secret society, chief or king". Hence proving who owns a ceremony is a crucial precondition of that ceremony. If the premier who stands on the platform as the high guest of the occasion and the receiver of a range of honors is not a real premier, then the ceremony turns into a mere parody. Thus, proving the ownership of the ceremony is the most important step in its organization. There are multiple ways to do so, but I think that the ultimate proof is the ceremony per se. If someone can mobilize the state apparatus to organize it and the people to participate in it, he fortifies his right to it. From that perspective, we can reevaluate the proliferation of ceremonial events that occurred in the first years of the dictatorship as a constant effort on the part of the dictatorship to prove its right to be acknowledged as the lawful owner of the national rituals.

The example of the 1971 celebrations marking one-hundred-and-fifty years of the 1821 Revolution (the founding event of the Greek state or the liberation of the nation from the bonds of Turkish slavery, as it is often described) is very illuminating of the effort the dictatorship had to put into such events. The festivities organized in 1971 were an excellent ceremonial occasion for the dictatorship to present itself as a regime that valued freedom. Freedom had a specific meaning in the dictatorial vocabulary, which owed a lot to the Cold-War culture. It was the right of the nation to combat its enemies, including internal enemies, that threatened its morale and destabilized it.

In 1970, a special committee was appointed to supervise the preparations, headed by the archbishop of the Orthodox Church of Greece, Ieronymos, and the vice-president of the government, Stylianos Pattakos. As the latter announced, the festivities would send a message about the worldwide significance of the 1821 Revolution and would be the occasion for the creation of a new movement of philhellenism, much like the movement of the foreign supporters of the 1821 revolution, which included eminent intellectuals such as Lord Byron, Shelley, and others.

However, Stylianos Pattakos argued that Greece did not want to inflame the passions over the "old enemies that now are allies", i. e. Turkey. Pattakos' statement illuminates the way the dictatorship's leadership was planning to benefit from the 1971 celebrations without causing unnecessary problems within NATO, where Turkey and Greece were allies, especially at a time when Papadopoulos was planning a new approach to Greek-Turkish relations over the Cyprus issue. Pattakos' statement indicates the precautions that the dictatorship had to take in the organization of the celebrations, so as not to be accused of being a militaristic regime that aggravated hostilities and thus destabilized the security of the South-East Mediterranean region.

At the beginning of 1971, the committee announced a wide range of celebratory events throughout Greece. The most central were set for the national holiday of March 25, the oldest annual state holiday in Greece, marking the 1821 revolution. According to the plan, on March 24, all the members of the so-called national government would gather at the Saint Lavra monastery in Kalavryta, 200 km away from Athens. In Greek national mythology, the monastery is the place where all the chiefs of the revolutionary army gathered and took the oath to launch the revolution of 1821. The planned ceremony had an obvious meaning. The new leaders of the "1967 revolution" would gather again to pay respect to the old heroes and renew their vows to bring about the rebirth of Greece. A second and even bigger event was planned for March 25, 1971. Atop an Athenian hill, the prime minister and leader of the dictatorship, Georgios Papadopoulos would lay the foundation stone for the biggest monumental project of the dictatorship, the so-called Nation's Vow. The Nation's Vow was a monumental church that the Greek people would offer to the "god of Greece", for his divine grace allowed the 1821 revolution to come to a successful end. According to the announcements, the vast edifice would be visible from miles away, and after its completion it would serve as the new cathedral of Athens as well as a place of official ceremony.

All the antidictatorial organizations reacted against the celebrations. Especially abroad, they organized a wide range of anti-celebrations, stressing that the dictatorship had no right to celebrate an anniversary that mainly expressed the ideal of freedom. These unofficial ceremonies reinterpreted the meaning that the dictatorship was trying to ascribe to the celebrations. For example, in London the dissidents – many of them centrists or even conservatives – gathered before the statue of Lord Byron at Hyde Park Corner, insinuating that the real philhellenes of their time could not back a dictatorship.

Within Greece, the manifestations against the celebration were more cautious; however, they sent strong messages to the dictatorship. For example, the leaders of the two major pre-dictatorial political parties, the right-wing ERE and the Center Union, issued a common statement about the Greek people who celebrated the 150 years of the 1821 revolution in exile and prison: "the community of the European countries, as well as the people of the USA, have founded their postwar progress on the principle of democracy – a principle that was defended with blood during the two world wars. Greece also participated in those wars with many sacrifices. On those sacrifices were laid the foundations of the Universal Declaration of Human Rights. [...] The dangerous road that our country took after April 21, 1967 undermines the historical mission and the moral lead of the Western World." In other words, the statement underlined the responsibility of the West, which tolerated the dictatorship's degrading the true meaning of democracy. Thus the celebratory occasion became a field of reinterpretation of the West's core values. Equally important was the fact that the statement was a gesture of reconciliation between the two major political rivals, who had been in bitter dispute prior to the dictatorship. According to the official narrative of the dictatorship, that dispute was the reason why the army had had to intervene in political life.

What was even more alarming for the regime was the fact that even countries such as the USA and West Germany addressed their congratulatory letters on the occasion not to the government or the viceroy appointed by the dictatorship but to the exiled king, an obvious gesture that they considered him as the lawful head of the Greek state.

At the same time, the regime received criticism from several internal fractions of the dictatorship. The so-called August 4 group, a small, openly fascist group that acted under the protection of Ioannis Ladas, one of the dictatorship's strongmen, criticized the decision of the organizing commission not to refer openly to the historical enemies of the nation – that is, the Turks – as a sign of moral degeneration. On another occasion, the ultra-conservative newspaper *Estia* wrote that some of the celebrations were meaningless pompous events. Its critique, which openly adopted a view projected by the dissidents, took aim at Dimitrios Tsakonas, a member of Georgios Papadopoulos' inner circle, and hence it amounted to almost open criticism of the regime's leader.

Such criticism must be understood within the context of the major leadership crisis that erupted between the regime's factions in 1971. With this in mind, it is easy to explain why the two events described above, the one in Kalavryta and the laying of the foundations of the Nation's Vow, were finally cancelled. Moreover, Georgios Papadopoulos did not even attend the military parade that was organized on March 25 due to health reasons, as it was officially announced. Hence the celebrations, instead of being a moment of exultation of the "1967 Revolution", became mired in controversy, contrasting proof that the dictatorship did not own the national celebrations. It is remarkable that from 1971 onwards, the dictatorship limited the national celebrations beginning with the central ceremony of the "1967 Revolution" in Athens. If the years from 1967 to 1971 can be described as a period of ceremonial inflation, the final phase, from 1971 up to 1974, was a period of ceremonial disinvestment. Accordingly, the dictatorship's major monumental project, the Nation's Vow, was never concluded.

In this article, I have tried to rethink the history of the 1967 dictatorship through the history of the regime's monumental and ceremonial projects. In doing so, I have also had to think the other way around, that is, about how the existing literature deals with ceremony when it comes to dictatorships. I suggest that an analytical approach that examines the dictatorial ceremonial projects only as propaganda, although valid, restrains the analytical framework. Ceremonies are intersecting fields in which different levels of politics overlap and interact. The case of the celebrations marking 150 years of the Greek Revolution is an obvious example of the political significance that ceremonies bear. It was planned as a cautious rebranding of the dictatorial regime so as not to disturb its international alliances; however, it was crippled by its internal controversies. Therefore, it gave the anti-dictatorial movement the necessary space to perform its own rituals of national reconciliation, which both empowered it and sent a strong message that Greek society did not need an oppressive guardian to be safe.

Moreover, it is a crucial event for understanding the fluctuations of the dictatorship's ceremonial politics. When we deal with ceremonies only as tools of propaganda, we fail to study the periods that an authority loses its interest in them, as our focus is on the big ceremonial occasions. However, especially for the study of the Greek 1967 dictatorship, it is equally important to inquire into both. The multiple approaches of the 1967 dictatorship to ceremonial practices provides insights into the impasses that the regime faced after the break in the post-civil-war anti-communist consensus, in the quest for a new sociopolitical equilibrium. The everchanging ceremonial practices of the dictatorship are a fruitful field for understanding the dictatorship as a work in progress.

Selected Bibliography

Antoniou, Dimitris, "Unthinkable Histories: The Nation's Vow and the Making of the Past in Greece," *Journal of Modern Greek Studies* 34 (2016) 1: 131–60.

Argyriou A. et al., *Nea Keimena* [New Texts]. Athens: Kedros, 1971.

Antoniou, D. et al., "Introduction: The Colonels' Dictatorship and Its Afterlives," *Journal of Modern Greek Studies* 35 (2017) 2: 281–306.

Clogg, Richard and George N. Yannopoulos, (eds.), *Greece Under Military Rule*. London: Basic Books, 1972.

Graeber, David, "Notes on the politics of divine kingship. Or, elements for an archaeology of sovereignty," in *On Kings,* edited by David Graeber and Marshall Sahlins. Chicago: HAU Books, 2017.

Laughlin, C., "A.M. Hocart on Ritual: On the Quest for Life, Ceremony, Governance and the Bureaucratic State," *Journal of Ritual Studies* 28 (2014) 1: 31–43.

Kallivretakis, Leonidas, "Greek-American Relations in the Yom Kippur War Concurrence," *The Historical Review – La Revue Historique* 11 (2014): 105–25.

Papadimitriou, Despoina, "George Papadopoulos and the Dictatorship of the Greek Colonels, 1967–1974," in *Balkan Strongmen. Dictators and Authoritarian Rulers of South Eastern Europe*, edited by Bernd J. Fischer, 393–424. London: Purdue University Press, 2007.

Van Steen, Gonda, *Stage of Emergency. Theater and Public Performance Under the Greek Military Dictatorship of 1967–1974*. UK: Oxford University Press, 2015.

Articles from the following newspapers: *New York Times, Eleytheri Ellada [Free Greece], Macedonia, Estia, 4 Avgoustou [4th of August].*

Florian Musil

Eine demokratischere Sicht auf die spanische Redemokratisierung der 1970er-Jahre

Die hier präsentierte und im Rahmen des Initiativkollegs „Europäische historische Diktatur- und Transformationsforschung" entstandene Dissertation „Demokratisierung ‚von unten': Die Zivilgesellschaft der Metropolregion Barcelona im Kampf um demokratische Rechte in der letzten Dekade des Franco-Regimes" beschäftigt sich mit der Zeit vor der politischen Reform Spaniens von einer rechtsradikalen Militärdiktatur in eine moderne liberale Demokratie westlichen Zuschnittes ab 1976. Die Dissertation befasst sich in einer Fallstudie mit der antifranquistischen Zivilgesellschaft im Großraum Barcelona im Allgemeinen und legt in einem zweiten Teil ein besonderes Augenmerk auf deren Arbeiterbewegung, da diese sowohl wegen der Mobilisierungszahlen bei ihren Aktionen wie der Zahl von Aktivisten in ihren Organisationen als auch in den wirtschaftlichen Auswirkungen ihres Handelns die größte und unmittelbar politisch wirkmächtigste soziale Bewegung innerhalb der prodemokratischen Zivilgesellschaft Barcelonas in dieser Zeit darstellt. Die Arbeit vergleicht diese Entwicklungen in Barcelona auch mit den Daten, politischen Konstellationen und Ereignissen in anderen Teilen Spaniens, um die Entwicklungen in Barcelona nicht einfach auf ganz Spanien zu extrapolieren, sondern sie in die Gesamtentwicklung einzuordnen, die Besonderheiten Barcelonas auszuweisen und allgemeine spanische Entwicklungen herauszuarbeiten.

Die Dissertation fügt sich in eine Reihe von Arbeiten der letzten zwei Jahrzehnte aus Spanien ein, die auf lokaler Ebene die Rolle der sozialen Bewegungen im Spätfranquismus aufarbeiten. Hier sind vor allem jene Arbeiten zu nennen, die aus dem *Centre d'Estudis sobre Dictadures i Democràcies* (CEDID) an der *Universitat Autònoma de Barcelona* hervorgegangen sind, aber auch eine Reihe anderer lokalgeschichtlicher Studien aus den verschiedensten Teilen Spaniens legt einen Paradigmenwechsel bei der Frage nach den Ursachen und dem Motor des spanischen Systemwechsels nahe. Größe und Einfluss der prodemokratischen Zivilgesellschaft in Spanien während der Demokratisierung werden dank dieser Regionalstudien immer deutlicher, sie belegen einen aktiven Beitrag der Zivilgesellschaft zur Disruption der politischen und sozialen Ordnung des Regimes und zeigen, wie die sozialen Bewegungen den Wunsch nach Demokratie, Rechtsstaatlichkeit und demokratischen Freiheiten in der Bevölkerung Spaniens verbreiteten. Dieser Paradigmenwechsel stellt aus mehreren Gründen eine demokratischere Sicht auf Spaniens letzte Demokratisierung dar. Er bringt die Rolle des *demos* – der Bevölkerung – stärker in den Fokus der Forschung. Es werden dabei massive qualitative und quantitative Daten zur sozioökonomischen Situation, zu Meinungen, Beweggründen und Lebensläufen erhoben bzw. sozialwissenschaftliche Daten aus der Zeit wieder in den historischen Diskurs eingebracht, die zugunsten von Politikerautobiografien lange wenig Beachtung fanden. Diese Daten helfen uns, ein differenziertes Bild des politischen Handelns aus der Bevölkerung zu zeichnen und endlich viele Stereotypen des „kleinen Mannes", die sich in Jahrzehnten des Blicks von oben im wissenschaftlichen Diskurs angehäuft haben, zu überwinden. So wird die Bevölkerung in der sich nun wandelnden historischen Erzählung immer mehr zu einem Bündel an (mal diversen, mal kollektiven) Handlungsträgern mit verschiedenen Gesichtern, Organisationen, Netzwerken und geistigen Strömungen und verliert dabei die lange zugeschriebene Rolle eines reinen Rezipienten bzw. Spielballs der Handlungen der großen Persönlichkeiten aus Regime, Kommunismus, Sozialismus und der westlichen Welt. Gleichzeitig werden durch diesen Paradigmenwechsel die Bevölkerung und vor allem die Zivilgesellschaft stärker in den wissenschaftlichen Prozess eingebunden, nicht nur als Forschungsobjekt bzw. als Zeitzeugen, sondern auch als Laienforscher, als Archivare, als Herausgeber historischer Publikationen oder Organisatoren historischen Gedenkens, die – wie es Verwaltung und Berufspolitik seit jeher tun – der Geschichtswissenschaft wichtige Impulse liefern.

1.   Die ursprüngliche Meistererzählung zur spanischen Demokratisierung der 1970er-Jahre

Das alte Paradigma sah hinter der politischen Demokratisierung der 1970er-Jahre eine besonders fähige und im Sinne des Allgemeinwohls handelnde Gruppe aus dem Franquismus und dem Königshaus, die Spanien vor allem aus dem Gedanken der Modernisierung und Effizienzsteigerung heraus in die Demokratie führte und das Land so in sich und mit seiner konfliktreichen Vergangenheit versöhnte. Dieses Narrativ deckt sich mit jenem des spanischen Königshauses und der durchführenden Regierung aus der Zeit der demokratischen Reformen sowie der Jahrzehnte danach und wurde in wenig veränderter Form auch von spanischen wie internationalen Massenmedien übernommen.

Abb. 1 und 2: Bildquelle: Online-Archiv des „Time Magazine". Juan Carlos | Nov. 3, 1975 (Cover Credit: LOOMIS DEAN); und Adolfo Suárez | June 27, 1977 (Cover Credit: DANIEL MAFFIA)

Anschauliche Beispiele dieses Blickwinkels auf die Demokratisierung geben uns die beiden oben abgebildeten Titelseiten des „Time Magazine". Die Titelseite links zum Tod Francos im November 1975 zeigt im Hintergrund Franco und vor ihm das neue Staatsoberhaupt, den von ihm eingesetzten König Juan Carlos, und baut so diese beiden als zentrale Protagonisten auf. Kein Wahlvolk, keine Opposition, keine Zivilgesellschaft findet hier Platz. Man vergleiche dies mit der Berichterstattung zum demokratischen Wandel in Osteuropa 14 Jahre später. Auf der Titelseite rechts daneben zu den ersten freien Wahlen im Juni 1977 zeigt das „Time Magazine" den Wahlsieger Adolfo Suárez, der ungefähr ein Jahr zuvor von dem im Bild hinter ihm stehenden König mit dem Auftrag zur Demokratisierung eingesetzt wurde, daraufhin das franquistische System auflöste und die wichtigsten Oppositionsparteien legalisierte. Das Bild zeigt ebenso wie jenes von Franco hinter Juan Carlos, auf welches Erbe und welchen staatsrechtlichen Rahmen diese neue demokratische Regierung zurückblickte und aufgesetzt wurde. Eine große Ausnahme bilden diesbezüglich die Berichte der Korrespondenten von *Le Monde* (José Antonio Nováis) und der *Frankfurter Allgemeinen Zeitung* (Walter Haubrich), die aber oft weniger zur Information der internationalen Öffentlichkeit dienten, denn als Mittel zum Schutz verfolgter Personen aus der Zivilgesellschaft.

Das in der internationalen Presse allgemein vorherrschende Narrativ „von oben" wurde nicht zuletzt durch die damals noch sehr stark vorhandenen Erzählstrukturen politikwissenschaftlicher Ansätze, vor allem der Transitionsforschung der Schule von Juan Linz und Alfred Stepan, gestützt, die in ihren Analysekategorien von Diktaturen und Demokratisierungen vor allem von den Regimen, deren Interna und deren Spitzen ausgingen, die Bevölkerung und sogar die diktatorischen Unterdrückungssysteme hingegen nur sehr peripher erwähnten. Aufgrund der damals dominanten wissenschaftlichen Diskurse ist es wenig verwunderlich, dass international renommierte Politikwissenschaftler – und nach ihnen bald ebenso hochdekorierte und international bekannte Historiker – in den beiden Jahrzehnten nach der spanischen Demokratisierung aus dieser Perspektive „von oben" ein Meisternarrativ in der internationalen Fachwelt formten, das diese Demokratisierung als aus dem Königshaus und Teilen des Regimes heraus initiiert, friedlich, vorbildlich und in großer Eintracht der Parteien durchgeführt darstellt.

Abb. 3: Bildquelle: persönliches Bilderarchiv Florian Musil

Ein prominentes Beispiel für diese Sichtweise zeigt das Bild oben: die Frontansicht der wichtigsten Monografie des spanisch-britischen Historikers Charles T. Powell zum Thema der spanischen Demokratisierung, in welcher der Autor schon zu Beginn darauf hinweist, dass sich „die Definition des Königs als ‚Motor des Wechsels'" durchgesetzt hat. Der Titel seines Buches stellt den König als Piloten dieser Demokratisierung und karikaturistisch als Tänzer in der Mitte Bildes dar, um ihn herum positioniert er Bilder von fünf Spitzenpolitikern aus dem Regime sowie von nur zwei Oppositionspolitikern, dem Sozialistenführer Filipe Gonzales und dem Kommunistenführer Santiago Carrillo, und als internationale Figur wählt er Augusto Pinochet, der eigentlich kaum Einfluss auf die spanische Demokratisierung hatte, sich aber gut in die Parade der bekannten Köpfe einreiht.

Es handelt sich hier nicht nur um das Phänomen einer Meistererzählung, wie sie einst Hayden White als eine allgemeingültige historische Darstellung beschrieben hat, die nicht nur Erklärungen und Daten liefert, sondern gleich eine fixe, für längere Zeit gültige Erzählung festlegt (englisch als *grand narrative* oder *monolitic narrative* bezeichnet), es handelt sich auch um eine Meistererzählung aus der Herrschaftsperspektive im Sinne der *master narratives* von Claude Lévi-Strauss, die er in seiner Arbeit den *slave narratives* gegenüberstellt.

Dieses in der internationalen akademischen Welt propagierte sehr positive Bild der spanischen Demokratisierung und ihrer Politiker dient zum Teil bis heute als offizieller Gründungsmythos und wichtigste demokratische Legitimation der konstitutionellen Monarchie Spaniens, ihres Königshauses und ihrer geltenden Verfassung. Der zivile Widerstand gegen das Regime fand – anders als bei den Demokratisierungen in Osteuropa – kaum Platz im Gründungsmythos der heutigen spanischen Demokratie bzw. wurde als Gefahr für eine sanfte Landung in der Demokratie dargestellt, mit dem Terrorismus der Epoche in engen Zusammenhang gebracht und als mögliche Provokation eines neuen Bürgerkrieges deskreditiert.

2. Zentrale Thesen der Dissertation

Die hier präsentierte Dissertation sieht den Ursprung des Systemwechsels nicht im Regime oder Königshaus. Das wird in der ersten These der Arbeit deutlich: *Bei der spanischen Redemokratisierung der 1970er-Jahre handelt es sich um „einen manifesten sozialen Wandel von unten".*

Mit der Kategorie des „manifesten Wandels von unten" bezieht sich die Arbeit auf das vierteilige Kategoriensystem möglichen sozialen und letztlich politischen Wandels des Soziologen Piotr Sztompka, der diese spezielle Kategorie als einen sozialen Wandel definiert, der zwar von der Regierung umgesetzt wurde, jedoch in Erfüllung von Ideen bzw. Wünschen, die zu diesem Moment schon in breiten Teilen der Bevölkerung präsent waren und wegen des Drucks ebenso breiter Teile der Bevölkerung, der Oppositionsparteien oder sozialer Bewegungen umgesetzt werden mussten. In den Ergebnissen der vorliegenden Studie zur Zivilgesellschaft in Barcelona zeigt sich klar, dass der notwendige Druck für die spanische Redemokratisierung der 1970er-Jahre „von unten" kam, auch wenn die letztendliche staatsrechtliche Demokratisierung durch eine vom König eingesetzte Regierung unter Adolfo Suárez erfolgte. Genaueres hierzu wird im Folgenden behandelt werden.

Mit der Verwendung des Terminus „Redemokratisierung" anstatt des für diese Zeit meist verwendeten Terminus „Demokratisierung" will der Autor in der Formulierung dieser These die wichtige, aber in der Forschung oft vernachlässigte historische Dimension demokratischer Kultur, Erfahrungen und Organisationsrepertoires in der spanischen Gesellschaft in die Diskussion einführen. Ein wichtiger Teil zu Beginn der Studie zeigt die lange Demokratiegeschichte Spaniens sowie seiner Bevölkerung und zivilgesellschaftlichen Organisationen auf. Im ursprünglichen Meisternarrativ für diesen Geschichtsabschnitt wird oft die Rückständigkeit der politischen Kultur Spaniens evoziert und damit klar eines der Legitimationsnarrative des Franquismus weitergeführt, welches der spanischen Bevölkerung Demokratieunfähigkeit unterstellt. Dass Spanien schon seit 1808, seit dem Unabhängigkeitskrieg gegen die napoleonische Besatzung, also fast 170 Jahre vor 1976, auf Perioden demokratischer Staatsverfassungen zurückblicken kann und eine noch viel längere Geschichte intensiver demokratischer Organisationsstrukturen im Bereich der Arbeitsorganisation und lokaler Selbstverwaltung bis hinein in die staatlichen Ständeversammlungen Kastiliens während der Neuzeit aufweist, wird im Meisternarrativ zur Demokratisierung der 1970er-Jahre fast immer ausgespart. Die letzte dieser demokratischen Perioden fand in der Zweiten Republik direkt vor dem Putsch der Militärs statt, der zum Bürgerkrieg und zur Franco-Diktatur führen sollte. Diese Demokratieerfahrungen und deren Gedächtnis bzw. deren Widerhall in den Organisationsstrukturen der spätfranquistischen Zivilgesellschaft sind klar zu erkennen.

Die zweite These der Studie lautet: *Die Zivilgesellschaft Barcelonas war der wichtigste Promotor demokratischer Praktiken und kognitiver demokratischer Handlungsrahmen in der Bevölkerung der Region.*

Es waren nicht das Regime in Form seiner falangistischen Organisationen oder seiner von Opus Dei dominierten Wirtschaftsreformregierung, das – wie in einigen Studien behauptet wird – die Gesellschaft demokratisierte. Gerade in Barcelona lebte der Großteil der Bevölkerung schon länger eine demokratische Kultur, die vor allem von der generell antifranquistisch geprägten Zivilgesellschaft im Großraum der Stadt wiederbelebt und verbreitet wurde.

These Nummer drei der Arbeit besagt: *Bei der Zivilgesellschaft Barcelonas im Generellen und der Arbeiterbewegung im Speziellen handelt es sich um ein Bündel nicht fremdbestimmter kollektiver Akteure.*

Die Forschung zu dieser Arbeit hat gezeigt, dass die Zivilgesellschaft Barcelonas im Allgemeinen sowie die Arbeiterbewegung im Speziellen keine Werkzeuge politischer Oppositionsparteien waren, auch wenn sie sehr stark mit diesen verwoben waren. Ihre Mobilisierungen und Aktionen folgten in den allermeisten und vor allem den wichtigsten Fällen sozialen und gesellschaftlichen Dynamiken und keinen Entscheidungen der Parteien.

3. Repression und Unterdrückung als identitäre Grundlage des Regimes

Um den Widerstand gegen den Franquismus verstehen zu können, müssen wir uns zunächst mit dem Charakter des Regimes und dessen Wirkung auf die Bevölkerung befassen. Die Unterdrückung der Kultur nationaler Minderheiten sowie der Emanzipation der Arbeiterschichten waren die grundlegende Motivation hinter dem Putsch der Militärs 1936, hinter dem ein Bündnis aus Klerus, Großgrundbesitzern, lokalen Honoratioren und Finanz- bzw. Industriebürgertum gestanden und der zur Diktatur geführt hatte. Der Wille zur Unterdrückung Andersdenkender und damit zur Repression war der wichtigste gemeinsame Nenner der sozioökonomischen Allianz hinter dem Franquismus. Wie viele rechtsradikale Diktaturen definierte sich diese stärker über den Gegner und Feindbilder als über gesellschaftliche Ideale. Franco selbst fasste dies zu Beginn des Bürgerkrieges 1939 mit den Worten zusammen: „Ich werde Spanien vor dem Marxismus retten, koste es, was es wolle. Ich werde nicht davor zurückschrecken, halb Spanien zu ermorden, wenn dies der Preis sein sollte, um das Land zu befrieden."[1]

Marxisten, Anarchisten und Regionalisten brachten in den Augen der Nationalen, wie sich die Putschisten nannten, Chaos und Schwäche in das Heimatland. Die Träger dieser Ideologien galt es physisch auszumerzen, um die gottgewollte und für die Spanier natürliche hierarchische Ordnung wiederherzustellen, die Spanien einst zur Weltmacht werden ließ. Gleichzeitig sollten die Sympathisanten der Verfolgten bzw. der demokratischen und linksgerichteten Ideologien durch den Terror der Repression und die Angst vor der Willkür der durch das Regime gefestigten Eliten für ihr restliches Leben in eine Schockstarre versetzt werden, um jeglichen Willen zu sozialer und politischer Organisation außerhalb der gelenkten und kontrollierten Bahnen des Regimes zu verhindern. Zu den angewandten Mitteln zählten u. a. Massenerschießungen politischer Gegner direkt nach der Einnahme neuer Ortschaften im Bürgerkrieg und massive standrechtliche Hinrichtungen in der Dekade nach dem Krieg. Anhänger der Republik mussten mit Gefängnisstrafen sowie Arbeits- und Konzentrationslager rechnen und wurden durch ein Gängelungssystem von Berufsverboten und Passierscheinen am wirtschaftlichen Vorankommen gehindert. Lokale Vertreter des Regimes wie auch die wirtschaftlichen Eliten konnten im Bürgerkrieg und dem frühen Franquismus ihrer Willkür gegenüber Regimegegnern freien Lauf lassen. Diese Maßnahmen büßten – seriösen Schätzungen zufolge – Hunderttausende Spanier mit ihrem Leben. Gleichzeitig wurde nationalen Minderheiten der Gebrauch ihrer Muttersprache in der Öffentlichkeit untersagt. Die letztgenannte Repressionsmaßnahme machte gerade in Barcelona viele ehemalige Unterstützer des Militärputsches zu Gegnern des Regimes.

Dieses Terror- und Gängelungssystem war durch die Dichte seiner Maßnahmen in seinen Resultaten so erfolgreich, dass sich bis zum Ende der 1950er-Jahre nur noch sehr vereinzelte verschworene Widerstandsgruppen organisieren konnten, die meist von der Repression gesprengt wurden. Proteste aus der Bevölkerung ereigneten sich in dieser Zeit nur noch in vereinzelten eruptiven Momenten auf lokaler Ebene. Von einer organisierten und vernetzten regimeunabhängigen Zivilgesellschaft oder sozialen Bewegungen kann darum in den

---

1 Übersetzung durch den Autor: „*Salvaré España del marxismo, cueste lo que cueste. No dudaría en matar media España, si tal fuera el precio a pagar para pacificarla.*" Aus Montse Armengou/Ricard Belis, Las Fosses del Silenci. Dokumentarfilm in zwei Teilen, Teil 1, 2003, um die Minute 2.

ersten zwanzig Jahren nach dem Ende des Bürgerkrieges nicht gesprochen werden.

4. Generationswechsel und Milderung in der Repressionspolitik

Der Widerstand der Generation der 1930er- bis 1950er-Jahre konnte somit fast vollständig gebrochen werden. Erst eine neu heranwachsende Generation am Ende der 1950er- und vor allem ab dem Ende der 1960er-Jahre – eine Generation, die den Terror der Nachkriegszeit nicht mehr kannte, von der jedoch einige zu Hause oder in ihrem Lebensumfeld mit sozialen Werten der Republik aufgewachsen waren – begann wieder außerhalb des Regimes vernetzt sozialpolitisch aktiv zu werden. Dieses neue Engagement traf auf veränderte politische Möglichkeitsstrukturen, wegen der Annäherung an den Westen konnte das Regime seine Repression nicht mehr so engmaschig und effektiv weiterführen. Die vier wichtigsten Mittel der franquistischen Repression während der zweiten Hälfte des Regimes waren: 1. der Einsatz purer körperlicher Gewalt, darunter Folter, Schläge und Schusswaffengebrauch gegen Demonstranten und Streikende; 2. jahrelange Gefängnisstrafen; 3. politische Kündigungen und Arbeitsverbote, die von Almosen abhängig machten oder in die Kriminalität trieben; 4. soziale Kontrolle durch dezidierte Bevorteilung regimeaffiner sozialer Schichten einerseits sowie soziale und kulturelle Exklusion der Arbeiterschicht andererseits.

So meinte Armando Varo, Kommunist und illegaler Gewerkschaftsführer der 1970er-Jahre, im Interview mit dem Autor:[2]

> „Der Bürgerkrieg, vor allem für die Generation von Camillo und Camacho [der Erstgenannte war Führer der spanischen Kommunisten, der Zweite Kopf der spanienweiten illegalen Gewerkschaft Arbeiterkommissionen], war ein beängstigender Ballast ihrer Vergangenheit. Klar! Ich bin 1947 geboren und für mich war das schon etwas Natürliches, einen Streik zu machen. Für sie war's etwas, wofür man vielleicht erschossen hätte werden können. Fakt ist, wir jungen Aktivisten bekamen ein Buch darüber, was uns auf der Polizeiwache erwarten könnte [...]. Wenn du dir dieses Buch durchgelesen hattest, dann hast du in Wirklichkeit bei der ersten Frage auf der Polizeiwache alles gesungen. [...] Aber verflucht! In den 60ern und den 70ern, klar brachten sie damals auch noch Leute um, aber sagen wir's so, nur ganz selten ist einer mit den Füßen voran aus einer Polizeiwache getragen worden, geschlagen auf jeden Fall schon, aber nicht getötet. Also ich war dreimal in der Situation und hier siehst du mich."

---

2 Übersetzung durch den Autor aus der Videodatei. Interview mit Armando Varo, geführt von Florian Musil, 5.6.2007, Aufnahme beim Autor. Das Thema des Interviews ist seine Zeit als Aktivist in Arbeiterkommissionen bei SEAT und in Barcelona allgemein und über die erlittene Repression und Polizeigewalt. Er war in den 1970er-Jahren auch Mitglied der Generalkoordinationskommission der gesamtspanischen Arbeiterkommissionen.

Die nun entstehende antifranquistische Zivilgesellschaft und auch die politischen Oppositionsgruppen, die ihre Mitglieder in erster Linie aus dieser neuen Zivilgesellschaft anwarben, wurden darum vor allem von jungen Menschen getragen. Dies spiegelt sich auch in den Akten des Regimes wider.

In den Archivbeständen des barcelonischen Zivilgouverneurs, des administrativen Oberhauptes der Provinz, konnte der Autor acht Listen mit den in der Provinz „wegen ihrer Aktenvermerke und Handlungen gegen das Regime hervorstechendsten Personen" vom Januar und Februar 1969 finden.

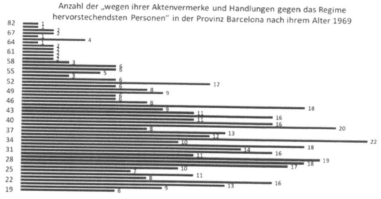

Abb. 4: Quelle: Dissertation des Autors

Es fällt auf, dass der Großteil der unter Beobachtung stehenden Aktivisten zwischen 27 und 45 Jahre alt waren, also 1936 zum Ausbruch des Bürgerkrieges entweder noch nicht auf der Welt oder höchstens zwölf Jahre alt. Nur 16 % der 468 Aufgelisteten waren 1939 am Ende des Bürgerkrieges und gar nur 5 % der Aufgelisteten 1931 bei der Ausrufung der Zweiten Republik über 20 Jahre alt, also in einem Alter, in dem politischer Aktivismus in der Republik schon möglich gewesen wäre. Diese Älteren sind zum Großteil dem Bürgertum zuzurechnen, wie Künstler, Anwälte, Wirtschaftstreibende und Industrielle, meist Christdemokraten oder Katalanisten. Arbeiter bzw. Mitglieder der Arbeiterkommissionen und die als Kommunisten Vermerkten sind in der Liste zumeist in ihren 20ern oder 30ern. Jugendliche unter 19 Jahren finden sich gar nicht in der Liste, diese gab es zwar zahlreich in den antifranquistischen Organisationen und Bewegungen, ihnen galt aber offensichtlich nicht das Interesse der Ermittler oder des Zivilgouverneurs.

5. Die wichtigsten Bewegungen innerhalb der neu erwachten antifranquistischen Zivilgesellschaft

Innerhalb dieser antifranquistischen Zivilgesellschaft gab es drei besonders mobilisierungsstarke soziale Bewegungen: die hier genauer untersuchte Arbeiterbewegung, sowie die Studierendenbewegung und die Nachbarschaftsvereine der Stadtviertel. All diese Bewegungen befassten sich mit konkreten gesellschaftlichen Missständen. Die Studentenbewegung forderte eine Demokratisierung des Unibetriebes, bildete von Barcelona aus eine spanienweite demokratische Studentenorganisation, die zwar die staatliche Studentenorganisation zur Auflösung zwang, selbst aber Anfang der 1970er-Jahre an der wieder aufflammenden staatlichen Repression zerbrach. Die Universitäten blieben jedoch auch nach dem Ende der spanienweiten demokratischen Studentengewerkschaft ein ständiger Ort großer Proteste gegen das Regime. Die sogenannte „Bürgerbewegung" gemeint ist die Bewegung der Nachbarschaftsvereine verfügte im Gegensatz zu den beiden anderen großen Bewegungen über keine spanienweiten Organisationen. Im Gegensatz zur Studierenden- und der Arbeiterbewegung konnte sich der Großteil ihrer Organisationen im legalen Rahmen der franquistischen Gesetzgebung bewegen. Die meisten ihrer Basisgruppen waren entstanden, weil die Arbeiterkommissionen Ende der 1960er von den Fabriken in die Arbeiterviertel expandierten und dort zunächst meist illegale Nachbarschafts- bzw. Bürgerkommissionen installierten, um gegen die schlechte infrastrukturelle Versorgung in den Arbeiterbezirken anzukämpfen. Später bildeten sich aus diesen legale Vereine oder diese Gruppen übernahmen schon vorhandene und vom Regime zugelassene Vereine lokaler Gewerbetreibender, die ursprünglich zur Organisation von Straßenfesten bestanden hatten. Zur Arbeiterbewegung werden wir später noch im Detail kommen.

Neben den drei großen Bewegungen und oft mit diesen verknüpft, bildete sich eine Reihe weiterer sachbezogener Bewegungen wie der Feminismus, der Pazifismus bzw. die Wehrdienstverweigerer, die Bewegung für eine egalitärere und alternative Schulausbildung, die Bewegung für eine bessere Gesundheitsversorgung in den Spitälern, aber auch berufsgruppenspezifische Bewegungen, Strömungen und Organisationen wie die prodemokratischen Netzwerke unter Künstlern, Journalisten, Architekten und Juristen, die einerseits die großen, kampfstarken Bewegungen mit ihrem Wissen und Dienstleistungen unterstützten, aber auch deklariert demokratische Fraktionen in ihren Berufskammern bildeten, um damit ein Zeichen gegen die geltende Ordnung zu setzen.

Sowohl die katalanistische Kultur- und Autonomiebewegung als auch der sozialkritische Katholizismus der Kirchenbasis waren nicht nur eigene Bewegungen, sondern, zusammen mit dem Marxismus in seinen verschiedenen Ausformungen, die bestimmenden ideologischen Strömungen innerhalb der barcelonischen Zivilgesellschaft, wie weiter unten ausgeführt wird.

6.   Die *Assemblea de Catalunya*

1971, also vier Jahre vor dem Tod Francos, gründete die katalanische Zivilgesellschaft zusammen mit den Oppositionsparteien eine gemeinsame illegale Dachorganisation, die *Assemblea de Catalunya* (Versammlung Kataloniens), eine Art immer wieder tagendes Zivilgesellschaftsparlament, das zum wichtigsten Koordinationsorgan der Großdemonstrationen am Ende des Franquismus werden sollte. Die *Assemblea de Catalunya* machte von Beginn an vier demokratiepolitische Forderungen zu ihrer zentralen Mission: 1. die Generalamnestie für politische Gefangene und Exilierte; 2. die Einführung der grundlegendsten demokratischen Freiheiten wie der Versammlungs-, Meinungs-, Vereinigungs- und Gewerkschaftsfreiheit sowie des Demonstrations- und Streikrechts, um, wie sie formulierte, „dem Volk den Zugang zur wirtschaftlichen und ökonomischen Macht zu garantieren"; 3. die Wiedereinsetzung der demokratischen Regionalverfassung Kataloniens und ihrer Institutionen aus den Zeiten der letzten Republik, was implizit die Forderung nach einer demokratischen Staatsverfassung ganz Spaniens bedeutete; und 4. strebte die *Assemblea de Catalunya* eine Koordination aller Völker der iberischen Halbinsel in deren Kampf um Demokratie an.

Die oben abgebildete Delegationsliste einer der Versammlungen der *Assemblea de Catalunya* bietet uns Einblick in den Aufbau und die Zusammensetzung dieser Dachorganisation der Zivilgesellschaft. Als Erstes sind etwas mehr als 20 politische Gruppen aufgelistet, von katholisch-konservativ wie der CDC über sozialistisch-katalanistische Parteien wie dem PSAN, Eurokommunisten wie dem PSUC und Sozialdemokraten wie dem PSC, gefolgt von den Delegierten von sechs Parteijugendorganisationen. Unter *O. Masses* („Massenorganisationen") stehen die illegalen Gewerkschaften. Unter *Diversos* („Diverse") finden wir zahlreiche Berufsverbände, von den Ingenieuren über die Geisteswissenschaftler bis zu den Anwälten. Aber auch der Verband der ehemaligen politischen Häftlinge und katholische NGOs wie *Pax Christi* oder *Solitaritat* (Organisation, welche finanzielle Hilfen für politische Häftlinge und deren Familien sammelte und verwaltete) finden sich in dieser Rubrik. Den *Diversos* folgen die *Comarques*, also die Landkreisdelegierten lokaler sogenannter demokratischer Versammlungen bzw. demokratischer Tische aus den verschiedenen Teilen Kataloniens, darunter auch eine dreiköpfige Delegation aus dem katalanischsprachigen Kleinstaat Andorra, aber auch aus dem Exil in London und der Schweiz. Und zuletzt finden wir unter *Barris* die Delegierten der Nachbarschaftsvereine der

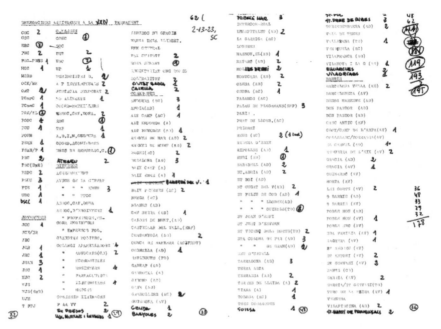

Abb. 5: Bildausschnitt eines maschinengeschriebenen und handschriftlich ergänzten Dokumentes: Arxiu Nacional de Catalunya (ACN). Fons Assemblea de Catalunya

verschiedenen Stadtviertel Barcelonas. Die Anzahl der Delegierten spiegelte hier jedoch nicht das wahre Kräfteverhältnis der einzelnen Organisationen innerhalb der Zivilgesellschaft wider. So sind Organisationen wie die mit Abstand mitgliederstärkste Partei (die kommunistische PSUC) mit drei Delegierten repräsentiert und die hegemoniale Gewerkschaftsorganisation der Arbeiterkommission gar nur mit einem Delegierten. Beide Organisationen waren wesentlich an der Gründung und dem Ausbau der *Assemblea de Catalunya* beteiligt, nahmen sich jedoch in dieser etwas zurück, um in Katalonien einen breiten zivilgesellschaftlichen Schulterschluss gegen das Regime gewährleisten zu können.

7.   Die prägendsten weltanschaulichen Strömungen in der Zivilgesellschaft Barcelonas

Die Zivilgesellschaft Barcelonas wurde vor allem von drei weltanschaulichen Strömungen dominiert: den beiden schon genannten des Katalanismus und des sozialkritischen Katholizismus sowie jener des Marxismus. Diese drei Weltanschauungen existierten nicht getrennt voneinander, sondern waren stark miteinander verwoben. Es gab zum Beispiel kommunistische Pfarrer, einer von ihnen wurde nach der Demokratisierung sogar kommunistischer Bürgermeister der Arbeitervorstadt Santa Coloma. Der stark kommunistische, spanischsprachig geprägte Dachverband der Arbeiterkommissionen (wichtigste illegale Gewerkschaftsorganisation) in Katalonien wiederum nahm in Bezug auf die Autonomieforderungen der Katalanen den Namen „Nationale Arbeiterkommission Kataloniens" an. Eine Großzahl der Aktivisten an der Basis der Arbeiterkommissionen kam ursprünglich aus katholischen Laienorganisationen. Manche katalanischen Priester wiederum predigten in hauptsächlich spanischsprachigen Arbeitervorstädten über die sozialen Ungerechtigkeiten des Regimes aus einem katalanistischen Opferparadigma der nationalen Unterdrückung heraus. Es gab aber auch weiterhin konservativ-katalanische Gruppierungen aus dem Bürgertum in der Zivilgesellschaft, die zwar durchaus katholisch geprägt waren, doch für den Marxismus und die Arbeiterbewegung nur geringe Sympathien aufbringen konnten. Die wichtigste Figur dieser Strömung war der spätere Langzeit-Regierungschef Kataloniens, Jordi Pujol i Soley.

Diese Vermengung der Weltanschauungen half, manifeste Dogmen und ideologische Gräben aus Zeiten des Bürgerkriegs und der Zweiten Republik zu überwinden. So war die Arbeiterbewegung in Barcelona in den 1970ern – im Gegensatz zu ihren anarchistischen bzw. sozialistischen Pendants in der Zweiten Republik – weder antiklerikal noch antikatalanistisch eingestellt. Die drei Weltanschauungen waren nun keine grundlegenden Gegensätze mehr, sondern förderten unterschiedliche, sich ergänzende Forderungen innerhalb der Zivilgesellschaft. Der Katalanismus forderte zunächst den freien Gebrauch der Muttersprache und die Förderung dieser in den Schulen sowie der katalanischen Kultur und des Brauchtums. Später kam die Forderung nach einer demokratischen Selbstverwaltung Kataloniens hinzu, das im Franquismus keine Verwaltungseinheit bildete, sondern in vier getrennte Provinzen unterteilt war. Der progressive Katholizismus setzte sich für mehr Mitmenschlichkeit, soziale Kohäsion und Menschenrechte ein und engagierte sich wesentlich im Kampf gegen die Repression und die Armut. Während der Marxismus die Emanzipation der arbeitenden Bevölkerung beförderte, indem er die Willkür der Unternehmer anprangerte und die verbotene unabhängige Koordination der Belegschaften in Interessenkonflikten zwischen Kapital und Arbeit förderte und als Grundrecht einforderte.

8.   Das Organigramm der Arbeiterbewegung im Großraum Barcelona

Nun zur Detailanalyse der Arbeiterbewegung, die sich im Großraum Barcelona in erster Linie in der neuen illegalen Gewerkschaftsorganisation der Arbeiterkommissionen organsierte. Diese war ursprünglich durch ein neues kollektives Handlungsrepertoire in Arbeitskonflikten vor allem während Tarifverhandlungen in den Arbeitshochburgen Asturiens und des Baskenlands entstanden. Den Arbeitern erschien es unmöglich, in diesen Verhandlungen ihren Wünschen Ausdruck und Nachdruck zu verleihen, da die staatliche Gewerkschaft, in der Arbeitgeber und Arbeitnehmer gemeinsam organisiert waren, eher als Gängelungsinstitution für die Forderungen der Arbeitnehmer fungierte. Es bildeten sich Belegschaftskommissionen, die mit dem Druckmittel illegaler Arbeitsniederlegungen Verhandlungen mit den Firmenleitungen an der offiziellen franquistischen Gewerkschaft vorbei erzwangen. Dieses kollektive Handlungsrepertoire verbreitete sich Anfang der 1960er-Jahre spanienweit in den Betrieben, in einigen als vorübergehende Verhandlungskommissionen, in anderen als ständige geheime Betriebsgruppen. An dieser Verbreitung waren illegale politische Parteien wie die katalanischen Kommunisten des PSUC, ihre spanische Schwesterpartei PCE oder auch sozialistische Kleinparteien wie der katalonische FOC federführend beteiligt, wenn auch viele der betrieblichen Aktivisten gerade in Katalonien aus den katholischen Arbeitervereinen kamen. Diese Kommissionen bzw. ihre Aktivisten vernetzten sich zunächst lokal und dann auch spanienweit. 1967 wurde landesweit die sogenannte *la general*, die Generalkoordinationskommission der Arbeiterkommissionen, mit Sitz in Madrid gegründet, die ab 1972 von Barcelona aus agierte, da die Gewerkschaftsspitzen aus den anderen Regionen im Zuge eines geheimen Treffens festgenommen und inhaftiert wurden, während die katalanischen Delegierten zu ihrem Glück zu spät gekommen waren und der Verhaftung entgingen.

In Katalonien selbst hatte es bis zum Ende der 1960er gedauert, bis sich das regionale Organigramm der neuen Gewerkschaftsorganisation herausgebildet hatte. An der Spitze stand die schon erwähnte Nationale Arbeiterkommission Kataloniens, die vor allem politisch agierte, da die regionale Eingrenzung auf Katalonien für Tarifverhandlungen irrelevant war. Unter ihr standen die für Tarifverhandlungen sehr wohl relevanten Lokalkoordinationskommissionen, so die wichtigste für Barcelona-Stadt oder jene für die Landkreise des Industriegürtels um Barcelona. Unter diesen gab es lokale Branchenkoordinationskommissionen sowie vorübergehende lokale Branchenforderungsplattformen, die vor allem bei den immer häufiger werdenden lokalen Flächenstreiks ab 1973 in den Industrievorstädten Barcelonas ins Leben gerufen wurden. Des Weiteren gab

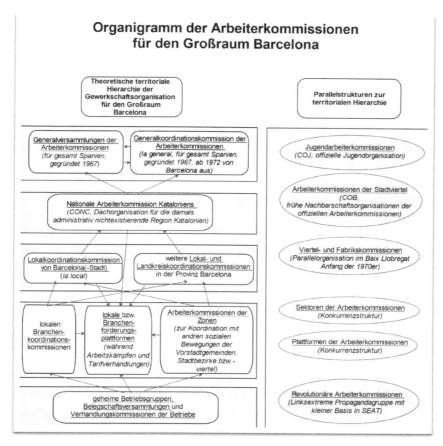

Abb. 6: Quelle: Dissertation des Autors

es die Arbeiterkommissionen der Zonen, die allgemeine soziale Kämpfe und Forderungen, zum Beispiel gegen die Inflation, mit den anderen sozialen Bewegungen koordinierten. In den einzelnen Betrieben gab es weiterhin geheime Betriebsgruppen, Belegschaftsversammlungen und Verhandlungskommissionen. Neben diesen Organisationseinheiten gab es noch Unterorganisationen wie die Jugendarbeiterkommissionen, die viele Studierende anzogen und vor allem im Freizeitbereich aktiv waren, sowie die Arbeiterkommissionen der Stadtviertel, die eine Zeit lang den sozialen Widerstand in den Wohnvierteln organisierten. Es existierten aber auch Parallelorganisationen, die die Bezeichnung Arbeiterkommission im Namen trugen, jedoch unabhängig waren.

9.   Kollektives Handlungsrepertoire der Arbeiterbewegung im Großraum Barcelona

So gut wie alle mobilisierungsstarken Aktionen der Arbeiterbewegung entstanden aus den Belegschaften der einzelnen Betriebe heraus. Sie breiteten sich zum Ende des Franquismus immer schneller durch Solidaritätswellen von einem Betrieb zum anderen aus und stellten als lokale Flächenbrände das Regime vor ernsthafte Probleme der öffentlichen Ordnung. Die höheren, meist politisch dominierten Einheiten dieser Hierarchie wie die Nationale Arbeiterkommission Kataloniens oder *la general* hatten keinen Einfluss auf das Streikverhalten, auch wenn diese immer wieder versuchten, Generalstreiks auszurufen, um das Regime zu Fall zu bringen, doch ohne Erfolg. Ihnen oblagen darum vor allem das Informationsmanagement und die breitere Öffentlichkeitsarbeit sowie Kampagnen für die in den Betrieben entstandenen Protestwellen. Kurzum, sie konnten Streikwellen befeuern, aber nicht gesteuert auslösen, um sie gezielt gegen das Regime zu verwenden.

Ein kollektives Handlungsrepertoire stand zu Beginn jedes betrieblichen Arbeitskampfs: die Belegschaftsversammlung. Sie war der Grundstein jeglicher kollektiven Entscheidungsfindung, ohne die kein Arbeitskampf möglich war. Sie diente zur Meinungserhebung und zum Meinungsaustausch der Belegschaften, zur politischen Schulung der Belegschaft durch die betriebliche Avantgarde und half, die Positionen zu vereinheitlichen und damit den Zusammenschluss der Belegschaft zu einem kollektiven Akteur zu gewährleisten. In ihr wurden auch alle Maßnahmen organisiert und deren Ergebnisse besprochen.

Einer Entscheidung zum Arbeitskampf folgte eine Reihe von möglichen Kampfmaßnahmen, die immer repressive Maßnahmen des Betriebs wie Kündigungen aus politischen Gründen oder Strafverfolgung nach sich ziehen konnten. Der Fächer der Repertoires im Arbeitskampf reichte von schwerer feststellbaren passiven Mitteln, wie akkordierte Senkung der Produktivität über friedlich aktive Mittel wie Betriebsbesetzungen oder Demonstrationen bis hin zu gewaltsamen Mitteln gegen Eigentum oder, was selten vorkam, gegen Personen wie vermeintliche Spitzel des Managements, Familienmitglieder von diesen oder die Polizei. Dabei darf aber nicht außer Acht gelassen werden, dass ähnliche persönliche Druckmittel während des Franquismus auch vom Management und der Polizei gegen Streikende und ihre Familien angewandt wurden.

Ein weiteres wichtiges Handlungsrepertoire der Arbeiterkommission war die Unterwanderung der staatlichen Gewerkschaft über die zur Wahl der Belegschaft stehenden betrieblichen Vertrauensmänner und überbetrieblichen Arbeitervertreter in den staatlichen Gewerkschaftsgremien. Diese Positionen waren in Verhandlungen wenig einflussreich, doch brachte die Infiltrierung der staatlichen Gewerkschaft den Arbeiterkommissionen und ihren Aktivisten drei zentrale Vorteile: Sie konnten sich nun offen unter den Belegschaften als Arbeitnehmervertreter bewegen; sie konnten Infrastrukturen der staatlichen Gewerkschaft wie deren Räume nützen; und sie konnten so die staatliche Gewerkschaft von innen ad absurdum führen. Diese Aktivisten wurden dabei jedoch immer wieder Opfer staatlicher Repression. Die Infiltration wurde nicht von allen Gruppen in der Arbeiterbewegung gutgeheißen. Gerade Sozialisten und Linksrevolutionäre sahen darin eine Stärkung des Regimes. 1975 konnte jedoch so die Liste der „einheitlichen und demokratischen Kandidaturen" der Arbeiterkommissionen zum großen Wahlsieger der staatlichen Gewerkschaftsvertreterwahlen in Katalonien aufsteigen und eine klar prodemokratische Willensbekundung der katalonischen Arbeitnehmer in der Öffentlichkeit manifestieren.

10. Mobilisierungsstärke der Arbeiterbewegung

Bis in die 1970er-Jahre hatte sich die Arbeiterbewegung Spaniens stark politisiert. Dies spiegelt sich auch in den von den Regimeorganisationen erhobenen Daten zu den Arbeitermobilisierungen wider.

Abb. 7: Quelle: Dissertation des Autors

Ging es 1963 bei über 70 % der Arbeitskonflikte spanienweit als Hauptthema um streng Finanzielles (Gehalt und Tarifverträge) und bei gerade mal 5 % um eher Politisches (sozialpolitische Themen und Solidarität gegen die Repression), wechselte dieses Verhältnis ab den 1970er Jahren. 1970 waren 73 % der Konflikte dem Wunsch nach politischer Einflussnahme geschuldet und nur noch 16 % waren rein monetär bedingt. In den letzten drei bis vier Jahren der Diktatur beinhalteten dann alle größeren Arbeitskonflikte zusätzlich dezidierte Forderungen nach demokratischen Freiheiten.

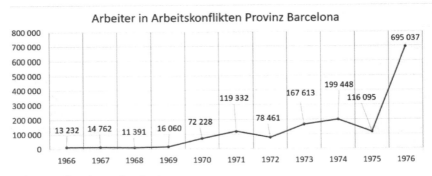

Abb. 8: Quelle: Dissertation des Autors

Gleichzeitig schnellten die Zahlen der an Arbeitskonflikten beteiligten Arbeitnehmer in die Höhe. Von 1966 bis 1974 verfünfzehnfachte sich die Zahl der an Arbeitskonflikten Beteiligten in der Provinz Barcelona. Der Anstieg der Repression wegen der sich abzeichnenden terminalen Krankheit des Diktators führte 1975 zu einem leichten Sinken der Beteiligung, doch mit dessen Tod im November dieses Jahres eskalierten die Mobilisierungszahlen unmittelbar. 1976, im Jahr der letzten franquistischen Regierung ohne Franco, stieg die Zahl der Beteiligten in der Provinz Barcelona um das Sechsfache im Vergleich zum Vorjahr an.

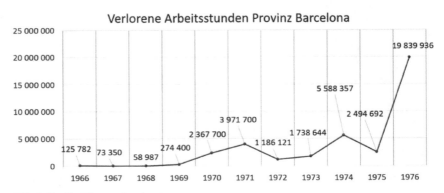

Abb. 9: Quelle: Dissertation des Autors

Es stieg nicht nur die Zahl der Beteiligten, sondern auch die Intensität der Konflikte. Die Zahl der verlorenen Arbeitsstunden in der Provinz Barcelona verachtfachte sich nach dem Tod Francos und mit ihr der wirtschaftliche Schaden.

Europavergleich: verlorene Arbeitstage pro 10.000 Personen der aktiven Bevölkerung

	1971	1972	1973	1974	1975	1976
ISLAND	3.554	1.340	1.591	10.365	6.948	34.439
PROVINZ BARCELONA	2.870	857	1.256	4.038	1.803	14.335
SPANIEN	722	493	909	1.469	1.525	10.582
FINNLAND	12.849	2.242	11.834	2.061	1.347	5.866
ITALIEN	7.474	9.847	11.828	9.832	13.732	12.817
MALTA	2.188	1.334	3.845	1.370	1.285	634
GROSZBRITANNIEN	5.271	9.299	2.799	5.737	2.338	1.277
IRLAND	2.423	1.831	1.829	4.883	2.617	6.876
GRIECHENLAND						2.439
BELGIEN	3.417	975	2.402	1.598	1.674	2.471
FRANKREICH	2.016	1.725	1.798	1.553	1.777	1.863
DÄNEMARK	89	94	16.888	797	433	910
TÜRKEI	315	436	444	734	443	216
PORTUGAL						
NIEDERLANDE	203	281	1.221	14	1	29
SCHWEDEN	2.337	29	33	160	1.018	69
NORWEGEN	62	85	78	2.181	85	943
ZYPERN	1.181	7.121	644	717	390	134
SCHWEIZ	25	7	-	9	6	66
BRD	1.685	25	212	395	26	201
ÖSTERREICH	12	48	512	23	18	2

Abb. 10: Quelle: Dissertation des Autors

Vergleicht man die Zahl der verlorenen Arbeitstage in der Provinz Barcelona mit der Streikstatistik der internationalen Arbeitsorganisation der UNO und berechnet die verlorenen Streiktage pro 10.000 Personen der aktiven Bevölkerung, übertraf 1976 nur Island als einziges europäisches Land die Streikdichte in Barcelona, da dort die gesamte weibliche Bevölkerung für mehr Rechte und bessere Bezahlung gestreikt hatte. Österreich zum Beispiel wies 1976 weniger als 0,2 Promille der Streikintensität Barcelonas auf.

Sehr großen Anteil an diesem enormen Anstieg der Streikstatistik 1976 in Barcelona hatten Flächenstreiks im Industriegürtel um die Stadt, die ganze Landkreise lahmlegten und zum Kampfgebiet zwischen Demonstranten und Polizei machten. All diese Streiks forderten neben anderen Themen auch eine politische Demokratisierung.

11. Die Reaktion des Königs

Um die Situation zu besänftigen, machte König Juan Carlos seine erste offizielle Reise als neues Staatsoberhaupt im Februar 1976 in die Provinz Barcelona, wo er vom Balkon des Rathauses der Arbeiter- und Streikhochburg Cornellà de Llobregat eine Rede an die Bevölkerung hielt:[3]

> „Wir, die Königin und ich, sind nach Cornellá in den Bajo Llobregat [Im Original wurde auch die kastilische und nicht die katalanische Ortsbezeichnung verwendet] gekommen, um euch kennenzulernen und damit ihr uns kennenlernt. Ich will, dass ihr wisst, dass der König die Probleme der Arbeitswelt als seine eigenen fühlt. Und das sind nicht einfach nur Worte. […] Ich sehe, dass ihr in diesem Gebiet, unter anderem, ernste Probleme […] mit urbanen und infrastrukturellen Einrichtungen habt, wie es auch in anderen Gebieten Spaniens der Fall ist. Ich bin auch gekommen, um euren Bestrebungen nach Vollbeschäftigung, Verbesserung der Sozialversicherung und einer volleren Beteiligung am politischen Leben zuzuhören. Seid versichert, dass all eure Rechte, als Bürger und Arbeiter, anerkannt und umgesetzt werden …"

Die Rede konnte jedoch die Arbeitermobilisierungen nicht verringern, schon wenige Tage später kam es im Großraum Barcelona und bald auch in Cornellà selbst zu weiteren Großdemonstrationen und Flächenstreiks.

Im Juni 1976, nach sieben Monaten Franquismus ohne Franco, bat der König den Regierungschef Arias Navarro, einen franquistischen Hardliner, um dessen Rücktritt und ließ darauf Adolfo Suárez González, einen gemäßigten Franquisten, als neuen Regierungschef einsetzen. Dieser begann unverzüglich mit dem Abbau der franquistischen Staatsstrukturen und ersetzte diese durch demokratische. Gleichzeitig baute Suárez geheime Kontakte zu den illegalen Oppositionsparteien auf und gewann diese für sein Projekt der Demokratisierung. Am 15. Dezember 1976 ließ er über sein demokratisches Reformgesetz in einem Referendum abstimmen und erhielt 94,45 % Zustimmung. Für den 15. Juni 1977 rief Suárez allgemeine freie Wahlen aus und legalisierte die im Untergrund relevanten Parteien, selbst die Kommunistische Partei, doch diese erst wenige Wochen vor den Wahlen und unter lautem Säbelrasseln der franquistischen Militärs. Suárez wurde als das Gesicht der Demokratisierung von den staatlichen Medien propagiert und seine neu gegründete Union der demokratischen Mitte aus gemäßigten Exfranquisten und bürgerlichen Antifranquisten wurden mit 34,44 % stärkste Partei. Durch das neue Wahlrecht, das Großparteien bevorteilt, wurde er erster Regierungschef der neuen konstitutionellen Monarchie. Die

---

3 Übersetzung durch den Autor. Zit. n. Casa de Su Majestad el Rey de España – Actividades y Agenda – Palabras de Su Majestad el Rey en Cornellá. Barcelona (Cornellá), 21. 2. 1976, URL: http://www.casareal.es/ES/actividades/Paginas/actividades_discursos_detalle.aspx?data=3 589 (abgerufen 13. 04. 2017).

Parteien, die dezidiert aus dem antifranquistischen Widerstand hervorgegangen waren, konnten knapp über 50 % der Stimmen auf sich ziehen, waren jedoch zu divers und zersplittert, um eine parlamentarische Mehrheit für eine Regierung bilden zu können.

12. Auswahlbibliographie

Marc Andreu i Acebal, El moviment ciutadà i la transició a Barcelona. La FAVB (1972–1986), phil. Diss., Universität Barcelona 2014.

Antoni Batista/Josep Playà Maset, La gran conspiració. Cronica de l'Assemblea de Catalunya, Barcelona 1991.

Georgina Blakeley, Building local democracy in Barcelona, Lewiston, NY 2004.

Eva Botella-Ordinas/Domino Centenero de Arce/Antonio Terrasa Lozano, Une tradition hispanique de démocratie locale. Les cabildos abiertos du XVIe siècle à nos jours, La vie des idées, URL: https://laviedesidees.fr/Une-tradition-hispanique-de.html (abgerufen 6.5.2022).

Antonio Cazorla Sánchez, Fear and progress. Ordinary lives in Franco's Spain, 1939–1975, Malden, MA 2010.

Xavier Domènech Sampere, Quan el carrer va deixar de ser seu. Moviment obrer, societat civil i canvi polític. Sabadell (1966–1976), Barcelona 2002.

Andrew Dowling, For Christ and Catalonia. Catholic Catalanism and Nationalist Revival in Late Francoism, in: Journal of Contemporary History 3 (2012), 594–610.

Friedrich Edelmayer (Hg.), Anarchismus in Spanien (Studien zur Geschichte und Kultur der iberischen und iberoamerikanischen Länder 12), Wien 2008.

Josep Fontana (Hg.), España bajo el franquismo, Barcelona 1986.

Konrad H. Jarausch/Martin Sabrow, „Meistererzählung" – Zur Karriere eines Begriffs, in: *dies.* (Hg.), Die historische Meistererzählung. Deutungslinien der deutschen Nationalgeschichte nach 1945, Göttingen 2011, 9–31.

Martí Marín i Corbera, La fàbrica, el barri, la ciutat i el país. La integració dels immigrants a Catalunya sota el franquisme, in: Jordi Font i Agulló (Hg.), Història i memòria. El franquisme i els seus efectes als països catalans, València 2007, 261–284.

Martí Marín i Corbera, Falange y poder local, in: Miguel À. Ruiz-Carnicer (Hg.), Falange. Las culturas políticas del fascismo en la España de Franco (1936–1975), Zaragoza 2013, 231–252.

Andreu Mayayo i Artal, La ruptura catalana. Les eleccions del 15-J del 1977, Catarroja 2002.

Memorial Democràtic (Hg.), SEAT 1950-1977. L'arquitectura de la Repressió, (Ausstellungskatalog), Barcelona 2011.

Stéphane Michonneau/Xosé M. Núñez Seixas (Hg.), Imaginarios y representaciones de España durante el franquismo, Madrid 2017.

Carme Molinero/Pere Ysàs, Productores disciplinados y minorías subversivas. Clase obrera y conflictividad laboral en la España franquista, Madrid 1998.

Carme Molinero/Pere Ysàs, Catalunya durant el franquisme, Barcelona 1999.

Carme Molinero/Pere Ysàs (Hg.), Construint la ciutat democràtica. El moviment veïnal durant el tardofranquisme i la transició, Barcelona 2010.

Florian Musil, Demokratisierung ‚von unten'. Die Zivilgesellschaft der Metropolregion Barcelona im Kampf um demokratische Rechte in der letzten Dekade des Franco-Regimes, Diss., Universität Wien, Wien 2017.

Florian Musil, Die Aufarbeitung der Franco-Diktatur als Werkzeug zur Wählermobilisierung, in: Linda Erker/Alexander Salzmann/Lucile Dreidemy/Klaudija Sabo (Hg.), Update! Perspektiven der Zeitgeschichte. Zeitgeschichtetage 2010, Innsbruck 2012, 564–572.

Florian Musil, Francos Spanien im Vergleich mit Fidel Castros Kuba. Möglichkeiten und Hindernisse für eine Demokratisierung in Kuba, Saarbrücken 2010.

Florian Musil, Internationaler Kongress „Die franquistische Diktatur: Institutionalisierung eines Regimes" vom 21. bis 23. April 2010 in Barcelona (Kongressbericht), in: diktaturforschung.univie.ac.at (2010).

Florian Musil, La Transición Democrática en España desde abajo. El ejemplo del Movimiento Estudiantil en Barcelona, in: Beatriz Ardesi de Taratuvíez et al. (Hg.), XIII Jornadas Interescuelas: Departamento de Historia, Catarmarca 2013.

Florian Musil, Los Movimientos Antifranquistas de Barcelona al final de la Dictadura. Propuesta para un esquema analítico de movimientos sociales contemporáneos, in: Alejandra Ibarra Aguirregabiria (Hg.), No es país para jóvenes. Actas del III Encuentro de jóvenes investigadores de la AHC, Vitoria-Gasteiz 2012, 1–20.

Florian Musil, Social and Political Victims Become the Founders of a New Democratic Civil Society under Dictatorial Rule, in: Revista Convergência Crítica 3 (2013), 10–25.

Oliver Rathkolb, Demokratie und Diktatur. Zeitgeschichtliche Reflexionen über zentrale Schlüsselbegriffe des 20. Jahrhunderts, Antrittsvorlesung vom 13. Januar 2009.

Borja de Riquer, La societat catalana al final del règim franquista, in: Pere Ysàs (Hg.), La transició a Catalunya i Espanya, Barcelona 1997, 49–65.

Adrian Shubert, A social history of modern Spain, London 2015.

Javier Tébar/José Fernando Mota Mun˜oz/Na`dia Varo Moral, TOPCAT 1963–1977. L'antifranquisme català davant el Tribunal de Orden Público TOPCAT, Broschüre des Forschungsprojekts: El Tribunal de Orden Público (TOP) i la repressió política sota la dictadura franquista a Catalunya, Barcelona 2010.

Pere Ysàs (Hg.), La transició a Catalunya i Espanya, Barcelona 1997.

Pere Ysàs, Disidencia y subversión. La lucha del régimen franquista por su supervivencia, 1960–1975, Barcelona 2004.

Lucile Dreidemy

Forever the First Victim? The Dollfuß Myth and the Long-Term Impact of Coalitional Historiography

The dispute over the interpretation of Engelbert Dollfuß's politics and person-ality has shaped the historical-political discourse of the Second Austrian Re-public like hardly any other. The conservative ÖVP has celebrated him as a heroic chancellor and resistance fighter against National Socialism, while the Social Democrats, Communists, and later the Greens have denounced the dictatorial and Fascist character of the regime Dollfuß initiated, and sought to rehabilitate the victims of his repressive policies. An oil painting of Dollfuß which had been placed in the club rooms of the ÖVP after 1945 became the focal point of the controversy for years. The last decade, however, brought some groundbreaking measures in the field of history policies. In January 2012, the so-called Abolition and Rehabilitation Act for the rehabilitation of the democratic victims of Aus-trofascism, which was called an "unjust regime" in the wording of the law, was passed with the support of all five parliamentary parties. The next historical-political "bang" followed in 2017, when the ÖVP took renovation work at par-liament as an opportunity to remove the controversial Dollfuß portrait.

With the portrait's removal, the central basis for the ritualistic controversy that had kept the Dollfuß myth alive throughout the Second Republic disappeared. Whether this measure could result in a definitive historicization of the figure of Dollfuß and an end to the myth can be doubted, given the characteristic muta-bility and adaptability of mythical discourses. Against this background, the re-moval of the controversial portrait appears to be a welcome occasion to take stock of the context-specific transformations of the Dollfuß myth since its creation in the years 1933–34 and of its historical-political consequences from its inception to the present day.

1.   Dollfuß, the Creator of His Own Personal Myth

An often underestimated dimension of the Dollfuß myth is that it did not originate with the posthumous cult of the dead leader but was actively shaped by Dollfuß and his followers as early as the dictatorial turn of 1933. Dollfuß's understanding of his political function went beyond that of an autocrat. This is evident in the fact that, from the time of the dissolution of parliament, he worked very consciously on his self-presentation and thus also de facto on the establishment of a personal myth. This can be seen first and foremost in his systematic tendency to transfigure his own path in life and to reinterpret its unpleasant or inglorious facets – or to conceal them. The most significant phase in Dollfuß's life was undoubtedly World War I, during which his engagement as an overzealous soldier was a way to compensate for both his illegitimate origins and his height (he was only 4'11"). The imprint of the war was reflected in the increasingly belligerent rhetoric that Dollfuß used after the dissolution of parliament and with which he portrayed himself, for instance as a warrior whom "physical danger does not shake much". In accordance with this militant rhetoric, Dollfuß began to appear increasingly often in public in the uniform of a *Kaiserschützenoberleutnant*. An example of this is the staging of his programmatic speech at Vienna's Trabrennplatz on September 11, 1933.

By resorting to the war uniform, Dollfuß undoubtedly imitated the appearance of the neighboring dictators. In comparison to Adolf Hitler or Benito Mussolini, however, Dollfuß seemed from the outset to be more concerned with defusing, or rather "humanizing", the image of the fearsome dictator by means of a humbler image. Accordingly, an essential characteristic of the Dollfuß cult was that, in contrast to Hitler or Mussolini, its mobilization strategy was based less on fear than on identification and sympathy. One might think, for example, of the numerous representations of Dollfuß in the role of husband and family man, as he was portrayed in the illustrated press, in propaganda brochures, and on postcards, even before his death. The decisive role that image propaganda played in the staging of the "humane leader" is also exemplified by the visual coverage of the first assassination attempt on Dollfuß on October 3, 1933, less than a month after the martial images of the uniformed dictator at the lectern in Vienna's Trabrennplatz. The media staging of Dollfuß in a state of shock and in his pajamas helped to reinforce the image of the simple, blameless man and sympathetic "victim chancellor."

"I am truly convinced that by God's providence I have now escaped grave danger," Dollfuß affirmed in his radio address following the putsch attempt. Even if he was undoubtedly convinced of this divine mission, it is also clear that this sense of duty and mission became an extremely favorable instrument with which to justify his dictatorial policy, since it presented him as an instrument of providence and henceforth minimized his own responsibility.

2.   The Beginnings of Dollfuß's Mythical Afterlife: The National Death Cult up to 1938

After his death, Dollfuß's sense of a mission led to something approaching the apotheosis of the dead "Führer." In line with the slogan "You are not dead to us" ("Du bist für uns nicht tot"), an imposing state cult was dedicated to the regime's founding father. On the political stage, the metaphor of immortality was materialized by omnipresent busts, reliefs, and portraits of the dead leader. This visual and sculptural staging of political immortality corresponds in many respects to the theory of the "Two Bodies of the King" advanced by the German historian Ernst H. Kantorowicz, according to which, as early as the Middle Ages, artificial, lifelike representations of the deceased ruler were placed in political and public spaces as symbolic placeholders in order to give overt character to the immortality of his spirit and his work. Through this mise-en-scène, the new leader Kurt Schuschnigg, in particular, was able to compensate for his own lack of charisma. By staging himself as the only legitimate successor to the eternal leader, he was also able to counteract the political ambitions of the *Heimwehr*. Additionally, the myth of the dead leader was used as a social model to demand from each individual a profession of loyalty not only to Dollfuß but also to the regime.

The apotheotic component of the cult of the dead leader was also demonstrated by the fact that Dollfuß's death was often compared with the death of Christ. The "Holy" Dollfuß thus took on the form of a savior, a renewer of Austria after the collapse of the Habsburg Empire and the presumed chaos of the postwar period. The association of Dollfuß and Christ correlates with the political instrumentalization of the Christ the King ideology, with which the regime under both Dollfuß and Schuschnigg legitimized the rejection of a pluralistic democratic society in religious terms. In an attempt to elevate Dollfuß to the status of a political saint, the propagandists also resorted to using the figure of Saint Engelbert. These sacral references became a central component of the regime's monument policy. Countless Dollfuß martyrs and crosses (but also statues of Saint Engelbert) were erected throughout Austria, memorial churches and chapels were built, and existing churches were rededicated. The appropriation of the existing cults of saints compensated for the failure of the canonization procedure that had been initiated in order to raise Dollfuß to the holy rank of his namesake on the basis of alleged miracles attributed to him, most notably the vague, nationalistic "miracle of Austria." Dollfuß did not become a saint in the strict Catholic sense, but the official and public worship nevertheless elevated him to the status of political pillar saint (*Säulenheiliger*).

The commemorative policies around the dead leader became a political refuge for the regime. The *Vaterländische Front* and the government tried in vain to hide the increasingly acute domestic and foreign policy crisis by increasing the number of symbolic acts of worship for the patriotic martyr. But apart from the Catholic-conservative rural areas where the official cult apparently found resonance – in many farmhouses, a picture of Dollfuß was placed in the household shrine (*Herrgottswinkel*) – the disproportionate commemorative policies could not curb the growing popular resentment towards the Austrofascist regime. On the contrary, it ultimately played into the hands of the much more profane and concrete Nazi mobilization propaganda.

3.   Dollfuß Myth and Worship during World War II

Immediately after the so-called Anschluss, most of the Dollfuß memorials were destroyed, and the official worship discourse was overwritten with a counter-cult for the thirteen executed Nazi *Juliputschisten*. The destruction of the symbols of the official cult was often used for political demonstrations of power and the public humiliation of local actors of the defeated regime. The climax of this symbolic assumption of power was the great Carnival procession in Vienna on February 19, 1939, which took the form of a final symbolic reckoning with the overthrown Austrofascist regime.

In spite of extensive destruction and repression measures, the Dollfuß cult continued to be cultivated underground by its followers and soon took on the form of a real act of political resistance. Through the influence of conservative exile circles, it was also exported abroad and adapted to the requirements of a new discursive context. This is when the myth of the "first resistance fighter" and "first victim of National Socialism" began to take shape, fully in line with the stance of conservative exile groups that sought international recognition of Austria as the first victim of National Socialism. A decisive role in this context was played by the legitimists under the leadership of pretender to the throne Otto Habsburg, who had arrived in the US in 1940. At his suggestion, July 25, 1942, was declared "Austrian Day" in several states and was celebrated as a day of remembrance of Dollfuß's death and Hitler's "first defeat".

After the 1943 Moscow Declaration, and especially in view of the required Austrian contribution to their own liberation, the mythical transfiguration of the dictator as a venerable resistance fighter gained even more argumentative weight. However, with the return of parliamentary democracy and the beginning of a groundbreaking grand coalition between the former political enemies after 1945, there was no longer any room for official worship of Dollfuß as a national martyr. The official "truce" nevertheless required a compatible memory between the former enemies. Two complementary paradigms played a decisive role in this new discourse: on the one hand, the so-called "thesis of shared guilt," and, on the other hand, the collective victim thesis.

4. The Dollfuß Myth in the Political Discourse of the Second Austrian Republic

Based on a one-sided interpretation of the Moscow Declaration, the myth of Austria as the first victim of National Socialism and the thesis of collective resistance in Austria became a central tenet in the self-representation of the grand coalition. These paradigms were meant to contribute simultaneously to domestic political reconstruction and to international rehabilitation. At the same time, the former civil war opponents agreed on the thesis of the shared guilt of the Christian Socials and Social Democrats for the destruction of the First Austrian Republic, in line with the narrative that the democrats had not been patriotic enough and the patriots had not been democratic enough. This paradigm was accompanied by the myth of the *Lagerstraße*, according to which the shared traumatic experience in the Nazi concentration camps had led to the former political enemies' reconciliation. These paradigms were particularly beneficial to the ÖVP because they made it possible to leave unmentioned the question of responsibility for the political repressions before 1938. In 1947, one final and fierce public debate took place during the trial of Austria's last foreign minister before the "Anschluss," Guido Schmidt, charged with high treason. The entire ÖVP elite was put on the witness stand. Although Schmidt was politically condemned, he was ultimately acquitted due to a lack of concrete evidence. All other functionaries of the Austrofascist regime also remained unindicted. Many of them were even reinstated to positions of state responsibility, such as the 1953–61 federal chancellor and ÖVP politician Julius Raab, often celebrated as the "State Treaty chancellor," who had been the leader of the Fascist home guard in Lower Austria from 1928–31 and who had accumulated several leadership roles in Austrofascism, including as a member of the leadership council of the *Vaterländische Front.*

The Dollfuß supporters in the ÖVP were also able to rely on the paradigm of shared guilt in order to rehabilitate Dollfuß's policy and to legitimize the continuation of Dollfuß veneration. A first step in this direction was taken when the official oil painting of Dollfuß from the time of the dictatorship was placed in the office of the new ÖVP parliamentary group. The *ÖVP-Kameradschaft der po-*

litisch Verfolgten und Bekenner für Österreich (ÖVP Comrade Group of the Victims of Political Persecution and Austrian Patriots), founded in 1948, became a genuine "Dollfuß lobby group" within the ÖVP and a decisive driving force of the Dollfuß cult. The Catholic Student Fraternity (*Cartellverband*) and the Peasants' League (*Bauernbund*), which had been among the central bearers of the official cult of the 1930s, also played an active part in the annual commemorations throughout the Second Republic.

As a reaction to the continuing Dollfuß veneration in the ÖVP, a counternarrative arose in the SPÖ that soon went beyond the factual-critical deconstruction of the conservative myth, acquiring its own mythical component. To draw on the "mythologics" theoretically advanced by Roland Barthes, a typical "second-order semiological system" emerged in which "a signified," in this case dictatorship, authoritarianism, and fascism, was associated with the "signifier" Dollfuß in a sort of self-evident way: Dollfuß became the personification of Austrofascism. The tendency to blame all evil on this single scapegoat clearly shows the extent to which the discursive memory of the Social Democrats was shaped by the traumas of the civil war generation. This tendency correlates with the observations made by the later SPÖ federal chancellor Bruno Kreisky, according to whom for the Social Democrats of the 1930s, the hatred of Dollfuß was stronger than the fear of everything else.

The Dollfuß cult gained new momentum under the ÖVP government of Joseph Klaus (1966–70). This was partly due to the influence of the radical-conservative "Reform" wing of the party and the *Cartellverband* in the government. As early as 1967, the government implemented an annual memorial mass for Dollfuß in the chapel of the federal chancellery. The further history of this mass is a striking example of the longer-term consequences of the grand coalition's policy of history. In 1970, Bruno Kreisky, himself a victim of the Austrofascist regime, became the head of an SPÖ government. His handling of the Austrofascist regime was marked by a blatant dichotomy between radical criticism and compromise-oriented piety. On the one hand, he clearly opposed the myth of shared guilt. On the other hand, he maintained the annual commemorative Dollfuß mass in the chancellery for the entire duration of his thirteen-year mandate. On the occasion of the fortieth anniversary of Dollfuß's death in 1974, he legitimized his government's reverent handling of Dollfuß's memory, subscribing to the notion that "The dead man is no longer our enemy."

This positioning reflects Kreisky's endeavoring to present himself as chancellor of the political middle ground. This forbearance was without a doubt part of a political strategy aimed at sending a clear signal to the ÖVP voters, but eventually it contributed in no small measure to making the homage to the dictator politically acceptable. Kreisky's successors, SPÖ chancellors Fred Sinowatz and Franz Vranitzky, followed Kreisky's example and thus maintained a stage for dubious political commemorative events at the chancellery. The mass was finally abolished in 2010 under chancellor Werner Faymann (SPÖ) – and even then only after the daily *Der Standard* had openly questioned this commemorative tradition.

While Kreisky and his Social Democratic successors in the federal chancellery chose to let piety prevail over confrontation, parliament often became the stage for open confrontation between the ÖVP and the SPÖ regarding the legacy of Austrofascism and, in particular, Dollfuß. A frequent source of controversy was the Dollfuß portrait in the parliamentary club of the ÖVP. Just as the official Dollfuß myth of the 1930s was cultivated via ritualized celebrations, henceforth it was largely these almost-ritualized Dollfuß controversies between the ÖVP and the SPÖ that kept the myth alive. Through the mediatization of these controversies, the myth also radiated increasingly into public discourse and ultimately survived the erosion of the partisan identities based on antagonistic historical narratives. A notable indication of the effectiveness of the Dollfuß myth beyond party lines is, for example, the widespread tendency in public discourse to personify the Austrofascist regime as Dollfuß while at the same time excluding the historical role of his successor, Schuschnigg. This cross-party tendency to reduce the historical discourse on Austrofascism to Dollfuß may be one reason why the ÖVP made the maintenance of the Dollfuß portrait in its parliamentary club a kind of unimpeachable matter of honor, although this stubborn defiance increasingly contradicted its own concessions regarding the dictatorial and repressive dimension of his policies.

5. The Scientification of Dollfuß Apologetics

In view of the continuous progress in research on Austrofascism from the 1960s and 1970s onward, Dollfuß's followers came under increasing pressure to justify themselves. They therefore adapted their argument to the new discursive mainstream. Those images that no longer corresponded to the new political and cultural zeitgeist were retouched. The "true German man" of the Austrofascist propaganda moved into the shadow of the anti-Nazi resistance fighter and the spiritual father of the Austrian nation, the "Führer" with a human face was transformed into the peasant democrat, and the hallowed victim ultimately became the "secularized" first victim of National Socialism. The political scientist Gottfried-Karl Kindermann played a pioneering role in this discursive evolution. From the early 1980s onward, he sought to rehabilitate the Austrofascist regime by presenting it as the first state that had resisted National Socialism, thus celebrating Dollfuß as its figurehead. The modern argumentation of Dollfuß supporters is also characterized by a segmented pattern of interpretation typical of mythical discourses. Accordingly, only those events and sources are consulted that support the authors' partisan pleas. This carefully selected version of the past is then treated as an objective, factual basis and, in a further step, transformed into a demand for "justice" for Dollfuß. Through this typical mixture of scientific categories and value judgments, every form of critical approach is finally branded – in a consistently paradoxical manner – as political propaganda and thus dismissed as unscientific. The benevolent Dollfuß biography by historian Gudula Walterskirchen of 2004 and her latest book, *The Blind Spots of History: Austria 1927–1938*, published in 2017, follows precisely this line of reasoning. Instead of, as she claims, opening up new perspectives, Walterskirchen seems to be primarily concerned with rehabilitating the politics of the bourgeois camp of the 1920s and 1930s. This is done, for example, by overemphasizing the Social Democrats' mistakes (a case in point being Karl Renner's "Yes" to the "Anschluss") or, as shown in the last book, by relying on meager and questionable sources to reinterpret the February struggles as an attempted coup orchestrated by the National Socialists. Proven experts, such as Emmerich Tálos, are again labeled "unscientific."

The political significance of these modern forms of apologetics is exemplified by the contradictory statements of the ÖVP politician Andreas Khol since the early 2000s. On the one hand, Khol was one of the first prominent ÖVP politicians to show groundbreaking impulses toward a critical assessment of the Austrofascist regime. In 2003, for example, as president of the Austrian Parliament, he explicitly distanced himself from the thesis of the "self-liquidation" of the parliament in March 1933. Instead, he spoke of a coup d'état and of an "authoritarian regime based on a juridical white lie." Ten years later, he even added: "Of course, Dollfuß was a dictator who was responsible for a coup and – today one would say – for state terrorism." Despite these critical insights, Khol never completely distanced himself from the victim and resistance narrative coined by Kindermann. In 2014, during a panel discussion at the Wien Museum about my monograph "The Dollfuß Myth. Biography of an Afterlife" (*The Dollfuß-Mythos. Eine Biographie des Posthumen*), Khol spoke of a revisionist study and in the same breath took up again the thesis of Dollfuß as the "first victim" of National Socialism, which had long since been overcome in the scientific mainstream discourse. This episode once again showed how much the emotional logic of the myth resists rational arguments. Even if more and more scientific findings about the Austrofascist regime are accepted by the ÖVP, Dollfuß remains, to quote Khol, a "pillar saint" of the party.

6. Traces of the Myth in the Austrian Memory and Museum Landscape

There are still about twenty Dollfuß monuments throughout Austria, most of them in Lower Austria and Tyrol. Instead of removing them, there has been a tendency in recent years to supplement them with explanatory plaques. This solution appears problematic in that these discreet additions alone cannot bring about a reversal of the functionality of these monuments – from signs of homage to critical memorials. Instead, they de facto legitimize the presence of symbols of veneration for a dictator, even in the present democratic context.

A similar compromise was initially chosen in 2014 for the Dollfuß portrait in the parliamentary club of the ÖVP. In the course of yet another debate about the painting, which took place during the commemoration of the eightieth anniversary of the uprising in February 1934, ÖVP representatives began to argue that the portrait should be retained out of a duty of remembrance and because it documented the party's critical reassessment of its past. In the light of this argument, the party decided to place a plaque beneath the portrait explaining that it was not honoring the leader but that "the good as well as the bad features" of his leadership needed to be told. The transition to dictatorship was once again presented as a response to the rise of Nazism, while other aspects of Dollfuß's ideology and political program, such as his anti-parliamentarianism, his negotiations with the Nazis, and his admiration for Mussolini, were not even hinted at. The text ended by recalling his death during an attempted Nazi coup, thereby reviving the old myth of the martyred chancellor. The decision to keep the portrait and add an explanatory note reaffirmed the legitimacy of the portrait's presence in the office of the conservative parliamentary group and de facto in the parliament itself – the very parliament that Dollfuß wanted to permanently abolish in 1933.

As in the case of the commemorative mass in the federal chancellery, it was an external event, namely necessary relocation as a result of renovation work at the parliament, which ultimately prompted the party to take down not only that very picture but also all historic portraits that had been hanging there. While the explanatory plaque had been publicly announced and justified by the party three years earlier, the removal of the portrait was done in a remarkably discreet manner, as if the "new" ÖVP was trying to sort out a problem without breaking too frontally with party tradition. The painting then became part of the exhibition *The Contested Republic. Austria 1918–1938* in the *Haus der Geschichte Niederösterreich* in Sankt Pölten, which opened in September 2017.

The portrait is indeed an ideal museum exhibit, as its long and controversial history lends it an incomparably expressive documentary and testimonial character. The process of the painting's creation takes us back to the phase of the creation of the *Führerkult* under Dollfuß. Its visual message (i.e., the dictator's relaxed pose as a modern bureaucrat) illuminates the characteristic features of the Austrofascist dictator's self-presentation and at the same time invites us to reflect on the longer-term effects of this self-staging on the later reception and interpretation of the regime. The portrait, which was reproduced under strict control after Dollfuß's death, is also exemplary of the diverse material forms of expression of the official, posthumous Dollfuß cult – from the classical portraits and reliefs to the most diverse devotional objects and memorabilia (i.e., post-cards, coins, mugs, calendars, etc.). But it is also a political history of the Second Republic that the portrait conveys to us. Its placement in the parliamentary club of the new ÖVP after 1945 raises the question of the political genealogy of the Austrian People's Party. The recurring debates from the 1970s on also shed light on the development of the historical-political discourse on Dollfuß and Austrofascism in the Second Republic on various levels: on the official level (especially regarding the impact of coalitionary historiography), in the context of party confrontations, but also in the context of internal party controversies in the ÖVP and the SPÖ. The added explanatory plaque in 2014 is also an example of the current compromise solutions in dealing with the remaining Dollfuß monuments; it therefore offers an ideal opportunity to discuss the consequences of consensual history policies.

However, none of these aspects were to be found in the chosen mise-en-scène. The curators were apparently anxious not to create a historical-political stir. The portrait was displayed together with several small plaques representing a variety of opinions expressed by politicians and academics. It was left to the visitors to form their own opinion on the basis of these statements or to come to the suggested conclusion that Dollfuß could be seen "one way or another" – or, in other words, that the interpretation of his historical responsibility is a matter of opinion, so to speak. After the end of the special exhibition in March 2019, the portrait was removed from the museum.

In the *Haus der Geschichte*, which opened in November 2018 in Vienna, a similar reserve dominates the discourse on Austrofascism. At the same time, recent academic publications on Dollfuß and Austrofascism exemplify this lack of stringency and critical examination, and instead reactivate old mythical themes (especially the thesis of shared guilt) and relativize the historic role of the Austrofascist regime in paving the way for a National Socialist takeover (cf. Pelinka and Höbelt 2018).

7. Conclusion and Outlook: The Persistent Dollfuß Myth, or the Long-Term Consequences of Coalitionary Historiography

At the beginning of 2019, the Facebook post from SPÖ Deputy Robert Laimer caused a brief media stir. The post was a collage based on two Dollfuß stamps, one of which had ÖVP chancellor Sebastian Kurz's head pasted over Dollfuß's. "Putschist chancellor, Austro-Fascism, Mussolini's Friend" stood under the original version; "Silent chancellor, Beer Capitalism, Kickl's Friend" stood under the altered picture. After the expected outcry from the ÖVP, the post was deleted. This incident suggests that the ritualistic Dollfuß dispute is far from over, even now that the controversial portrait has been taken down. Such media-political flashes in the pan are, however, nothing but anecdotal.

The much more explosive relevance of the Dollfuß myth is demonstrated by the seemingly unbridgeable gap between the rational grasp of Dollfuß's anti-democratic policies and the persistent overemphasis on his victim status. In recent decades, the modern Dollfuß apologetics have promoted the image of a historical "light and shadow figure" as an apparent concession to the progress of historical research. Due to its consensual dimension, this topos has now also established itself in the memory discourse. A striking example of this impact is the fact that the chairman of the Federation of Social Democratic Freedom Fighters, Victims of Fascism and Active Anti-Fascists, Gerald Netzl, attended the memorial service for Engelbert Dollfuß at Hietzing Cemetery in July 2019. The contrasting positions of Laimer and Netzl again point to the structural dis-integration of Austrian social democracy's historical basic line, namely the struggle against fascism and the antagonism toward the bourgeois camp.

The compromise solutions regarding the remaining Dollfuß monuments, a social democratic functionary participating in a Dollfuß ceremony in 2019, the over-cautious treatment of Dollfuß in the newly opened *Häuser der Geschichte,* and the revival of revisionist tendencies in academic publications about the Austrian First Republic and Austrofascism: all these examples bear witness to the far-reaching impact of the *Koalitionsgeschichtsschreibung* that emerged in the early postwar period. From the perspective of promoting knowledge, this con-sensual narrative is sterile. From a historical-political perspective, it is even dangerous. The last authoritarianism survey from 2007 warns of the devastating consequences of such historical relativism. At that time, barely half of the thousand respondents associated Dollfuß with the establishment of a dictator-ship in Austria.

Regarding this recent evolution and in light of the growing influence of the "post-truth" paradigm in political discourse, it is high time there was a radical critique of this coalitionary mode of writing history and that historians reasserted their accountability and responsibility by acknowledging and engaging with scientific findings instead of just alluding to different opinions.

8.   Selected Bibliography

Bischof, Günter et al. (eds.), *Myths in Austrian History. Construction and Deconstruction.* Innsbruck: University Press, 2020, (Contemporary Austrian Studies 29).

Dreidemy, Lucile, *Der Dollfuß-Mythos. Eine Biographie des Posthumen.* Vienna: Böhlau, 2014.

Dreidemy, Lucile, "Austrofaschismus," in *100 x Österreich. Neue Essays aus Literatur und Wissenschaft,* edited by Monika Sommer et al., 29–33. Vienna: Haus der Geschichte Österreich, 2018.

Dreidemy, Lucile, "A Dictator with a Human Face? The Portraits of the Austrian Chancellor Engelbert Dollfuß," in *The Political Portrait. Leadership, Image and Power,* edited by Luciano Cheles and Alessandro Giacone, 98–115. New York: Routledge, 2020.

Höbelt, Lothar, *Die Erste Republik 1918–1938. Das Provisorium.* Vienna: Böhlau, 2018.

Liebhart, Karin, *Zur Funktion von Mythen für politische Inszenierungen,* PhD diss. University of Vienna, 1998.

Mattl, Siegfried, "Vergangenheitspolitik und Geschichtsrevisionismus – Februaraufstand 1934, Dollfuß-Mord und Austrofaschismus," in *Geschichte macht Herrschaft. Zur Politik mit dem Vergangenen,* edited by Florian Wenninger, 215–226. Vienna: Braumüller, 2007.

Pelinka, Anton. *Die gescheiterte Republik: Kultur und Politik in Österreich 1918–1938.* Vienna: Böhlau, 2018.

Rathkolb, Oliver, *Fiktion 'Opfer' Österreich und die langen Schatten des Nationalsozialismus und der Dollfuß-Diktatur.* Innsbruck: Studien Verlag, 2017.

Tálos, Emmerich, "Deutungen des Österreichischen Herrschaftssystems 1934–1938. Am Beispiel des 'Ständestaats-Paradigmas'," in *Geschichte macht Herrschaft. Zur Politik mit dem Vergangenen,* edited by Florian Wenninger, 199–213. Vienna: Braumüller, 2007.

Walterskirchen, Gudula, *Engelbert Dollfuß. Arbeitermörder oder Heldenkanzler,* 2nd. ed. Purkersdorf: BuchPurkersdorf, 2017.

Walterskirchen, Gudula, *Die blinden Flecken der Geschichte. Österreich 1927–1938.* Vienna: Kremayr & Scheriau, 2017.

Filip Zieliński

The "Golden Age" Narrative of Interwar Poland and Its Effects on Democratization in 1989. A Case Study in History Politics

1.   History Politics[1]

The term history politics[2] implies that this is a subject that will benefit from an interdisciplinary approach, including – at least – political science and history. When taking the historian's point of view, it is important to go beyond merely fact-checking the narratives about the past put forth by politicians and claiming that they are abusing history for political ends. From the perspective of the political system, the métier of political scientists, this "abuse" is, in fact, functional and – as I would like to argue in this paper – it can have fundamental consequences for politics.

Indeed, history can be used in politics to legitimize decisions in public that were in fact taken "behind the scenes", for reasons that have nothing to do with history. This in itself would already be sufficient reason to argue for the subject's relevance. But far from it – history politics affect fundamental aspects of political systems and processes: Not only do narratives about the past legitimize decisions but they sometimes also *help make* these decisions; they *inform* them, and thus the outcomes of political processes, including law-making. This happens very much in the same way that narratives in general help individuals make sense of their own past and future when acting in the present. Furthermore, history politics contributes to the process of constructing group identities, which includes politically relevant groups such as the political unit, organizations such as political parties, and other political institutions. Finally, it affects the legitimacy of a specific political regime, which becomes particularly urgent in times of transformation, i. e. in the process of change from one political regime to another.

1 The author thanks Claudia Kraft (University of Vienna) for her comments on an earlier draft of this paper.
2 German: *Geschichtspolitik* or *Erinnerungspolitik*, Polish: *polityka historyczna*.

2.   First Sidenote: Methodology

What makes the subject both fascinating and complex is the fact that all these different narratives that *inform and legitimize decisions and group identities* are inter-related, are part of an ongoing discourse. Furthermore, when analyzing narratives that were recorded and mediated, for instance via text, we are left to hypothesize about the intentions and interpretations of the sender, and even more so about the perceptions on the part of the audience. The latter question is of crucial importance when assessing the political impact of history politics.

Finally, when analyzing historical narratives in contemporary politics, for example by examining transcripts of parliamentary sessions, we face the challenge of identifying and then analyzing the relevant content in a vast amount of data. Methodologically, it is not satisfactory to pick out, in an unsystematic manner, a handful of quotations by leading politicians in order to construct far-reaching conclusions.[3] The methodologically stringent method of quantitative content analysis, on the other hand, allows reliable conclusions, but this comes at the expense of these conclusions being very limited in scope and complexity. One possible way out of this dilemma is to combine both approaches, quantitative and qualitative ("mixed methods"). Secondly, it seems to be reasonable to analyze various media of history politics, as opposed to an isolated analysis, e.g. only street names, monuments or speeches.

For this reason, my dissertation, which deals with history politics in the Polish parliament in the years after 1989,[4] analyzed *all* instances of historical references in the parliament that could be found (and not only those one might look for in order to confirm a conclusion that was determined *a priori*): in the building and surroundings of the parliament itself, in "commemorative laws", in the coat of arms, the name of the state, and in references in all plenary session protocols for a certain time period in order to be able to systematically analyze which narratives were used by whom and in which context in order to provide a more solid basis for the discourse analysis that followed.

---

3 See for example the following studies: Christoph Steinbach, "Historische Argumentation in politischen Reden und Leitartikeln zum 30. Jahrestag der deutschen Kapitulation von 1945," in *Geschichte in der Öffentlichkeit*, edited by Wilhelm van Kampen et al. (Stuttgart: Klett, 1979), 237–63; Katherina Oehler, *Geschichte in der politischen Rhetorik. Historische Argumentationsmuster im Parlament der Bundesrepublik Deutschland* (Hagen: Rottmann, 1989); Wolfgang Bach, *Geschichte als politisches Argument. Eine Untersuchung an ausgewählten Debatten des Deutschen Bundestages* (Stuttgart: Klett-Cotta, 1977); Matthias Rensing, *Geschichte und Politik in den Reden der deutschen Bundespräsidenten 1949–1984* (New York: Waxmann, 1996).
4 Filip Zieliński, *Demokratie erzählt. Geschichtspolitik im polnischen Parlament nach der Wende von 1989*, unpublished PhD thesis, Universität Wien, 2017. http://doi.org/10.25365/thesis.51825 (7 May 2022).

3. Second Sidenote: Theory

When it comes to analyzing history politics, it is much more useful to focus on *narratives*, as opposed to the notion of *memory*, which, at least for my research, has proved to be a dead-end. The notion of "memory" ("memory politics"/ "Erinnerungspolitik" etc.) does not help explain *how* such narratives connect the past with the present and the future and thus make the past politically relevant. While it has been suggested that analogies[5] serve this role, actual historical references in politics, in fact, rarely take the form of analogies in the strict sense, while the more general, metaphorical sense of the term does not help explain the creative and discursive aspects of the phenomenon.

A historical monument, for example, becomes politically relevant only when and so far as it is linked to historical narratives, which, by definition, are able to create a horizon spanning across past, present and future while making *sense* of otherwise meaningless, contingent "events" which are always accompanied by the claim to speak the truth about what actually happened (as opposed to fiction). In the case of a monument, the narratives are usually implied and the monument itself serves merely as a "marker", or the narrative is explicated on a label next to it. Locals will be able to link it to historical narratives based on their education, a tourist might need a tour guide in order to decipher it, and politicians might argue about whether or not it (i. e. a narrative it represents) is in line with a master narrative linked to the political community's identity. In other words, there is no history politics without narratives.

German philosopher of history Jörn Rüsen offers an excellent and useful theoretical framework here for understanding what historical narratives are, their typical forms and social functions. This includes Rüsen's typology of narratives – exemplary, traditional, genetic, and critical – which serves as a "grammar" that helps us analyze historical narratives and discourses about the past within the political system.

4. History Politics: an Example

In 2010–12, I analyzed the narratives about the past within the Polish parliament, a) based on such "markers", including architecture and symbols found within the building itself, the national flag, and the title of the state, and b) explicit narratives such as those presented in texts, including legal documents and inscriptions.

---

5 Horst-Alfred Heinrich, "Kollektive Erinnerungen im politischen System," in *Geschichtspolitik und kollektives Gedächtnis. Erinnerungskulturen in Theorie und Praxis*, edited by Harald Schmid (Göttingen: V&R unipress, 2009), 77–93.

Interestingly, the interwar period, and more specifically: the Second Republic of Poland, which existed within this timeframe, stands out as the most prevalent item of reference. For example, the largest and most visible commemorative plaque in the Sejm (the first chamber of the Polish parliament) honors and lists the names of the members of the Sejm of the Second Republic who "gave their life for Poland in the Second World War", thus creating a direct narrative link between the parliaments of the Second and Third Republic while excluding its history in-between.[6] Turning to a different medium for another example: If we examine the commemorative "laws" adopted by the parliament in 1989–2010, the interwar period stands out as the timeframe with the most commemorations.[7]

These are examples of many cases in which the Polish parliament of the Third Republic directly referred to (and still does refer to) the Second Republic as its predecessor. Tellingly, the regime in-between is not included in the count of state names but instead is referred to as the *Polska Rzeczpospolita Ludowa*[8] (People's Republic). These findings confirm – and provide an empirical basis for – other studies, including historian Claudia Kraft, who coined the term of the "factoring-out-narrative" (*Ausklammerungsnarrativ*). As I will argue later in this paper, upon closer inspection, the process in which this narrative became dominant was politically conflictual, as the narrative was criticized and/or alternative narratives were proposed by certain actors and parties. The narrative's dominance was functional for democratization, but so was the discourse around it.

What is the political function and relevance of such a narrative? Does it not ignore the many continuities of pre- and post-1989 politics in Poland? It does indeed, which is exactly why it is useful: It *creates* a clean break between the old and the new regime, declaring the People's Republic as a period of foreign, Soviet rule and therefore deviance from the "normal" condition of sovereign, national statehood. It is a classic "golden age" narrative of the traditional type, if we follow Rüsen's typology, which means that it offers the return to a glorious past as a sensible direction for the future.

---

6 The plaque was established as late as 2005 but it was certainly inspired by the one commemorating the senators of the Second Republic who died in the war, which can be found in the Senate's building. The latter was established in 1999, but Senator Roman Ciesielski proposed the idea for such a commemorative endeavor during a session of the Senate as early as July 1989. Other plaques commemorate, for example, the tragic plane crash near Smolensk on 10 April 2010 or the visit of Pope John Paul II on 11 June 1999.

7 These "laws", which are mostly prepared for anniversaries, are symbolic in the sense that they usually have no legal effect beyond codifying a certain narrative, thus constituting a commemorative medium under direct control of the parliament. From the point of view of history politics analysis, it is interesting to look at the discussions and voting that accompany the adoption of these laws.

8 *Polska Rzeczpospolita Ludowa* (PRL) was the official name of the Polish state in 1952–1989.

As outlined above, history politics, i. e. narratives about the past that become relevant within the political system, serve the functions of a) legitimizing, and potentially also informing decisions, and b) constructing identities of individuals and – more importantly here – groups. How does this theoretical framework, which is derived from Rüsen's works, translate to the narrative of the Second Republic as the golden age?

5.   Decisions

Before we turn to the exemplary conclusions, three important theoretical preliminary notes are necessary. First, when it comes to the justification of decisions in politics, and in parliaments specifically, be it by history politics or any other means, it would be naive to take explanations presented by politicians in public statements, including parliamentary assemblies, at face value. Instead, decisions are often made elsewhere, e. g. behind the closed doors of a non-public party group meeting. A speech in parliament, in this perspective, does not serve its hypothetical or formal purpose of persuading other MPs, but merely to legitimize a decision vis-á-vis the public, mostly via the media. This brings us to the second issue, which is that most political statements, including parliamentary sessions, reach audiences that are very limited in size. Finally, when it comes to analyzing the effects of history politics specifically, it is important to keep in mind the capacity of the audience to interpret a given narrative. For example, a comparison with available sociological research[9] of the "memory culture" in Poland suggests that many of the names of historical persons mentioned by Polish deputies in plenary sessions analyzed within this project were known only to a very narrow audience.

That being said, it is striking how directly the "golden age" narrative seems to have influenced Polish deputies' adapting the existing legal framework in order to set up the new, democratic, post-communist regime. When we analyze all references to the interwar period in all transcripts of plenary sessions of the *Sejm* in 1989–92,[10] it is striking how often deputies have argued for (or against) a specific legal decision using numerous variations of the "golden age" narrative, i. e. saying that a legal provision is desirable simply because it had existed in the interwar period but was then changed in the People's Republic. So much so that this practice of law-making in itself became a topic of discussion, for example

---

9 Surveys carried out by *Centrum Badania Opinii Społecznej* (CBOS) and studies by Barbara Szacka and Piotr T. Kwiatkowski. For details, see: Zieliński, "Demokratie erzählt, " 285–9.
10 Content analysis of all transcripts of the Sejm's plenary sessions from 4 July 1989 to 4 June 1992, a total of 37,584 standard pages of text (9 million words).

when a deputy criticized how "[t]he press law of the interwar period served as a model for this proposal, it was simply copied word-for-word. This happened in an unprecise and unclear manner. One may suspect that the authors did not think through the practical implications if we relaxed censorship without providing for new and clear regulation."[11] This statement is seconded by another deputy: "These are the consequences of a hasty combination of fragments of the realities of the press in the interwar period, when censorship sometimes resulted in newspapers being published with sections left blank, with the current requirements of liberalizing the press system on the eve of the 21st century."[12]

The "golden era" narrative was invoked in a broad range of contexts, reflecting the general topics of law-making in these three years of the Polish democratization process, namely: the economy, finances, the state budget (25% of all citations analyzed); administration, institutions, parties, parliament, elections (25%); social issues, ecology, health (12%), foreign policy and diplomacy (9%); civil and criminal law, security (8%); history, veterans, orders (8%); the constitution (7%); education, culture and religion (6%). Additional research would help establish the effects of history politics on law-making more precisely, both in terms of the legal texts and regarding the individual motivations of the law-makers: Was their decision to use a specific narrative always determined by their current political goals? Or were their actions determined by a dominant narrative that had become part of the parliament's 'culture' and 'habitus'? After all, if we look at it from a pragmatic point of view: These MPs, many of them lacking experience in politics, found themselves under considerable pressure, both from the domestic electorate and foreign partners, to restructure the entire legal framework (including the constitution itself) as quickly as possible. The previous regime (and with it, it's laws) had become objectionable. How were they to adapt the constitution and laws to a new reality that had not yet arrived, but was supposed to be created? Obviously, established liberal democracies served as a useful model in many ways, including for law-making. But it is difficult to imagine a political community which continues to identify as a *nation* state orientating itself solely towards foreign role models (not to mention the practical difficulties of translating the laws). In addition to, and to balance out, this orientation towards "the West", Poland's *own* history of democratic statehood, i. e. the Second Republic, offered a useful and readily available repository of examples and "best practices" in a situation of great uncertainty. One might object that such solutions had to be anachronistic and would have undesirable effects, seeing

---

11 Transcript of the plenary session of the Sejm on 1 February 1990, statement by Aleksander Luczak (PSL *Odrodzenie*).
12 Transcript of the plenary session of the Sejm on 1 February 1990, statement by Dobrochna Kędzierska-Truszczyńska (PZPR).

that the "realities" of the Second and Third Republic are, indeed, different from each other. On the other hand, one may argue that the "golden age" narrative was of the utmost importance to the process of democratization itself, as it was useful in explaining how this was a sensible future direction for Poland to take at a time when the previous regime had become unsustainable for reasons both domestic and foreign. What would democratization in Poland after 1989 have looked like if Poland and its politicians had not had its own democratic history to look back to for orientation?

6. Identities

In the previous section, we already touched upon the question of how the "golden age" narrative was part of the process of constructing a group identity on the level of the *nation state*. In addition to the political community as whole, the parliament is also the arena in which *political parties* (and individual politicians) create and demonstrate their identities. As Claudia Kraft notes: "As a consequence of the negotiated character of regime change, of the lack of a differentiated spectrum of political parties and the fact that the former opposition had first and foremost been a social, and especially cultural, movement, disputes about [Poland's] recent history served the purpose of differentiating between different political and societal interest groups."[13]

As a result of the political transformation from autocracy to democracy in 1989, existing political institutions such as the parliament again took center stage, having served as a mere facade for decades. The senate, the second chamber of the parliament, was restored. News media, now liberalized, covered the ever-changing and hence confusing landscape of political parties, their deputies and policies. The symbolic and material regime change of 1989 and the dominance of the "golden age" narrative had an effect on the group identities of political parties, and vice versa.

The dominant role of the Polish United Worker's Party (PZPR) diminished rapidly with elections held in 1989 and 1991. At the same time, the "golden age" narrative dominated history politics, a master narrative that strongly contradicted that of the party's history and identity and must therefore have decreased the party's legitimacy. (The PZPR disbanded in January 1990, some of its delegates moving to new successor parties.) Consequently, these PZPR and post-

13 Claudia Kraft, "Geschichte im langen Transformationsprozess in Polen," in *GegenErinnerung. Geschichte als politisches Argument im Transformationsprozeß Ost-, Ostmittel- und Südosteuropas*, edited by Helmut Altrichter (Munich: Oldenbourg, 2006), 145. Citation translated into English by FZ.

PZPR delegates were critical of the golden age narrative, but much less so than one might expect: The narrative had become dominant across political camps (see graph 1).

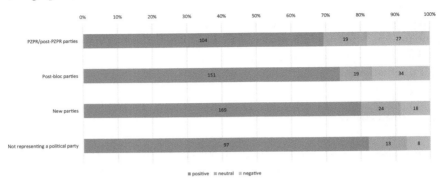

Graph 1: Positive, neutral, and negative attitudes towards the interwar period in statements by Members of Parliament (the Sejm) during plenary sessions in 1989–1991. Amounts provided = total numbers of quotations analyzed.

The following words of Stanisław Gabrielski of the soon to be dissolved "Polish United Workers' Party" (PZPR), which is unusual in its relatively high level of reflection on the golden age narrative and history politics in general, encapsulates the contradiction between the golden age narrative and the PZPR's identity perfectly. He proposes a "narrative of inclusion" as an alternative to the "golden age" narrative, as do some of his colleagues, but without success:

> Ladies and Gentlemen, I am deeply worried by a certain tendency that has come up in our discussions here in the parliament, that is the attempt to completely strike through the past four decades. … [This] period of twenty years [of the interwar period, 1918–39], of which we speak so nicely today, it had grand, noble aspects that need to be honored. But in these twenty years, there was also Bereza Kartuska [an internment camp for political prisoners established by the Sanacja regime, 1934–39] and the Brest trials [the trial of eleven opposition politicians, 1931–32]. This should not be forgotten.
> I know that in these forty years [1945–89] there were bad things that we need to get rid of, and my party [PZPR] also explicitly distances itself from these. But there were also valuable things which should be appreciated. And when we talk about creating a certain new project for the future [i. e. the constitution], […] we cannot achieve this if we cross out these forty years. I suggest that this new project should be a constructive synthesis of everything that is most valuable in our national, historical heritage, with present-day progress.[14]

---

14 Discussion about changing the Polish constitution. Transcript of the plenary session of the Polish Sejm on 27 December 1989.

The legitimacy and identities of the two former bloc parties *Stronnictwo De-mokratyczne* (SD) and *Zjednoczone Stronnictwo Ludowe* (ZSL) were also affected by the regime change. Interestingly, it was the SD's politicians who pushed hardest for a change of the name of the state (from *Polska Rzeczpospolita Lu-dowa*, as it had been known since 1952, back to *Rzeczpospolita Polska*) and of the national coat of arms (the coat of arms of the Second Republic was reinstated, with minor adjustments; most importantly, this meant that the white eagle again wore a crown, which had been "taken away" by the previous regime). The SD were keen for these changes to take effect before the end of 1989 (and indeed the law was passed on 29 December 1989), while their coalition partner, the governing parliamentary group *Obywatelski Klub Parlamentarny* (OKP)[15] and its leader Bronisław Geremek were reluctant to make this symbolic change in a situation where most of the factual changes, including a new constitution, still had to be accomplished. By that time, the SD consisted mostly of new delegates, while those who had already sat in parliament before 1989 presented the SD's history as that of a democratic, oppositional party that had been fighting for democratic values all along and reinforced their commitment to pre-1945 Polish democracy. In fact, however, the role of the SD, the ZSL, and other bloc parties before 1989 was limited to creating the illusion of a multi-party democracy in which the interests of various social groups (beyond those of workers) were represented.

The ZSL adopted a similar strategy of readapting the party's pre-war past and identity. In November 1989, it changed its name to the PSL *Odrodzenie* (Revival), thus claiming to be the standard-bearers of the pre-1949 traditions of the Polish People's Party PSL (a highly problematic narrative in light of the violent dis-mantling of said party by the communist regime in the 1940s). This brought them in conflict with other contenders, including the PSL *Wilanowskie*, which was initiated by people who had already been active in the PSL in 1945–49. In May 1990, the PSL *Odrodzenie* merged with the PSL *Wilanowskie* and others to form the PSL, thus uniting many of the agrarians into a party that exists to this day and continues to refer to the pre-1949 traditions of Polish agrarian parties. This way, the (infra)structures of the ZSL could be retained while the symbolic changes and the incorporation of former anti-communist agrarians provided much-needed legitimacy within the new political context. In parliament, this was accompanied by lengthy and heated debates about the history of agrarians and their parties in Poland, which served as a way to both unite and differentiate political camps on the new and still obscure arena of political parties.

Consequently, when we move further away from the macro level of the nation state and parliament, down to the level of party identities, or even individual

---

15 The OKP had come to power after the bloc parties had joined its ranks. This parliamentary group originated in the anti-communist *Solidarność* movement.

politicians' identities, the narratives become even more differentiated and less concordant. As we have seen, the "golden age" narrative was dominant, but far from undisputed (e.g. the "integration narrative"), and many smaller "battle grounds" of history politics could be observed on the sidelines. For example, when opportune, agrarians would remind people of the fact that their interwar predecessors were among those imprisoned by Józef Pilsudski's *Sanacja* regime in the *Bereza Kartuska* prison (at the cost of simultaneously questioning the democratic qualities of the Second Republic). Or, to provide another glimpse into the intricacies of Polish history politics during these years: The act of "returning the crown" to the white eagle of the national coat of arms was far from conflict-free and had been preceded by relentless debates about several visual elements and their implications, including the question of whether the crown should be with or without a cross on top, or the meaning of the alignment of some of the eagle's feathers, since they resembled a five-pointed star – and thus could be interpreted as symbols of communism. By creating criteria of inclusion and exclusion, of sameness and difference, these debates were useful in helping to construct much-needed party identities.[16]

7. Summary and Conclusion

The "golden age" narrative, i.e. the idea that the Third Republic (since 1989) is a direct successor of the Second Republic (1918–45), which is perceived in highly positive terms, while dismissing or ignoring the People's Republic (1945–89) as a period of foreign rule, was the dominant, albeit controversial, historical narrative within the Polish parliament in its early years of post-1989 democratization. When the People's Republic ended in 1989, this narrative presented democratization as "redemocratization", as a sensible part of Poland's own national history of statehood, thus increasing the legitimacy of this new political regime and thereby contributing to its persistence.

One might argue, firstly, that it was useful in "masking" the many factual continuities of pre- and post-1989 Poland by creating a clear but merely symbolic break (together with many other symbolic acts in Poland and beyond which presented 1989 as an "annus mirabilis") and that its national dimension helped people accept a change that was, in fact, brought about and later influenced by foreign actors to a substantial extent. On the other hand, the findings of this

---

16 Narratives about a shared past constitute an important means of constructing the group identity of a political party, in addition to name, political program, visual identity etc. See: Michael Waller, "Party Inheritances and Party Identities," in *Stabilising Fragile Democracies. Comparing New Party Systems in Southern and Eastern Europe*, edited by Paul Lewis and Geoffrey Pridham (London: Routledge, 1996), 23–44.

research project, which relies largely on Jörn Rüsen's theory of history and on quantitative and qualitative analysis of textual and material sources, suggests that history politics did in fact bring about results of both a symbolic and a material nature, including law-making and the construction of group identities such as those of political parties. The influential "golden age" narrative, as well as the many other narratives that make up the history of history politics of that time, have not only legitimized, but also informed many decisions of Polish lawmakers across all political issues of the time. Furthermore, they have influenced the construction and differentiation of identities of post-1989 political parties, which is, after all, a prerequisite of democracy itself.

Historic narratives create a horizon spanning past, present and future; they are as much about the past as they are about what we do in the present in order to arrive at a future that is constructed by the narrative. The golden age narrative is a good case in point for the political effects of such narratives.

As far as further research is concerned, it would be worthwhile to compare this aspect of post-1989 democratization with the cases of Bulgaria, Czechoslovakia, Estonia, Latvia, Lithuania, Hungary, and Romania. How did narratives about their pre-communist political history influence democratization processes, and vice versa?

8. Selected Bibliography

Altrichter, Helmut (ed.), *GegenErinnerung. Geschichte als politisches Argument im Transformationsprozeß Ost-, Ostmittel- und Südosteuropas.* Munich: Oldenbourg, 2006.

Bock, Petra and Edgar Wolfrum (eds.), *Umkämpfte Vergangenheit. Geschichtsbilder, Erinnerung und Vergangenheitspolitik im internationalen Vergleich.* Göttingen: Vandenhoeck & Ruprecht, 1999.

Cichocki, Marek, *Władza i pamięć.* Kraków: Biblioteka Myśli Politycznej, 2005.

Demandt, Alexander, *Geschichte als Argument. Drei Formen politischen Zukunftsdenkens im Altertum.* Konstanz: Univ.-Verl., 1972.

Faber, Karl-Georg, "Zum Einsatz historischer Aussagen als politisches Argument," *Historische Zeitschrift*, 221 (1975) 2: 265–303.

François, Étienne, Kornelia Kończal et al. (eds.), *Geschichtspolitik in Europa seit 1989. Deutschland, Frankreich und Polen im internationalen Vergleich.* Göttingen: Wallstein Verlag, 2013.

Fritz, Regina (ed.), *Nationen und ihre Selbstbilder. Postdiktatorische Gesellschaften in Europa.* Göttingen: Wallstein Verlag, 2008.

Heinrich, Horst-Alfred and Michael Kohlstruck (eds.), *Geschichtspolitik und sozialwissenschaftliche Theorie.* Stuttgart: Steiner, 2009.

Kraft, Claudia, "Der Umgang mit der mehrfachen Diktaturerfahrung im östlichen Europa. Die Europäische Erinnerung an das 'Jahrhundert der Diktaturen'," *Der Bürger im Staat* 56 (2006): 177–83.

Kwiatkowski, Piotr Tadeusz, *Pamięć zbiorowa społeczeństwa polskiego w okresie trans-formacji*. Warsaw: Wydawnictwo Naukowe "Scholar", 2008.

Nijakowski, Lech M., *Polska polityka pamięci. Esej socjologiczny*. Warsaw: Wydawnictwo Akademickie i Profesjonalne, 2008.

Rathkolb, Oliver and Imbi Sooman (eds.), *Geschichtspolitik im erweiterten Ostseeraum und ihre aktuelle Symptome – Historical Memory Culture in the Enlarged Baltic Sea Region and its Symptoms Today*. Göttingen: V&R Unipress, 2011.

Ruchniewicz, Krzysztof, "Die polnische Geschichtspolitik nach 1989", *Polen-analysen* 20 (2007): 2–8.

Rüsen, Jörn, *Zeit und Sinn. Strategien historischen Denkens*. Frankfurt am Main: Fischer-Taschenbuch-Verlag, 1990.

Rüsen, Jörn, *Zerbrechende Zeit. Über den Sinn der Geschichte*. Köln: Böhlau, 2001.

Schmid, Harald (ed.), *Geschichtspolitik und kollektives Gedächtnis. Erinnerungskulturen in Theorie und Praxis*. Göttingen: V&R unipress, 2009.

Szacka, Barbara, *Czas przeszły, pamięć, mit*. Warsaw: Wydawnictwo Naukowe "Scholar", 2006.

Traba, Robert, *Przeszłość w teraźniejszości. polskie spory o historię na początku XXI wieku*. Poznań: Wydawnictwo Poznańskie, 2009.

Troebst, Stefan (ed.), *Postdiktatorische Geschichtskulturen im Süden und Osten Europas. Bestandsaufnahme und Forschungsperspektiven*. Göttingen: Wallstein Verlag, 2010.

Zerubavel, Eviatar, *Time Maps. Collective Memory and the Social Shape of the Past*. Chicago: Univ. of Chicago Press, 2004.

Zieliński, Filip, *Demokratie erzählt. Geschichtspolitik im polnischen Parlament nach der Wende von 1989*, unpublished PhD thesis, Universität Wien, 2017, http://doi.org/10.25365/thesis.51825 (7 May 2022).

Johannes Thaler

Drei gegensätzliche Deutungen des Faschismus und ihre Synthese. Politische Praxis – Ideologie – Genese

Die hier folgenden Überlegungen dienten dazu, einen Arbeitsbegriff „Faschismus" zu schaffen, um ihn im Rahmen eines Diktaturvergleichs zur Anwendung zu bringen.[1] Ziel war es, eine möglichst effiziente Faschismusdefinition zu erarbeiten, um faschistische Elemente in vom Konservatismus geprägten Diktaturen aufzeigen oder widerlegen zu können. Es werden drei Deutungsansätze des Faschismus untersucht, ihre Unterschiedlichkeit und gegenseitigen Widersprüche werden erläutert, in weiterer Folge aber ihre wechselseitige Komplementarität dargestellt, Lücken aufgezeigt und Vorschläge zu ihrer Erweiterung gebracht. Einander ergänzend zeichnen sie ein Gesamtbild des Wesens faschistischer Bewegungen und Regime. Es geht um die praxeologische Faschismusdefinition Sven Reichardts,[2] die Definition eines *fascist minimum* von Roger Griffin[3] und schließlich um die Darstellung der historischen Genese faschistischer Ideologie durch Zeev Sternhell.[4]

---

1 Siehe Johannes Thaler, Faschismus, katholische Kirche und kleinstaatliche Diktaturen. Ein Vergleich von Litauen und Österreich in der Zwischenkriegszeit, phil. Diss., Universität Wien 2016. Die Dissertation entstand im Rahmen des Initiativkollegs „Europäische historische Diktatur- und Transformationsforschung" am Institut für Zeitgeschichte der Universität Wien.

2 Zeev Sternhell/Mario Sznajder/Maia Asheri, Die Entstehung der faschistischen Ideologie. Von Sorel zu Mussolini, Hamburg 1999.

3 Roger Griffin, The Nature of Fascism, London 1991; Roger Griffin/Werner Loh/Andreas Umland/Walter Laqueur (Hg.), Fascism Past and Present, West and East. An International Debate on Concepts and Cases in the Comparative Study of the Extreme Right (Soviet and Post-Soviet Politics and Society 35), Stuttgart 2006.

4 Sven Reichardt, Faschistische Kampfbünde. Gewalt und Gemeinschaft im italienischen Squadrismus und in der deutschen SA, Köln 2009.

1.   Reichardts praxeologische Faschismusdefinition

Reichardt gründet seine praxeologische Faschismusdefinition auf eine aus-
führliche Darstellung von Gewaltakten der deutschen SA und der italienischen
squadristi und hebt die Bedeutung der Gewalt für die politische Praxis faschistischer Bewegungen hervor. Nicht Ideologie und weltanschauliche Überzeugungen sieht Reichardt für den Faschismus als wesentlich, sondern die Praxis der
Gewalt, die für faschistische Verbände als einigendes Band diente. Er orientiert
sich dabei unter anderem an einer Aussage Benito Mussolinis, der im Oktober
1919 beteuerte, die Faschisten hätten keine vorgefasste Doktrin, sondern ihre
Doktrin sei die Tat.[5] Reichardt bezweifelt in diesem Sinne ausdrücklich, ob dem
Faschismus überhaupt irgendein konsistenter ideologischer Kern zugesprochen
werden könne:

> „Eine ideologische Verortung der faschistischen Bewegungen scheint angesichts un-
> terschiedlichster Traditionen, innerer Widersprüche, mangelnder Kohärenz und der
> Wandelbarkeit der Bewegungen eher zur Verwirrung beizutragen. Solche Versuche der
> Bestimmung ideologischer Traditionen und Gemeinsamkeiten enden letztlich darin,
> zuzugestehen, daß dem Faschismus kein konsistenter ideologischer Kern zugesprochen
> werden kann."[6]

In diesem Sinne formuliert Reichardt die These, dass der Faschismus „die Zweck-
Mittel-Relation des politischen Handelns umkehrte"[7]: Nicht die politische
Handlung stand im Dienst der politischen Überzeugung, sondern umgekehrt, die
politische Überzeugung wurde in den Dienst der politischen Handlung gestellt.
Die typische faschistische Handlung war Reichardt zufolge die Gewalt: „Handeln
bedeutet bei den untersuchten paramilitärischen Kampfbünden zuerst gewaltsame Aktion. Damit rückt ein zentrales Merkmal des Faschismus in den Vordergrund. Sowohl am Anfang wie am Ende des europäischen Faschismus stand
Gewalt."[8] Gewalt war, Reichardts Ansatz zufolge, für den Faschismus ein Wert für
sich und diente drei Zwecken:

> „erstens der Lahmlegung des politischen Gegners durch direkte Gewalt, zweitens dem
> inneren Zusammenhalt der Kampfbünde durch das ‚Kampferlebnis' selbst und drittens
> der öffentlichen Demonstration faschistischer Stärke und Ordnung. Neben diesen drei
> Hauptzwecken war der gewalttätige Aktivismus in der Anfangszeit dazu geeignet, die
> faschistischen Bewegungen in der Öffentlichkeit bekannt zu machen."[9]

---

5 Reichardt, Kampfbünde, 25.
6 Ebd., 23.
7 Ebd., 25.
8 Ebd., 11.
9 Ebd., 135–138.

Die Gewalthandlungen wurden in diesem Sinne zum Selbstzweck jenseits aller Ideologie.

2. Griffins *fascist minimum*

Roger Griffin stellt sich gegen eine Beschreibung der faschistischen Phänomenologie und erhebt den Anspruch zum ideologischen Kern des Faschismus, *fascist minimum,* vorzudringen. Griffin nähert sich dem Faschismus nicht über dessen politische Praxis, sondern über die Ideologie.[10] Eine von Griffins bekanntesten Formulierungen lautet: „Fascism is a political ideology whose mythic core in its various permutations is a palingenetic form of populist ultra-nationalism.“[11] Den von ihm gewählten Begriff der „Palingenesis" (Wiedergeburt) bezeichnet Griffin als „generic term for the vision of a radically new beginning which follows a period of destruction or perceived dissolution".[12] Die von den Faschisten angestrebte „Palingenesis" grenzt er klar von dem Begriff einer konservativen oder reaktionären „Restauration" ab. Gemeint ist damit nicht eine rückwärtsgewandte Nostalgie (also die Wiedergeburt von etwas bereits Dagewesenem), sondern „a radically non-restorationist sense of a ‚new birth' occurring after a period of perceived decadence".[13] Zwar finde man, Griffin zufolge, den Gedanken der nationalen Wiedergeburt auch in anderen Ideologien, im Faschismus habe sie jedoch einen besonderen Stellenwert: „Fascism radically diverges from liberalism, socialism, conservatism and most religious ideologies by making the ‚revolutionary' process central to its core myth."[14] Zum Begriff des „Ultranationalismus" führt Griffin aus: „I am using ‚ultra-nationalism' [...] to refer to forms of nationalism which ‚go beyond', and hence reject, anything compatible with liberal institutions or with the tradition of Enlightenment humanism which underpins them."[15]

Er unterscheidet zentrale Inhalte einer Ideologie, die er als „ineliminable (uncontested, definitional)" bezeichnet, von variablen, den zeitlichen und örtlichen Umständen geschuldeten Inhalten, die er als „eliminable (contested, va-

---

10 Explizit betont dies Griffin in: Roger Griffin, Fascism's New Faces (and Facelessness) in the ‚Post-Fascist' Epoch, in: Roger Griffin/Werner Loh/Andreas Umland/Walter Laqueur (Hg.), Fascism Past and Present, West and East. An International Debate on Concepts and Cases in the Comparative Study of the Extreme Right (=Soviet and Post-Soviet Politics and Society, 35), Stuttgart 2006, 29–67, 39.
11 Griffin, Nature, 26, 44; Griffin, New Faces, 41.
12 Griffin, Nature, 33.
13 Ebd., 35.
14 Ebd., 39.
15 Ebd., 37.

riable)" beschreibt.[16] Die zentralen Inhalte des Faschismus fasst er in seiner Minimaldefinition zusammen. Andere Merkmale des Zwischenkriegsfaschismus waren, Griffin zufolge, variabel und der speziellen politischen und gesellschaftlichen Situation der Zeit geschuldet, wie etwa das Aufkommen von Massenparteien und uniformierten Paramilitärs sowie das charismatische Führertum, das staatsmännische Qualitäten mit denen eines militärischen Führers vereinte.[17]

3. Sternhells Entstehungsgeschichte faschistischer Ideologie

Anders als Reichardt bzw. in gewisser Übereinstimmung mit Griffin vertritt Zeev Sternhell die Ansicht, dass der Faschismus ausgehend von seiner Ideologie verstanden werden sollte. Sternhell will in diesem Sinne „die wahre Bedeutung der Ideologie für die Ausbreitung des Faschismus nachweisen, jenes politischen und kulturellen Phänomens, das sich geistig stets als völlig autonom erwies".[18] Er widerspricht damit einer verbreiteten Auffassung, die dem Faschismus keine eigenständige oder nur eine sehr inkohärente Ideologie zuspricht. Sternhell kommt zu dem Ergebnis, dass der Faschismus

> „insgesamt ein konsequentes, logisches und gut strukturiertes Ganzes war. […] Sein intellektuelles Rüstzeug machte ihn autonom, und seine Theorien waren nicht weniger homogen als die des Liberalismus oder Sozialismus. Die Unstimmigkeiten und Widersprüche, die das faschistische Denken durchzogen, waren nicht zahlreicher oder gravierender als jene, die sich seit hundert Jahren bei den Liberalen oder Sozialisten fanden."[19]

Sternhell zufolge wäre es außerdem verfehlt, den Faschismus ideologisch als ein Produkt des Ersten Weltkriegs zu begreifen: „Im Zwischenkriegsfaschismus, unter dem Regime Mussolinis wie in allen anderen faschistischen Bewegungen Westeuropas, gibt es nicht eine einzige Idee von Belang, die nicht im Laufe des Vierteljahrhunderts vor August 1914 langsam herangereift wäre."[20]

In seiner Arbeit „Die Entstehung der faschistischen Ideologie" untersucht Sternhell den Ursprung des Faschismus, den er in der revolutionären Linken des späten 19. Jahrhunderts verortet. Im Faschismus erkennt er eine antimaterialistische und antirationalistische Revision des Marxismus: „Es ist unerlässlich, diesen wesentlichen Aspekt der Faschismusdefinition hervorzuheben, denn die Kristallisation der Grundideen des Faschismus, seiner Philosophie und Mytho-

---

16 Griffin, New Faces, 39.
17 Ebd., 46.
18 Sternhell/Sznaijder/Asheri, Ideologie, 14.
19 Ebd., 23.
20 Ebd., 17.

logie bleibt unverständlich, wenn man sie nicht auch als Revolte *marxistischen Ursprungs* gegen den Materialismus begreift."[21] Vom revolutionären marxistischen Milieu übernahmen, Sternhell zufolge, Vordenker des Faschismus den revolutionären Gestus sowie Gewaltkult und -bereitschaft. Einen solchen Vordenker des Faschismus sieht er im französischen Marxismus-Revisionisten George Sorel, auf dessen Ideen sich um die Jahrhundertwende die Sorelianer, später die revolutionären Syndikalisten und schließlich, in weiterentwickelter Form, die Faschisten stützten.[22]

Wesentlich für die Entstehung der faschistischen Ideologie, argumentiert Sternhell, war die Synthese dieser Marxismus-Revision mit einem revolutionären Nationalismus. Diesen Vorgang beschreibt er wie folgt: Die von Marx als zwangsläufig charakterisierte proletarische Revolution war ausgeblieben, der Lebensstandard der arbeitenden Schichten war im letzten Drittel des 19. Jahrhunderts deutlich gestiegen – eine Revolution zeichnete sich somit auch für die nähere Zukunft nicht ab.[23] Die Arbeiterklasse war den revolutionären Denkern und Anführern aufgrund der verringerten wirtschaftlichen Not „abtrünnig" geworden. Diese suchten daher eine neue revolutionäre Einheit – und fanden sie in der Nation. Den Revisionisten des Marxismus war es, Sternhell zufolge, wichtiger, den revolutionären und gewaltbereiten Gestus des Marxismus zu erhalten, als die Interessen der Arbeiterschaft zu vertreten. „Das versagende Proletariat sollte durch jene aufstrebende Macht der modernen Welt ersetzt werden, die aus dem Fortschritt, den Unabhängigkeitskriegen und der kulturellen Integration geboren war: durch die Nation. Alle ihre Klassen sollten zusammengeschweißt werden im gemeinsamen Kampf gegen die bürgerliche, demokratische Dekadenz."[24] Sternhell betont wiederholt, dass der faschistische Kult von Heroismus und Gewalt vom Marxismus übernommen wurde[25] und gegen die bürgerliche Ordnung und die liberale Demokratie gerichtet war.[26]

Wesentliche Elemente waren bei Georges Sorel Gewaltverherrlichung und ein in den Mythos getriebener Nationalismus: „Mythos und Gewalt stellten bei ihm Schlüsselelemente dar, keine Mittel, sondern dauerhafte Werte. Gleichzeitig sollten sie die Massen mobilisieren, wie es die moderne Politik erforderte."[27] Diese für den Faschismus wesentliche Symbiose von Ideen war Sternhell zufolge,

---

21 Ebd., 16; Zeev Sternhell/Mario Sznajder/Maia Ashéri, Naissance de l'idéologie fasciste, Saint-Amand 1994, 21. Der hier kursiv gestellte Zusatz ist im französischen Originaltext zu lesen (*„révolte d'origine marxiste"*), nicht aber in der deutschen Übersetzung.
22 Sternhell/Sznajder/Asheri, Ideologie, 16.
23 Ebd., 28.
24 Ebd., 45.
25 Ebd. 22–23, 66–67.
26 Ebd., 22–23, 133–135, 140–141, 297–298.
27 Ebd., 42.

wie bereits erwähnt, schon vor dem Ersten Weltkrieg vollzogen: „Dieser Prozess war vor dem Krieg beendet und stand in keinem Zusammenhang mit ihm."[28]

4.　　Gegensätze der Deutungen

Bei den hier dargestellten Theorien handelt es sich um sehr unterschiedliche und teilweise einander widersprechende Ansätze zur Beschreibung faschistischer Bewegungen und Regime. Griffin hebt Reichardts Arbeit als eine der wenigen im deutschsprachigen Raum hervor, die sich des neuen Konsenses *(new consensus)* der englischsprachigen Literatur annimmt und in einer profunden Studie den Faschismus als kulturelle und anthropologische Gesamtrevolution untersucht.[29] Allerdings ist anzumerken, dass Reichardts Deutung, „daß dem Faschismus kein konsistenter ideologischer Kern zugesprochen werden kann",[30] Griffins und auch Sternhells Ansatz diametral widerspricht, die den Faschismus aufgrund seiner Ideologie zu begreifen versuchen. Reichardt vertritt die These, „daß der Faschismus nicht essentialistisch von seinem ‚Wesen' (Walter Laqueur) oder seiner ‚Natur' (Roger Griffin) her begriffen werden kann".[31] Er müsse vielmehr „als politische Handlung und als politisch-kultureller Ausdruck analysiert" werden.[32]

Auch Griffin anerkennt die Bedeutung von Gewalt für faschistische Regime in der Gestalt von Verfolgung und Krieg,[33] selbst wenn er die Destruktivität des Faschismus nicht im Sinne Reichardts als Selbstzweck auffasst: „The destruction which is necessitated both in theory and in practice by the fascist revolution is seen by its activists not as an end in itself but as the corollary of the regenerative process by which society is to be purged of decadence."[34]

Ein wesentlicher Unterschied zwischen Reichardts und Griffins Ansatz ist Reichardts Historisierung des Faschismusbegriffs. Reichardt begrenzt ihn auf die Epoche der 1920er- und 1930er-Jahre, die er als „Epoche der faschistischen Herausforderung"[35] bezeichnet. Griffin hingegen betont die „starke darwinistische Fähigkeit zu kreativer Mutation"[36] des Faschismus. Er definiert ein „faschistisches Minimum", das ermöglichen soll, faschistische Bewegungen zu an-

---

28　Ebd.
29　Griffin, New Faces, 33.
30　Reichardt, Kampfbünde, 23.
31　Ebd., 25.
32　Ebd.
33　Griffin, Nature, 5.
34　Ebd., 44–45.
35　Reichardt, Kampfbünde, 29–30.
36　Griffin, New Faces, 56.

derer Zeit in neuem Gewand zu erkennen und offenzulegen. Griffin verfolgt das Ziel, mit seiner Minimaldefinition auch moderne Spielarten des Faschismus zu erfassen, die nicht mit Massenparteien, uniformierten Paramilitärs und charismatischen Führern auftreten. Allerdings hebt Reichardt trotz der von ihm befürworteten Historisierung des Faschismus auch dessen Wandlungsfähigkeit hervor: „Der Faschismus war keine statische Erscheinung. Im Gegenteil: Im Faschismus zeigt sich ein enormes Wandlungs- und Entwicklungspotential, das nicht schon in den Anfängen der faschistischen Bewegungen zu erkennen war."[37]

Reichardts Postulat der Umkehrung der Zweck-Mittel-Relation im Faschismus und der vorrangigen Bedeutung von Gewalt und Aktion vor jeder Ideologie ist wiederum mit Sternhells Ansatz schwer zu vereinen. Für Sternhell ging die intellektuelle Auseinandersetzung der politischen Aktion voraus: Nachdem die Vorläufer der faschistischen Ideologie „zum autonomen System geworden waren, gingen sie dem Handeln voraus, das sie anführen und zur Veränderung der Gesellschaft nutzen wollten. [...] Die Theorie lieferte der Revolution ein perfektes Programm."[38]

Mit Sternhells Versuch, den Faschismus über seine ideologischen Ursprünge und deren Entwicklung zu begreifen, geht Reichardt schärfer ins Gericht als mit Griffins Minimaldefinition. So schreibt er im Hinblick auf Sternhells Arbeit: „Die Gleichsetzung der inkohärenten kulturellen Ursprünge des Faschismus mit einem angeblich ideologischen Programm führt [...] zu einer monokausalen ideengeschichtlichen Vereinfachung. Dadurch wird vor allem der gesamte Bereich der Praxis und der Handlungsebene ignoriert."[39]

Was Griffin als „palingenetischen Ultranationalismus" bezeichnet, hat bei Sternhell eine Entsprechung, wenn er den faschistischen Nationalismus und seine Vorläufer als einen „vom Konservatismus abgeschnittenen Nationalismus" bezeichnet.[40] Die von den Faschisten angestrebte „Palingenesis" grenzt Griffin deutlich von konservativen oder reaktionären Bewegungen ab.[41] Bei Sternhell hat dies seine Entsprechung in der Betonung der modernistischen Züge. Der Faschismus war „darauf bedacht, die Vorteile des Fortschritts zu erhalten. Nie trat er für eine Rückkehr zu einem hypothetischen ‚Goldenen Zeitalter' ein."[42] Griffin stimmt mit Sternhell auch darin überein, dass der Faschismus nicht nur über seine Antihaltungen, also im negativen Sinne, zu definieren ist.[43] Allerdings

---

37 Reichardt, Kampfbünde, 27.
38 Sternhell/Sznaijder/Asheri, Ideologie, 44.
39 Reichardt, Kampfbünde, 23–24.
40 Eigene Übersetzung aus dem Französischen: *„un nationalisme coupé du conservatisme".* Sternhell/Sznaijder/Ashéri, Naissance, 63.
41 Griffin, Nature, 35.
42 Sternhell/Sznaijder/Asheri, Ideologie, 18.
43 Griffin, New Faces, 39.

kritisiert er auch, Sternhell führe eine allzu starke Dichotomie zwischen Faschisten und Demokraten ein und ignoriere dadurch andere politische Strömungen.[44] Darüber hinaus gehe Sternhell zu wenig auf gesellschaftliche und nationale Besonderheiten, auf den Stellenwert der Aktion für den Faschismus und auf die praktische Umsetzung der Ideologie ein.[45]

5. Schlüsse: Vorschlag der Erweiterung von Reichardts Deutung faschistischer Gewalt, kritische Betrachtung und Synthese der Deutungen

Reichardts Theorie zur Bedeutung der gewaltsamen Aktion als zentrales Element des Faschismus bezieht sich in seinem Werk ausschließlich auf die Bewegungsphase des Faschismus: Der italienische Squadrismus 1921 und 1922 wird mit der deutschen SA der Jahre 1929–1932 verglichen.[46] Die Phase der Machtergreifung und die Regimephase (Schieder)[47] bzw. die Phase der Radikalisierung (Paxton)[48] werden in Reichardts praxeologischer Faschismusdefinition nicht berücksichtigt. Die Bedeutung der Gewalt könnte jedoch durchaus allgemeiner gefasst und auf die Regime- und die Radikalisierungsphase des Faschismus angewandt werden. Der Hang faschistischer Regime zu Repression und Verfolgung im Inneren sowie ihr Drang zu Krieg und Eroberung nach außen könnten ebenso in diesem Kontext der Gewalt als politischer Praxis interpretiert werden wie die Verbrechen des Holocaust. In eine solche allgemeinere Deutung der faschistischen Gewalt passt Reichardts oben zitierte Aussage, dass sowohl der Anfang wie das Ende des europäischen Faschismus von Gewalt geprägt waren.[49]

Ein Brückenschlag zum Ansatz Roger Griffins wäre dabei die Annahme, dass ein „palingenetischer Ultranationalismus" (Griffin) in der Praxis unweigerlich zur Gewaltbereitschaft bzw. zu einem zentralen Stellenwert der Gewalt im politischen Handeln führt. So betont Griffin etwa, dass der „nationalen Wiedergeburt" in der faschistischen Ideenwelt eine destruktive Phase der Zerstörung bestehender Strukturen vorangehe. Reichardt wiederum anerkennt die Bedeutung der „erlösten Nation" (Palingenesis) als Handlungsziel faschistischer Bewegungen und räumt ein, dass dieses Denken „mobilisierende Wirkung"[50] entfaltet

---

44 Griffin, Nature, 6–7.
45 Ebd.
46 Reichardt, Kampfbünde, 15.
47 Wolfgang Schieder, Der italienische Faschismus 1919–1945, München 2010; ders., Faschistische Diktaturen. Studien zu Italien und Deutschland, Göttingen 2008.
48 Robert O. Paxton, The Anatomy of Fascism, New York 2004.
49 Reichardt, Kampfbünde, 11.
50 Ebd., 36.

habe. Es habe faschistische Ideale hervorgebracht, die „für die Mobilisierung rebellischer Gefühle und Leidenschaften von Bedeutung"[51] waren.

Ebenso könnten die für den Faschismus typischen Antihaltungen (Antisozialismus, Antiliberalismus, Antiparlamentarismus u. a.) vor dem Hintergrund des zentralen Stellenwerts der Gewalt gedeutet werden. Von der Forschung werden diese Antihaltungen häufig damit begründet, dass der Faschismus im Vergleich mit anderen politischen Strömungen wie Sozialismus, Liberalismus oder Konservatismus erst sehr spät auf der politischen Bühne Europas erschien und sich deswegen besonders gegen die bereits etablierten politischen Strömungen behaupten musste.[52] Diese Antihaltungen könnten ihren Ursprung vielmehr in der stark auf Destruktivität gerichteten Grundhaltung des Faschismus haben, aus der heraus auch der Gewalt ein zentraler Stellenwert erwuchs.

Hinsichtlich Griffins Minimaldefinition des Faschismus sei an dieser Stelle kritisch festgehalten, dass diese – ungeachtet ihres nicht zu bestreitenden wissenschaftlichen Wertes – die ursprüngliche, etymologische Bedeutung des Begriffs „Faschismus" ignoriert bzw. ihr sogar widerspricht. Das italienische *fascio*, in wörtlicher Übersetzung und im alltäglichen Sprachgebrauch ganz einfach „das Bündel", wurde – politisch aufgeladen – im späten 19. Jahrhundert auf linke sozialrevolutionäre Gruppen von ArbeiterInnen und BäuerInnen angewandt. Die Bezeichnung wurde von Mussolini später im Zuge des Ersten Weltkriegs für die ihm nahestehenden gewaltbereiten, kriegsbejahenden und rechtsgerichteten sozialistischen Verbände verwendet, die schließlich in seinen 1919 in Mailand gegründeten *Fasci di Combattimento* („Kampfverbände") eine erste offizielle politische Ausprägung fanden.[53] Es entwickelte sich damit eine weitere politische Aufladung des Begriffs. Als geeignetes Symbol wurde auf die altrömischen *fasces* („Rutenbündel") mit eingeflochtener Axt und herausstehender Klinge zurückgegriffen. Dieser *fascio* war einerseits ein Symbol für die Staatsgewalt und stand auch für den faschistischen Gewaltkult. Andererseits war er als „Bündel" auch symbolischer Ausdruck für die faschistische Gemeinschaft, unter der die gewaltbereite paramilitärische Truppe, weitergehend aber auch die Partei und die idealisierte Nation verstanden wurden.[54] Die beiden wesentlichen Aspekte des Symbols der *fasces*, Gewalt und Gemeinschaft, denen der Faschismus sogar seinen Namen verdankt, reduziert Griffin gemeinsam mit anderen Merkmalen

---

51 Ebd.
52 Vgl. Juan José Linz, Totalitäre und autoritäre Regime (Potsdamer Textbücher 4), Potsdam 2009, 198; auch zu finden in: Sternhell/Sznaijder/Asheri, Ideologie.
53 Siehe auch Mussolinis eigene Ausführungen: Benito Mussolini, La Dottrina del Fascismo (1932), in: Edoardo Susmel/Duilio Susmel (Hg.), Opera Omnia di Benito Mussolini, Band 34, Firenze 1967, 114–138.
54 Ebd.

auf „eliminable concepts", sie werden also scheinbar nicht als wesentliche Aspekte des Faschismus gesehen.[55]

Zu Sternhell soll hier noch angemerkt werden: So überzeugend er die Entstehung faschistischer Ideologie analysiert, so wenig erfolgreich ist sein Versuch, den deutschen Nationalsozialismus typologisch vom Gesamtphänomen des Faschismus zu trennen.[56] Er beruft sich darauf, dass im deutschen Fall der biologische Determinismus beziehungsweise der Rassismus in seiner extremsten Form das Wesen der Bewegung ausmachten. Für den Faschismus hingegen sei der Rassismus keine notwendige Voraussetzung: „Der Rassismus ist […] keine notwendige Voraussetzung für den Faschismus, er trägt jedoch zum faschistischen Eklektizismus bei."[57] Wolfgang Schieder betont, dass sich Sternhell mit dieser Position nicht durchsetzen konnte.[58] Jüngere Meilensteine in der Faschismusforschung wie die Studien Reichardts und Paxtons verdeutlichen, dass der Nationalsozialismus in der einschlägigen Forschung weiterhin als Variante eines faschistischen Regimes gedeutet wird.

Trotz der Unterschiedlichkeit und teilweise Gegensätzlichkeit der hier beschriebenen Ansätze zur Untersuchung des Faschismus scheint es, dass sich mithilfe von Sternhells Überlegungen der theoretische Ansatz von Reichardt mit jenem von Griffin in Einklang bringen lässt. Bei näherer Betrachtung wird deutlich, dass die historische Genese der faschistischen Ideologie, wie Sternhell sie beschreibt, den *missing link* zwischen den beiden anderen Theorien darstellt. Verfolgt man die Entwicklung faschistischer Ideen in den Jahrzehnten vor dem Ersten Weltkrieg, so wird deutlich, wie der Kult der Gewalt (Reichardt) einerseits und der „palingenetische Ultranationalismus" (Griffin) andererseits in die junge politische Bewegung einflossen. Vom revolutionären Syndikalismus hatten sich die frühen Faschisten den Gewaltkult entlehnt, während das Ideal des Klassenkampfs durch den Nationalismus ersetzt wurde. Von diesen beiden Aspekten, die Sternhell historisch herleitet, untersucht Reichardt den Aspekt der Gewalt, während Griffin die besondere Ausprägung des Nationalismus im Faschismus hervorhebt.

6.   Auswahlbibliografie

Roger Griffin, *The Nature of Fascism*. London 1991.
Roger Griffin / Werner Loh / Andreas Umland / Walter Laqueur (Hg.), Fascism Past and Present, West and East. An International Debate on Concepts and Cases in the Com-

---

55 Griffin, New Faces, 39.
56 Sternhell/Sznaijder/Asheri, Ideologie, 15–16.
57 Ebd., 16.
58 Schieder, Diktaturen, 12. Ähnlich auch: Griffin, Nature, 6–7.

parative Study of the Extreme Right (Soviet and Post-Soviet Politics and Society 35), Stuttgart 2006.

Juan José Linz, Totalitäre und autoritäre Regime (Potsdamer Textbücher 4), Potsdam 2009.

Sven Reichardt, Faschistische Kampfbünde. Gewalt und Gemeinschaft im italienischen Squadrismus und in der deutschen SA, Köln 2009.

Zeev Sternhell /Mario Sznajder /Maia Asheri, Die Entstehung der faschistischen Ideologie. Von Sorel zu Mussolini, Hamburg 1999.

Johannes Thaler, Faschismus, katholische Kirche und kleinstaatliche Diktaturen. Ein Vergleich von Litauen und Österreich in der Zwischenkriegszeit., phil. Diss., Universität Wien 2016.

Katharina Ebner / Kathrin Raminger

Documentation

The Doctoral College (DC) "European Historical Dictatorship and Trans-formation Research" was a joint project of the Departments of Contemporary History, Political Science, East European History, and Byzantine and Modern Greek Studies of the University of Vienna. Twelve doctoral fellows from various disciplines conducted research on the authoritarian regimes of the interwar period as well as on those under the communist regime after 1945 in Bulgaria, Greece, Latvia, Lithuania, Austria, Poland, Portugal, Romania, Spain, Hungary, and the Soviet Union. The focus was on a comparative analysis of the causes of the establishment of dictatorships in several Central and Eastern European states after the wave of democratization as a result of World War I, the examination of the resulting political and socio-cultural patterns, and the strategies of coping with the past after the end of the regimes in question. The aim was an inter-disciplinary approach to these questions from a historical perspective against a background rooted in social and political sciences.

Website: https://diktaturforschung.univie.ac.at/en/home/

Faculty

Univ.-Prof. Mag. DDr. Oliver Rathkolb (Spokesman) (Department of Con-temporary History)
PD Mag. Dr. Karin Liebhart (Department of Political Science)
Univ.-Prof. Dr. Oliver Jens Schmitt (Department of East European History)
Univ.-Prof. Dr. Maria A. Stassinopoulou (Department of Byzantine and Modern Greek Studies)

Fellows and Research Topics[1]

- Katharina Ebner: Ideologietransfer des italienischen Faschismus nach Wien und Budapest unter Berücksichtigung der Rolle der römisch-katholischen Kirche (2016)
- Alena Haubenhofer: Europabilder in Litauen und Lettland (2016)
- Inga Kokalevska: Das Androgyne und die Diktatur
- Florian Kührer-Wielach: Siebenbürgen ohne Siebenbürger? Staatliche Integration und neue Identifikationsangebote zwischen Regionalismus und nationalem Einheitsdogma im Diskurs der Siebenbürger Rumänen. 1918–1933 (2013)
- Florian Musil: Demokratisierung 'von unten': Die Zivilgesellschaft der Metropolregion Barcelona im Kampf um demokratische Rechte in der letzten Dekade des Franco-Regimes (2017)
- Wolfram Niess: Die politische Rechte in Bessarabien (1918–1944)
- Inga Paslaviciute: Petitionen an das Regime. (Rhetorische) Strategien in der Kommunikation mit der kommunistischen Bürokratie in der Litauischen Sozialistischen Sowjetrepublik 1953–1989 (2020)
- Kathrin Raminger: Visuelle Repräsentationen von (Ohn-)Macht. Kunstausstellungen als politisches Instrument. Die iberischen Diktaturen Francos und Salazars im Vergleich (2017)
- Nathalie Patricia Soursos: Fotografie und Diktatur. Eine Untersuchung anhand der Diktaturen Ioannis Metaxas' in Griechenland und Benito Mussolinis in Italien (2015)
- Johannes Thaler: Faschismus, katholische Kirche und kleinstaatliche Diktaturen. Ein Vergleich von Litauen und Österreich in der Zwischenkriegszeit (2016)
- Filip Zielinski: Demokratie erzählt. Geschichtspolitik im polnischen Parlament nach der Wende von 1989 (2017)

Associated Fellows

- Lucile Dreidemy: Denn ein Engel kann nicht sterben. Engelbert Dollfuß 1934–2012. Eine Biographie des Posthumen (2012)
- Linda Erker: Die Universität Wien im Austrofaschismus – zur politischen Vereinnahmung einer Hochschule: im Vergleich mit der Universität Madrid im Franco-Faschismus (2018)

---

1 Original titles of the projects. Year of graduation in brackets.

- Eleni Kouki: Politics of the Regime of the 21st of April to Control the National past: Historical Celebrations and Monuments (2016)
- Tobias Reckling: Foreign Correspondents in Francoist Spain, 1945–1975 (2016)
- Florian Wenninger: "… werden wir mit aller Brutalität vorgehen." Zum Polarisierungsprozess der Zwischenkriegszeit in Österreich und seinen Nachwirkungen (2015)

Chronological Table

- Winter semester 2009: Launch of the Doctoral College "European Historical Dictatorship and Transformation Research"
- 8 March 2010: Official inauguration with an opening speech by Rector Georg Winckler, followed by a lecture entitled "Authoritarian Movements Then and Now" by Barbara Coudenhove-Kalergi, and a poster session
- 14 June 2010: Guest lecture by Eveline List (Universität Wien) and Peter Angerer (Universität Wien): "Dynamics of Mass Psychology and its Effectiveness in Dictatorships"
- 28 June 2010: Guest lecture by Herlinde Pauer-Studer (Universität Wien): "Transformations of Normativity: The Nazi System from the Perspective of Moral Philosophy"
- 24 October 2011: Guest lecture by Carlo Moos (Universität Zürich): "Italian Fascism's Search for a Role Model"
- March 2011: Workshop "Authoritarian Regimes and Inter-War Europe: Austria Under Dollfuss/Schuschnigg, Gömbös-Hungary During the Horthy Era and Salazar's *Estado Novo*. Comparison, Memory, Continuities" with António Costa Pinto (Universidade de Lisboa), Anton Pelinka (CEU Budapest), József Vonyó (University of Pécs)
- May 2011: Workshop "Visual History/Visual Culture" with Birgit Mersmann (Jacobs University Bremen), Almira Ousmanova (European Humanities University Vilnius), Tasoula Vervenioti (Hellenic Open University), Sandra Grether (Humboldt Universität zu Berlin) and Benedikt Vogeler (Humboldt Universität zu Berlin).
- May 2011: Workshop "Phases of Transformation and their Preconditions in Lithuania, Romania and Moldova in Comparison" with Joachim Tauber (Nordost-Institut – Institut für Kultur und Geschichte der Deutschen in Nordosteuropa e. V., Lüneburg), Hans-Christian Maner (Johannes Gutenberg-Universität Mainz), Svetlana Suveica (Leibniz-Institut für Ost- und Südosteuropaforschung, Regensburg), Alvydas Nikžentaitis (Lithuanian Institute of History)

- June 2011: Workshop "Memory Culture and History Politics in Post-Dictatorial Societies" with Walther L. Bernecker (Friedrich-Alexander-Universität Erlangen-Nürnberg) and Stefan Troebst (Leibniz-Institut für Geschichte und Kultur des östlichen Europa, Leipzig)
- 7–8 November 2011: International Conference "Images of Power/Representations of the Past", organised by the DC
- 7 November 2011: Public Lecture by Klaus von Beyme (Ruprecht-Karls-Universität Heidelberg): "End of Transformation – End of Democracy?"
- 24–25 November 2011: International Conference "Public Sphere, Ideology, Transformation of Power", organised by the DC
- 9 May 2012: Received the award "Successful Congress Organizer 2011" from the City of Vienna
- 23 May 2012: Federal president of the Republic of Austria, Dr. Heinz Fischer, visits the DC

Scientific Output

Monographies

Lucile Dreidemy: *Der Dollfuß-Mythos. Eine Biographie des Posthumen.* Wien – Köln – Weimar: Böhlau, 2014.
Linda Erker: *Die Universität Wien im Austrofaschismus. Österreichische Hochschulpolitik 1933 bis 1938, ihre Vorbedingungen und langfristigen Nachwirkungen.* Göttingen: V&R unipress, 2021.
Florian Kührer-Wielach: *Siebenbürgen ohne Siebenbürger? Zentralstaatliche Integration und politischer Regionalismus nach dem Ersten Weltkrieg.* Munich: de Gruyter Oldenbourg, 2014.
Kathrin Raminger: *Politik der Bilder. Offizielle Ausstellungen im Franquismus und ihre politischen Funktionen (1936–1951).* Weimar: VDG, 2011.

Publications as editor

Linda Erker with Veronika Duma, Veronika Helfert and Hanna Lichtenberger: *Perspektivenwechsel. Geschlechterverhältnisse im Austrofaschismus, Österreichische Zeitschrift für Geschichtswissenschaften* (ÖZG) 3 (2016).
Lucile Dreidemy and Florian Wenninger: *Das Dollfuß/Schuschnigg-Regime 1933–1938. Vermessung eines Forschungsfeldes.* Wien – Köln – Weimar: Böhlau, 2013.
Florian Kührer-Wielach with Angela Ilić, Irena Samide, and Tanja Žigon: *Blick ins Ungewisse. Visionen und Utopien im Donau-Karpaten-Raum. 1917 und danach.* Regensburg: Verlag Friedrich Pustet, 2019.

Florian Kührer-Wielach with Sarah Lemmen: *Transformation in East Central Europe. 1918 and 1989 – a Comparative Approach.* Special issue of the *European Review of History* 23 (2016) 4.

Book chapters

Lucile Dreidemy und Florian Wenninger: "Einleitung," in *Das Dollfuß/Schuschnigg-Regime 1933–1938. Vermessung eines Forschungsfeldes,* edited by Florian Wenninger and Lucile Dreidemy, 7–13. Wien – Köln – Weimar: Böhlau, 2013.

Lucile Dreidemy: "Dollfuß – biographisch. Eine Längsschnittanalyse des biographischen Diskurses über Engelbert Dollfuß," in *Österreich 1918–1938. Interdisziplinäre Bestandaufnahme und Perspektiven,* edited by Ilse Reiter-Zatloukal et al., 230–44. Wien – Köln – Weimar: Böhlau 2012.

Lucile Dreidemy: "'Aus der Geschichte lernen … und gegen die Rotfront kämpfen!' Das Dr. Engelbert Dollfuß-Museum in Texingtal, Niederösterreich," in *Zeit-/Geschichte ausstellen in Österreich. Bestandsaufnahme und Recherche,* edited by Dirk Rupnow and Heidemarie Uhl, 369–92. Wien – Köln – Weimar: Böhlau, 2011.

Lucile Dreidemy: "Botz verstehen! Verdienst und Grenzen von Provokation und Empathie im Kontext öffentlicher Geschichtspolitik," in *Politische Gewalt und Machtausübung im 20. Jahrhundert. Zeitgeschichte, Zeitgeschehen und Kontroversen. Festschrift für Gerhard Botz,* edited by Heinz Berger et al., 695–707. Wien – Köln – Weimar: Böhlau 2011.

Katharina Ebner: "Karl Anton Prinz Rohan und der italienische Faschismus in Österreich," in *Bananen, Cola, Zeitgeschichte. Oliver Rathkolb und das lange 20. Jahrhundert,* Volume 1, edited by Lucile Dreidemy et al., 191–201. Wien – Köln – Weimar: Böhlau, 2015.

Katharina Ebner: "Politische Katholizismen in Österreich 1933–1938 – Aspekte und Desiderate der Forschungslage," in *Das Dollfuß/Schuschnigg-Regime 1933–1938. Vermessung eines Forschungsfeldes,* edited by Florian Wenninger and Lucile Dreidemy, 159–221. Wien – Köln – Weimar: Böhlau, 2013. (peer reviewed)

Linda Erker with Katharina Kniefacz: "'Es ist halt alles eine Blickwinkelfrage!' Zur umstrittenen Verleihung des Ehrendoktorates der Universität Wien an den Staatsrechtler Ernst Forsthoff (1965)," in *Zuviel der Ehre? Interdisziplinäre Perspektiven auf akademische Ehrungen in Deutschland und Österreich,* edited by Alexander Pinwinkler and Johannes Koll, 275–306. Wien – Köln – Weimar: Böhlau, 2019.

Linda Erker: "Studierende der Universität Wien und ihr Antisemitismus in der Zwischenkriegszeit," in *Antisemitismus in Österreich 1933–1938,* edited by Gertrude Enderle-Burcel and Ilse Reiter-Zatloukal, 785–806. Wien – Köln – Weimar: Böhlau, 2018.

Linda Erker with Klaus Taschwer: "'Eine wirklich befriedigende Lösung der Judenfrage!' Antisemitische Personalpolitik an der Universität Wien vor und nach 1933," in *Antisemitismus in Österreich 1933–1938,* edited by Gertrude Enderle-Burcel and Ilse Reiter-Zatloukal, 751–67. Wien – Köln – Weimar: Böhlau, 2018.

Linda Erker: "Violencia y poder en las universidades de Viena y de Madrid durante el austrofascismo y el franquismo," in *Extremos. Visiones de lo extremo en literatura, historia, música, arte, cine y lingüística en España y Austria,* edited by Georg Pichler, 337–54. Berne: Peter Lang, 2017.

Linda Erker: "Expulsions prior to the Anschluss: students in the inter-war years," in *Die Universität. Eine Kampfzone*, edited by Werner Hanak-Lettner, 211–13. Vienna: Picus – Jüdisches Museum Wien, 2015.

Linda Erker with Herbert Posch: "Mehr als 2.230 Studierende ausgeschlossen / Studieren 1938–1945 / Vertriebene Studierende / Studieren im Widerstand," in *Bedrohte Intelligenz. Von der Polarisierung und Einschüchterung bis zur nationalsozialistischen Vertreibung und Vernichtung. Ausstellung und Zeitung zur Ausstellung*, edited by Franz-Stefan Meissel and Thomas Olechowski, 32–39. Vienna: Universität Wien, 2015.

Linda Erker: "'Jetzt weiß ich ganz, was das 'Dritte Reich' bedeutet – die Herrschaft schrankenloser, feiger Brutalität.' Eine Momentaufnahme der Universität Wien im Oktober 1932," in *Bananen, Cola, Zeitgeschichte: Oliver Rathkolb und das lange 20. Jahrhundert*, Band 1, edited by Lucile Dreidemy, et al., 177–90. Wien – Köln – Weimar: Böhlau, 2015.

Linda Erker: "Hochschulen im Austrofaschismus und im Nationalsozialismus: Ein kooperatives Lehrprojekt der Österreichischen HochschülerInnenschaft," in *Der lange Schatten des Antisemitismus*, edited by Oliver Rathkolb, 245–51. Göttingen: V&R unipress, 2013. (Zeitgeschichte im Kontext 8).

Florian Kührer-Wielach: "(Was) Minderheiten schaffen. 'Eigen-sinnige' Lebenswelten und ethnonationale Blockbildung am Beispiel 'Großrumäniens'," in *Zerfall, Trauma, Triumph. Das Epochenjahr 1918 und sein Nachleben in Zentral-, Ostmittel- und Südosteuropa*, edited by Steffen Höhne, 327–62. Munich: Oldenbourg Verlag, 2020.

Florian Kührer-Wielach: "Viziunea de la Alba Iulia şi realitatea interbelică. O perspectivă (trans)regional," in *România şi evenimentele istorice din perioada 1914–1920. Desăvârşirea marii unirii şi întregirea României*, edited by Victor A. Voicu, 165–75. Bucharest: Academia Română, 2018.

Florian Kührer-Wielach: "'Maniu, schläfst du?' Ethnoregionalistische Diskurse nach dem Ersten Weltkrieg an einem Fallbeispiel," in *Umbruch mit Schlachtenlärm. Siebenbürgen und der Erste Weltkrieg*, edited by Harald Heppner, 339–53. Wien – Köln – Weimar: Böhlau, 2017. (Siebenbürgisches Archiv 44).

Florian Kührer-Wielach: "A Counter-Community Between Regionalism und Nationalism: State-Building and the Vision of Modernisation in Interwar Romania," in *(Re)Constructing Communities in Europe, 1918–1968. Senses of Belonging Below, Beyond and Within the Nation-State*, edited by Stefan Couperus and Harm Kaal. London: Routledge, 2016.

Florian Kührer-Wielach: "Siebenbürgen als administrative Einheit und diskursives Konzept," in *Das Südosteuropa der Regionen*, edited by Oliver Jens Schmitt and Michael Metzeltin, 349–409. Vienna: Verlag der Österreichischen Akademie der Wissenschaften, 2015.

Florian Kührer-Wielach: "Zwischen 'mongolischem Zorn' und der 'tschechoslowakischen Sonne der Freundschaft'. Eine siebenbürgische Perspektive auf die Rumänen jenseits der Grenze. Ungarn und die Tschechoslowakei im Vergleich," in *Die Pariser Vororte-Verträge im Spiegel der Öffentlichkeit*, edited by Harald D. Gröller and Harald Heppner, 1–16. Vienna-Berlin: Lit Verlag, 2013. (Transkulturelle Forschungen an den Österreich-Bibliotheken im Ausland 7).

Florian Kührer-Wielach: "Von Dieben und Doktoren. Die Rumänisierung Kronstadts. Das Beispiel der Jorgastraße," in *Kronstadt und das Burzenland. Beiträge von Studium*

Transylvanicum zur Geschichte und Kultur Siebenbürgens, edited by Bernhard Heigl and Thomas Sindilariu, 44–53. Kronstadt: Aldus, 2011.

Florian Musil: "La Transición Democrática en España desde abajo: El ejemplo del Movimiento Estudiantil en Barcelona," in *XIII Jornadas Interescuelas / Departamento de Historia,* edited by Ardesi de Taratuvíez, Beatriz et al. Catarmarca: Universidad Nacional de Catamarca, 2013.

Florian Musil: "Anti-Francoist Social Movements in Barcelona," in *Societats en canvi: Espanya i Portugal als anys setanta,* edited by Manuel Loff and Carme Molinero. Bellaterrra: Universitat Autònoma de Barcelona, 2012.

Florian Musil: "Die Aufarbeitung der Franco-Diktatur als Werkzeug der Wählermobilisierung," in *Update! Perspektiven der Zeitgeschichte. Zeitgeschichtetage 2010,* edited by Linda Erker, Alexander Salzmann, Lucile Dreidemy, and Klaudija Sabo, 564–72. Innsbruck–Vienna–Bozen, 2012.

Florian Musil: "Los movimientos antifranquistas de Barcelona al final de la dictadura: Propuesta para un esquema analítico de movimientos sociales contemporáneos," in *"No es país para jóvenes." Actas del III Encuentro de Jóvenes Investigadores de la AHC,* edited by Alejandra Ibarra. Bilbao, 2012.

Kathrin Raminger: "Verehrung wider Willen: António de Oliveira Salazar. – Die visuelle Repräsentation eines unsichtbaren Diktators," in *Visualisierungen von Kult,* edited by Marion Meyer and Deborah Klimburg-Salter, 138–173. Wien – Köln – Weimar: Böhlau, 2014.

Nathalie Patricia Soursos: "Griechenland. Von der Krise des Parlamentarismus bis zum Scheitern der Demokratie (1922–1936)," in: *Nach dem 'Großen Krieg.' Vom Triumph zum Desaster der Demokratie 1918/19 bis 1939,* edited by Steffen Kailitz, 358–406. Göttingen: V&R, 2017. (Schriften des Hannah-Arendt-Instituts 62).

Nathalie Patricia Soursos: "Diktatoren-Kitsch," in *Renaissancen des Kitsch,* edited by Christina Hoffmann and Johanna Öttl, 71–88. Vienna–Berlin: Turia + Kant, 2016. (Antikanon 1).

Johannes Thaler: "Legitimismus. Ein unterschätzter Baustein des autoritären Österreich," in *Das Dollfuß/Schuschnigg-Regime 1933–1938. Vermessung eines Forschungsfeldes,* edited by Florian Wenninger and Lucile Dreidemy, 69–86. Wien – Köln – Weimar: Böhlau, 2013.

Articles

Lucile Dreidemy: "Die Staatsoperette. Satire als Geschichtspolitik," in *Images et discours de la nation. Arts et identité collective dans les pays de langue allemande depuis 1945, Revue d'Allemagne et des pays de langue allemande* 45 (2013) 2, edited by Emmanuel Béhague: 265–83. (peer reviewed)

Lucile Dreidemy: "Engelbert Dollfuß 1934–2009. Reflexionsansätze zu einer Biographie des Posthumen," in *zeitgeschichte* 37 (2010) 3: 153–62; also published in: *BIOS, Zeitschrift für Biographieforschung, Oral History und Lebensverlaufsanalysen* 22 (2009) 2: 207–17. (peer reviewed)

Katharina Ebner, with Sandra Grether and Benedikt Vogeler: "Feindbilder nach 1945. Zur Kontinuität von Feindbegriffen in Deutschland, Österreich und der Sowjetunion," *zeitgeschichte* 38 (2011) 6: 364–83. (peer reviewed)

Linda Erker: "La Universidad de Viena en el austrofascismo," in *La Universidad europea bajo las dictaduras, AYER* 1 (2016) 101, edited by Carolina Rodríguez-López, 79–104. (peer reviewed).

Linda Erker: "Jüdische Studierende im Nationalsozialismus – von Ausgrenzung und Vertreibung," *GEDENKDIENST. Verein für historisch-politische Bildungsarbeit und internationalen Dialog* 4 (2012): 1–2.

Eleni Kouki: "The Unknown Soldier of Athens and the quest for a new monumental style during the Interwar period in Greece", *ARCHEIOTAXIO* (2011) 13: 152–163.

Florian Kührer-Wielach: "'A fertile and flourishing garden.' Alexandru Vaida-Voevod's Political Account Ten Years after Versailles," in "Romania and the Paris Peace Conference (1919). Actors, Scenarios, Circulation of Knowledge," edited by Svetlana Suveica, *Journal of Romanian Studies* 1 (2019) 2: 135–52.

Florian Kührer-Wielach: "The Transylvanian promise: political mobilisation, unfulfilled hope and the rise of authoritarianism in interwar Romania," in *Transformation in East Central Europe. 1918 and 1989 – a Comparative Approach*, edited by Florian Kührer-Wielach and Sarah Lemmen, *European Review of History* 23 (2016) 4: 580–94.

Florian Kührer-Wielach: "Die Eingliederung Siebenbürgens in den rumänischen Staat. Erwartungen, Erfolge und Enttäuschungen," *Zeitschrift für Siebenbürgische Landeskunde* 36 (2013): 92–100.

Florian Musil: "Franco-ellenes társadalmi mozgalmak Barcelonában: Hogyan váltak a rezsim szociális és politikai áldozatai az új demokratikus civil társadalom megalapítóivá a diktatórikus rendszer uralma idején," *Eszmélet, Hungarian quarterly magazine for social critique and culture* (2013) 99: 86–100.

Florian Musil: "Social and Political Victims Become the Founders of a New Democratic Civil Society under Dictatorial Rule," *Revista Convergência Crítica* (2013) 3 <https://periodicos.uff.br/convergenciacritica/article/view/36425> (19 August 2021).

Inga Paslaviciute: "'Privatisierung des Staates' und 'Politisierung des Privaten' als Kommunikationsstrategien der Petitionen in der Litauischen Sozialistischen Sowjetrepublik 1953–1964," in *Staat oder privat? Akteure und Prozesse zwischen Staaten und Gesellschaften in Osteuropa. Beiträge für die 18. Tagung junger Osteuropa-Experten. Arbeitspapiere und Materialien, Forschungsstelle Osteuropa Bremen*, 109 (2010): 69–71.

Kathrin Raminger: "Fortschritt in abstrakter Form: Eine US-amerikanisch – spanische Annäherung in Bildern (1951–1964)," *ILCEA, Revue de l'Institut des langues et cultures d'Europe et d'Amerique, 16/2012* (La culture progressiste à l'époque de la guerre froide), Éditions Littéraires et Linguistiques de l'Université de Grenoble <http://ilcea.revues.org/index1327.html> (19 August 2021). (peer reviewed)

Nathalie Patricia Soursos: "The dictator's photo-albums. Private and public photographs in the Metaxas-dictatorship," *Journal of Modern European History* 16 (2018): 509–25. (peer reviewed)

Nathalie Patricia Soursos: "Fotografie und Diktatur – Eine Untersuchung anhand der Diktatur Ioannis Metaxas' in Griechenland und Benito Mussolinis in Italien," *Fotogeschichte* 129 (2013): 67.

Johannes Thaler: "Ally and Opposition. The Legitimist Movement under the Dollfuß-Schuschnigg-Dictatorship," *Austrian History Yearbook* 45 (2014): 167–85

Johannes Thaler: "Litauens 'Eiserner Wolf' als faschistischer Wehrverbund," in *Verräter und Überzeugungstäter / Traitors and True Believers,* edited by David Feest and Florian Kührer-Wielach, *Nordost-Archiv. Zeitschrift für Regionalgeschichte* XXVI (2019): 88–111.

Newspaper articles

Lucile Dreidemy: "Totenkult für einen Diktator," *Die Zeit,* 30, 2011, pp. 10–11.

Lucile Dreidemy: "Wirklich Hitlers erstes Opfer?," *Der Standard,* 25 July 2009, p. 34.

Reviews

Florian Musil: Pamela Beth Radcliff, Making Democratic Citizens in Spain: Civil Society and the Popular Origins of the Transition, 1960–78, *zeitgeschichte* 3 (2012).

Kathrin Raminger with Tobias Reckling: Legacies of War and Dictatorship in Contemporary Portugal and Spain, Alison Ribeiro de Menezes and Catherine O'Leary (eds.) (2011), Oxford: Peter Lang (Iberian and Latin American Studies: The Arts, Literature and Identity, 1), xvii + 270 pp, *International Journal of Iberian Studies* (IJIS) 26 (2013) 1–2: 120–21.

Nathalie Patricia Soursos: Wolfgang Schieder, Mythos Mussolini. Deutsche in Audienz beim Duce, München 2013, *zeitgeschichte* (2014) 1: 64–65.

Lectures

Lucile Dreidemy: Public Lecture: "Engelbert Dollfuß 1892–2012, Rückblick auf eine der umstrittensten Persönlichkeiten der österreichischen Zeitgeschichte," Linz, Wissensturm, March 2012.

Lucile Dreidemy: Keynote Lecture at the Conference "Museumsanalyse im deutschsprachigen Raum:" "Eine Gedenkstätte über den Umweg eines Museums, das Engelbert-Dollfuß-Museum in Texingtal, Niederösterreich," Österreichische Akademie der Wissenschaften, Vienna, October 2011.

Lucile Dreidemy: Guest Lecture: "Engelbert Dollfuß 1934–2009. Die Vita eines Mythos," Department of Contemporary History, Universität Innsbruck, January 2011.

Florian Kührer-Wielach: "Habsburgs Wiedergänger auf der Siegesstraße. 'Großrumänien' 1918–1940," Series of Lectures "Modernisierung und Fortschritt? Die Zwischenkriegszeit in Ostmittel- und Südosteuropa," Schweizerische Osteuropabibliothek, Bern, 18 October 2018.

Florian Kührer-Wielach: "O cetate fără cetățeni? România Mare de la Alba Iulia la Grivița," University Museum Iași, 2015.

Florian Musil: "Propuestas metodológicas para la investigación de los movimientos sociales," Seminari permanent del Grup de Recerca sobre l'Època Franquista (GREF-CEFID), Universitat Autònoma de Barcelona, 13 November 2012.

Nathalie Patricia Soursos: "Der Faschismus in Griechenland. Die Metaxas-Diktatur, ihre Vorgänger und Vorbilder," Geh Denken! Verein Gedenkdienst, Vienna, 12 December 2016.

Nathalie Patricia Soursos: "Der lächelnde Diktator. Die Fotografie in der Metaxas-Diktatur," Photoinstitut Bonartes, Vienna, 28 April 2016.

Nathalie Patricia Soursos: "Die Metaxas-Diktatur und die Beziehungen nach Deutschland – Spurensuche anhand von Fotografien," Evangelische Gemeinde, Athens, 27 February 2013.

Conference talks

Lucile Dreidemy: "30 Jahre danach – Der Skandalfilm 'Staatsoperette' oder die mühsame Hinterfragung der Mythen und Tabus rund um die diktatorische Wende in Österreich," International Conference "Images de la nation, Contribution de l'oeuvre d'art à la réflexion sur l'identité dans les pays de langue allemande," Université de Strasbourg, December 2011.

Lucile Dreidemy: "Scenes and Actors of Engelbert Dollfuss's Representations in Austrian Memory Politics since 1945," International Conference of the Doctoral College for European Historical Dictatorship and Transformation Research "Images of Power/ Representations of the Past", Universität Wien, November 2011.

Lucile Dreidemy: "Engelbert Dollfuss 1934–2009 – The Changing Face of a 'Small' Political Icon," International Workshop "Hegemony and the image," Universität Klagenfurt, May 2011.

Lucile Dreidemy: "Dollfuß – biographisch. Eine Längschnittsanalyse der Dollfuß-Biographik," Conference "Österreich 1933–1938," Universität Wien, January 2011.

Lucile Dreidemy: "'A dead man leads us!' Collective mourning as a political weapon in panic situations." International Graduate Conference "Panic and Mourning," Universidade Católica Portuguesa, Lisbon, October 2010.

Lucile Dreidemy: "Herausforderungen der Geschichtswissenschaft im Umgang mit dem Dollfuß-Mythos," Doctoral Workshop "Rationalität und Formen des Irrationalen im deutschen Sprachraum vom Mittelalter bis zur Gegenwart," MISHA, Strasbourg, June 2010.

Lucile Dreidemy: "Engelbert Dollfuß 1934–2009. Reflexionsansätze zu einer Biographie des Posthumen," International Conference "Zeitgeschichtetage 2010. Update! Perspektiven der Zeitgeschichte," Universität Wien, May 2010.

Lucile Dreidemy: "Kulturelle Hegemoniestrategien des Austrofaschismus," International Conference "Kulturelle Transfers – Mythen der Erneuerung. Vienna um 1930," Wien Museum, January 2010.

Lucile Dreidemy: "Engelbert Dollfuß-Biographik: Zwischen Mythos und Geschichte," International Conference "Identität und Lebenswelt. Praxis der historischen Biographieforschung," Haus der Geschichte des Ruhrgebiets, Bochum, December 2009.

Lucile Dreidemy: "Engelbert Dollfuß-Biographien: Zwischen Mythos und Geschichte," Annual Conference of the German Studies Association, Washington D.C., October 2009.

Katharina Ebner: "Strategies of Ideological Transfer – Italofascist Propaganda in Interwar Austria and Hungary," International Conference of the Doctoral College for European Historical Dictatorship and Transformation Research "Public Sphere, Ideology, Transformation of Power," Universität Wien, 24 November 2011.

Katharina Ebner: "The Reception of the Papal Encyclical Quadragesimo anno (1931) and the Dollfuss/ Schuschnigg-Regime: the Example of Karl Anton Prince Rohan (1898–1975)," 35th Annual Conference of the German Studies Association (GSA), Louisville, Kentucky, 23 September 2011.

Katharina Ebner: "Ideological Transfer of Italian Fascism – the Role of the Austrian Catholic Church in Youth Education," 5th Graduate Conference on European History (GRACEH) "Transfers and Demarcations," European University Institute (EUI), Florence, 30 April 2011.

Katharina Ebner: "Zur Rezeption der päpstlichen Enzyklika Quadragesimo anno (1931) am Beispiel von Karl Anton Prinz Rohan (1898–1975)," Editorial Workshop "Vergleich und Transfer," Cluster of Excellence "Religion und Politik," Universität Münster, 24 March 2011.

Katharina Ebner: "Ideologietransfer des italienischen Faschismus am Beispiel Österreichs und Ungarns und der Beitrag der Katholischen Kirche," Doctoral Conference "Mitteleuropäische Perspektiven," Andrássy University, Budapest, 24 September 2010.

Linda Erker: "(K)ein Karriereknick? Reintegration der 'Ehemaligen' im akademischen Milieu," Conference "Die 'Ehemaligen' NS-Kontinuitäten – Transformationen – Netzwerke nach 1945," Vienna, 2016.

Linda Erker: "Relegierte Interbrigadistas. Österreichische Freiwillige mit Disziplinarverfahren an der Universität Wien im Austrofaschismus," International Symposium "Der Spanische Bürgerkrieg als Antihumanistisches Laboratorium. Engagierte Intellektuelle im Spannungsfeld von Avantgarden und Faschismen in Österreich, Italien und Spanien," Vienna, 2016.

Linda Erker: "Relegierte Interbrigadistas. Von der Universität Wien in den Spanischen Bürgerkrieg," International Symposium "Camaradas. Österreicherinnen und Österreicher im Spanischen Bürgerkrieg 1936–1939," Graz, 2016.

Linda Erker: "Faschistische Universitäten? Die Universität Wien im Austrofaschismus und die Universität Madrid im Franquismus," International Colloquium, Freising, 2016.

Linda Erker: "Antisemitism in Austria between 1918 and 1938," Conference "Right Wing Politics and the Rise of Anti-Semitism in Europe 1935–1940," Institut für Zeitgeschichte (IfZ), Munich, 2016.

Linda Erker: "Studierende Antisemiten an der Universität Wien (1933–1938)," Conference "Antisemitismus in Österreich 1933–1938," Vienna, 2015.

Linda Erker: "Gewalt an der Universität Wien im Austrofaschismus und an der *Universidad Central de Madrid* im frühen Franquismus," IX. Workshop der Historischen Spanienforschung, Georg-von-Vollmar-Akademie, Kochel am See, 2014.

Linda Erker: "Die gewaltvolle Geschichte der Universität Wien im Austrofaschismus und der *Universidad Central de Madrid* im frühen Franquismus," Workshop "Universitätsgeschichte im 19. und 20. Jahrhundert," Universität Münster, 2014.

Linda Erker: "Die Universität Wien im Austrofaschismus," Workshop of the FSP Diktaturen, Gewalt, Genozide, Department of Contemporary History, Universität Wien, 2012.

Alena Haubenhofer: "Divided Nation? Integration of Post-Soviet Latvia's Society Reflected in the Press," 17th Annual World Convention of the Association for the Study of Nationalities, Columbia University, New York, 21 April 2012.

Alena Haubenhofer: "The discourses on Europe in the press of Lithuania and Latvia after 1990," Conference "Communicating European Integration of History of European Integration Research Society," Humboldt Universität zu Berlin, 30 March 2012.

Alena Haubenhofer: "Latvia – the Case of Permanent Collective Identity Crisis?," Conference "Crisis: Interruptions, Reactions and Continuities in Central and Eastern Europe," SSEES University College London, 17 February 2012.

Alena Haubenhofer: "Brussels Sprout, Eurobureaucrats and the Promised Land – The Images of Europe in Political Cartoons of Lithuania and Latvia (2003–2009)," International Conference of the Doctoral College for European Historical Dictatorship and Transformation Research "Images of Power / Representations of the Past," Universität Wien, 7 November 2011.

Alena Haubenhofer: "Images of Europe in Lithuania and Latvia," Conference "Imagining Europe: Perspectives, Perceptions and Representations from Antiquity to the Present," University of Leiden, 27 January 2011.

Eleni Kouki: "When a dictatorship remembers a previous dictatorship: The promotion of Ioannis Metaxas by the 1967 junta in Greece," International Conference of the Doctoral College for European Historical Dictatorship and Transformation Research "Images of Power / Representations of the Past," Universität Wien, 7–9 November 2011.

Eleni Kouki: "War photographs re-used: An approach to the photograph collection of the Memorial Museum of the Battle of Sarantaporo," Conference "Greek (Hi)stories through the Lens: Photographs, Photographers & their Testimonies," Centre for Hellenic Studies and Department of Byzantine & Modern Greek Studies, King's College, London, 9–11 June 2011.

Eleni Kouki: "The hero and the crowd. The Unknown Soldier monument in Athens," Social History Forum "New approaches to Greek society during the interwar period (1922–1940)," 14–16 January 2011, Athens.

Florian Kührer-Wielach: "Demokratie der Krisen. Rumäniens Integrationsprozess zwischen den Weltkriegen," Scientific Symposium of the Plattform zeithistorische Archive "Die Krisen der Demokratie in den 1920er und 1930er Jahren," Österreichisches Volkskundemuseum, Vienna, 3–5 November 2021.

Florian Kührer-Wielach: "Viziunea de la Alba Iulia şi realitatea interbelică. O perspectivă (trans)regional," Conference "Romania and the Historical Events in the Period 1914–1920," Ateneul Român, Bucharest, 18 September 2018.

Florian Kührer-Wielach: "'Ein fruchtbarer und blühender Garten.' Großrumäniens erstes Jahrzehnt nach dem Ersten Weltkrieg," Humboldt-Kolleg "World War I and Beyond: Human Tragedies, Social Challenges, Scientific and Cultural Responses," Bucharest, 17 September 2018.

Florian Kührer-Wielach: "On Clowns and Hooligans. Romania 1918–1948–1989," International Conference "1918–1938–2018: Dawn of an Authoritarian Century?," Schloss Eckartsau, 4–7 September 2018.

Florian Kührer-Wielach: "Transylvania in transition: national integration, political regionalism, and minority issues after World War I," Conference "#Romania100: Looking Forward through the Past," Society for Romanian Studies (SRS), 25–30 June 2018.

Florian Kührer-Wielach: "Ethno-Elitists into Regio-Nationalists. The Transylvanian Case," IARCEES 40th Annual Conference "Individuals and Institutions in Europe and Eurasia," Maynooth University, 2016.

Florian Kührer-Wielach: "Die Rumänische Nationalpartei, ihre Protagonisten und die Integration Siebenbürgens in den rumänischen Staat. Institutionelle Zentralisierung und politischer Regionalismus in der Krise," Conference "Politische Mobilisierung in Ostmittel- und Südosteuropa," Herder-Institut, Marburg, 13–14 June 2013.

Florian Kührer-Wielach: "Regionalism as a Means of Opposition? Transylvanian Romanians after the Treaty of Trianon," International Conference of the Doctoral College for European Historical Dictatorship and Transformation Research "Public Sphere, Ideology, Transformation of Power," Universität Wien, 24–25 November 2011.

Florian Kührer-Wielach: "Transylvania without Transylvanians? National Unification and Intra-national Demarcation. 1918–1938," 5th Annual Graduate Conference in European History "Transfers and Demarcations," Florence, 28–30 April 2011.

Florian Musil: Colóquio Internacional "O Colapso das Ditaduras: Sul da Europa, América Latina, Leste Europeu e África do Sul," Universidade Federal do Rio de Janeiro, 24–26 October 2012.

Florian Musil: 8th Workshop "Historische Spanienforschung," Kochel am See, 14–16 September 2012.

Florian Musil: "East and West – European Dictatorships in the Twentieth Century and their Aftermath," Department of Political Science, Universität Wien, 9 June 2012.

Florian Musil: 43rd Annual Meeting: Association for Spanish and Portuguese Historical Studies, Tufts University, Medford MA, 22–25 March 2012.

Florian Musil: International Conference of the Doctoral College for European Historical Dictatorship and Transformation Research "Public Sphere, Ideology, Transformation of Power," Universität Wien, 24–25 November 2011.

Florian Musil: General Conference of the European Consortium for Political Research, University of Iceland, Reykjavík, 25–27 August 2011.

Inga Paslaviciute: "Letters to Power: Criticism of the Party and State Institutions in the Case of the Petitions to the Central Committee of the Lithuanian Communist Party 1953–1964," History Lab Annual Conference "Institutions," Institute of Historical Research, London, 12–13 June 2013.

Inga Paslaviciute: "'Kritik' und 'Selbstkritik' im Spiegel der Petitionen an das Zentralkomitee der Litauischen kommunistischen Partei in der Litauischen Sozialistischen Sowjetrepublik 1953–1964," Tag der Politikwissenschaft, University of Graz, 29–30 November 2012.

Inga Paslaviciute: "Petitionen an das Regime. (Rhetorische) Strategien in der Kommunikation mit der kommunistischen Bürokratie in der Litauischen Sozialistischen Sowjetrepublik," Conference "Linkstotalitarismus und Realsozialismus," Universität Wien, 12 December 2010.

Kathrin Raminger: "Francoist cultural diplomacy in the name of *Hispanidad* and the political instrumentalisation of al-Andalus: The Exposición de Arte Español in Cairo

(1950)," Conference of the Carl Justi-Association "Das kulturelle Erbe von al-Andalus und die Nationale Identität," Humboldt Universität zu Berlin, 27–29 October 2017.

Kathrin Raminger: "'Saber ser português:' Exhibition Politics, Artistic Representation and the Construction of an Imperial Portuguese Identity during the Salazarist Estado Novo (1933-1974)," 33rd Annual Conference of the Association for Contemporary Iberian Studies (ACIS), King's College, London, 4–6 September 2012.

Kathrin Raminger: "Salazarism and Francoism: Portuguese-Spanish bilateral relations as mirrored by their exhibition politics (1936–1974)," I International Graduate Conference on Portuguese Modern and Contemporary History "Portugal in the last two centuries," Centro de Estudos de História Contemporânea, Instituto Universitário de Lisboa, 21–23 June 2012.

Kathrin Raminger: "*Imperio* and *Portugalidade*. Exhibition-Politics and Ideology in the Portuguese Estado Novo. The Salazar-Years (1932-1968)," International Conference of the Doctoral College for European Historical Dictatorship and Transformation Research "Images of Power / Representations of the Past," Universität Wien, 7–8 November 2011.

Kathrin Raminger: "Abstracción y modernidad. Consecuencias políticas y artísticas del intercambio cultural entre España y los Estados Unidos en el marco de la Guerra Fría, International Conference "La Culture 'progressiste' pendant la Guerre Froide (1945–1989),'" Institut des langues et des cultures d'Europe et d'Amérique, Université Stendhal, Grenoble, 15–16 September 2011.

Nathalie Patricia Soursos: "'The first peasant.' Ioannis Metaxas and the politicized view of Greek peasantry," Conference "Rural History 2017," European Rural History Organisation, University of Leuven, 11–14 September 2017.

Nathalie Patricia Soursos: "The dictator's photo-albums. Private and public photographs in the Metaxas-Dictatorship," Conference "Photographing under Dictatorships of the Twentieth Century: Public Spheres and Photographic Practice," Humboldt Universität zu Berlin, 26–28 October 2016.

Nathalie Patricia Soursos: "Feste im Regime des Vierten August. Zur Inszenierung der Diktatur des Ioannis Metaxas (1936–1941)," 6th Workshop of the HKF Visuelle Kulturgeschichte – Kulturen und Medien des Visuellen, Department of Art History, Universität Wien, 4 December 2015.

Nathalie Patricia Soursos: "Griechenland. Von der Krise des Parlamentarismus bis zum Scheitern der Demokratie (1922–1936)," Conference "Nach dem 'Großen Krieg.' Vom Triumph zum Desaster der Demokratie 1918/19–1939," Hannah-Arendt-Institut, Dresden, 6–8 October 2014.

Nathalie Patricia Soursos: "The dictator in dialogue with the mass: Photographic sources of a conversation," Conference "The 4th of August regime and the Greek society. A fascist experiment. Social history forum," University of Athens, 27–28 September 2014 (in Greek).

Nathalie Patricia Soursos: "The King and his Dictator. Photographs of the Power Play in Italy and Greece (1936-1945)," International Conference of the Doctoral College for European Historical Dictatorship and Transformation Research "Images of Power – Transformation of the Past," Universität Wien, 7–8 November 2011.

Nathalie Patricia Soursos: "Fotografie und Diktatur. Die Bildpropaganda in Italien und Griechenland 1936–1941," Workshop of the FSP Diktaturen, Gewalt, Genozide, Department of Contemporary History, Universität Wien, 7 October 2011.

Nathalie Patricia Soursos: "Photography and Dictatorship – A Research on the Cases of Ioannis Metaxas in Greece and Mussolini in Italy," Conference "(Hi)stories through the Lens," Centre for Hellenic Studies, King's College, London, 9–11 June 2011.

Johannes Thaler: "Conservative Dictatorships and Fascist Paramilitary – A Comparison of Interwar Political Crisis in Lithuania and Austria," 11th International Postgraduate Conference on Central and Eastern Europe Conference: "Crisis: Interruptions, Reactions and Continuities in Central and Eastern Europe," School of Slavonic and East European Studies, University College London, 15–17 February 2012.

Johannes Thaler: "Habsburg Legitimism and Austrofascism – Ideological Stronghold or Opposition?," German Studies Association 35th Annual Conference, Louisville/Kentucky, 22–25 September 2011.

Johannes Thaler: "Petty State Dictatorships in Interwar European Politics: The Cases of Austria and Lithuania," International Conference of the Doctoral College for European Historical Dictatorship and Transformation Research "Public Sphere, Ideology, Transformation of Power," Universität Wien, 24–25 November 2011.

Filip Zieliński: "Voting on History. Laws Enacted by the Polish Parliament to Commemorate the Past," International Conference of the Doctoral College for European Historical Dictatorship and Transformation Research "Images of Power / Representations of the Past," Universität Wien, 7–8 November 2011.

Filip Zieliński: "Vom Nutzen und Nachteil der Geschichtspolitik – Geschichtspolitik als *politics* im Transformationsprozess Polens," Conference "Brauchen Demokratien Geschichte?", Arbeitskreis Politik und Geschichte in der Deutschen Vereinigung für Politische Wissenschaft, Bonn, 1–2 July 2011.

Abstracts

Authoritarian Regimes in the Long Twentieth Century. Preconditions, Structures, Continuities – Contributions to European Historical Dictatorship and Transformation Research

Lucile Dreidemy
Forever the First Victim? The Dollfuß Myth and the Long-Term Impact of Coalitional Historiography

The dispute over the interpretation of Engelbert Dollfuss's politics and personality has shaped the historical-political discourse of the Second Austrian Republic like hardly any other. An oil painting of Dollfuss which had been placed in the club rooms of the ÖVP after 1945 became the focal point of the controversy for years. With the portrait's removal in 2017, the central basis for the ritualistic controversy that had kept the Dollfuss myth alive throughout the Second Republic disappeared. Whether this measure could result in a definitive historicization of the figure of Dollfuss and an end to the myth can be doubted, given the characteristic mutability and adaptability of mythical discourses. Against this background, the removal of the controversial portrait appears to be a welcome occasion to take stock of the context-specific transformations of the Dollfuss myth since its creation in the years 1933–34 and of its historical-political consequences from its inception to the present day.
Keywords: Dollfuss, myth, fascism

Katharina Ebner
Ideology Transfer of Italian Fascism. Fascist Transmission Belts in Vienna and Budapest

The "seizure of power" by Italian Fascism in 1922 served as a model for many sympathising movements in post-war Europe. This leading function of Italian Fascism serves as the starting point for this transfer-historical investigation. Italy's protective power over Austria and Hungary between 1927 and 1936 also aimed to create a philo-fascist climate in the Austrian and Hungarian public spheres, and for Austria in particular, to fascistize the political system. Fascist Italy used channels of mediation, so-called Fascist transmission belts, to spread Fascist ideology in Vienna and Budapest. Through the comprehensive reconstruction of these channels, it can be shown that the Italian goals of this Fascism export were aimed at specific target groups and were closely linked to local reception processes. Although the positive reception phases of fascism coincided in Austria and Hungary, the Fascist mediating institutions encountered different reception preconditions. The rise of National Socialism marked a fascist challenge in Europe to which Italy had to respond. Therefore, country-specific goals for the export of fascism were subject to change in accordance with the priorities of Italian foreign policy.
Keywords: fascism, transfer, ideology

Linda Erker
The University of Vienna from 1933 to 1938 and the Dictatorship of Many Names. A Contribution to Fascism Studies

This article is based on the doctoral dissertation *The University of Vienna under Austrofascism. Austrian Higher Education Policy 1933 to 1938, its Preconditions and Long-Term Effects* (published as a monograph in 2021). While there are countless studies on Austria's universities after the so-called Anschluss in 1938, there has barely been any discussion of the university's history during the five years prior to it. This astonishing research gap is resolved by my study, which shows how much the University of Vienna was harmed during the Dollfuss/ Schuschnigg dictatorship. On the one hand, radical austerity measures were imposed and used for political and anti-Semitic "purges" of the teaching staff. On the other hand, the regime intervened in university and student self-administration by means of new laws. This self-inflicted provincialization in some areas was seamlessly continued after 1945, as former Austrofascist functionaries were (again) appointed to the university leadership.
Keywords: University of Vienna, Austrofascism, anti-Semitism, Fascism Studies

Eleni Kouki
What Can the Study of Monuments and Ceremonies Tell Us About a Dictatorship? The Case of the Dictatorship of April 21 in Greece. 1967–74

The Dictatorship of April 21 holds a particular significance in the Greek political discourse. Its fall in 1974 was the first step toward the foundation of the Third Hellenic Republic, the most stable period of democracy in Greece's history. However, many facets of the dictatorship remain undiscussed, especially regarding the features of the regime. If the past is a foreign country, following Lowenthal's well-known dictum, can we use the dictatorship's ceremonies and monuments as a new path for exploring the characteristics of the regime and pose new questions? This article is an attempt to reevaluate the dictatorship's quest for legitimacy through its ritual politics. Moreover, it is also an attempt to explore rituals not as a mere reflection of power, but as political acts with tangible effects.
Keywords: Greece, Dictatorship of April 21, ceremonies

Florian Kührer-Wielach
Habsburg Revenants on Victory Road. Greater Romania's Integration Process 1918–33

This article examines the post-imperial transformation of the Kingdom of Romania after World War I, when its territory and population had doubled. The article first explores the months following the nominal unification of Romanian, Hungarian, Austrian, and Russian territories into "Greater Romania" beginning in late 1918 before describing the main aspects of institutional integration of the newly formed state. Three main processes are identified: centralization, Romanianization, and nationalization. These years are dominated by a power struggle encompassing all levels of society, essentially between "old" and "new" Romanian elites. This is followed by analysis of the moment when the "Habsburg" opposition, united with the socially agitated peasant party, first gained confidence and then power only to lose both within a few years. This moment of general disappointment, aggravated by the effects of the Great Depression, marked the final turn toward increasingly authoritarian politics in Romania.
Keywords: Romania, transformation, authoritarianism

Florian Musil

Democratization 'From Below'. Civil Society in the Metropolitan Area of Barcelona in their Struggle for Democratic Rights in the Final Decade of the Franco Regime

Spain's democratization – the *transición* – is mostly examined 'from above'. Countless historians have analyzed how the great players in this process – moderate Francoists in the government and the democratic opposition leaders – brought about the democratic transformation of the Francoist regime after the dictator's death. Attention is usually drawn to the skill and peacefulness of these big players, while the multitudes of Spaniards are often described as the receiving mass of these processes. This article focuses on the other aspect of democratization in Spain: the struggle of the anti-Francoist social movements for democracy, which was at times far from peaceful due to the repression on the part of the Francoist police and military, even after the death of Franco himself. The study consists of two main parts. The first focuses on civil society before the transformation of Spain's political system in the metropolitan area of Barcelona as one of the spearhead regions in this struggle for democracy. The second part consists of a broad scale movement analysis of the workers' movement within this metropolis. It is shows that social mobilization was an important agent in the social change to democracy.
Keywords: social movements, civil society, democratization

Inga Paslavičiūtė

Petitions to the Regime. (Rhetorical) Strategies in Communication with the Communist Bureaucracy in the Lithuanian Soviet Socialist Republic 1953–89

As part of fragmented Soviet publicity, petitions were tolerated by the state and became an established way for citizens to exert influence. The system of petitions, complaints and statements by the people addressed to various institutions of state and party can be considered a field of communication between the state and society. The politically and ideologically organized state regime felt a responsibility to conduct communication with the citizens in order to gain insights into their concerns and needs (control function) and to keep control of the "socialist democracy" (valve function). The investigation of the petitions will help track the boundaries of (dis)loyalty with the state regime due to the fact that the petitions demonstrate the extent to which an absolute claim to control pushed "the voice of the people" to (non)conformity and contributed to the regime's destabilization. In fact, it became a false reality: for the Communist Party, citizens played an active, creative role in building the

socialist ideal, while for the authors, such attempts to write about their needs were often a last cry for help.
Keywords: East European History, LSSR History, petitions

Kathrin Raminger
Visual Representations of Hegemony. Art Exhibitions as Political Instruments in the Iberian Dictatorships of Franco and Salazar

Applying a comparative hermeneutic approach, the article analyses the political functions of official exhibitions of visual arts in the Iberian dictatorships of Francisco Franco and António de Oliveira Salazar from their origins in the interwar period until their collapse in 1974/75. Presuming that images do play a fundamental role in the discursive construction of hegemonic social reality, the dissertation focuses on the contribution of art exhibitions to the constitution of hegemony and dominance as two major pillars on which these long-lasting rightwing dictatorships built their legitimacy. Official art exhibitions are regarded as a visual means of communication and representation and therefore as powerful political instruments. Their analysis is based not only on archival material concerning their organisation, but also on their visual reconstruction using photographs and exhibition catalogues. The article demonstrates that the Spanish Franco regime successfully relied on art exhibitions as political instruments in its cultural diplomacy, seeking legitimation in international acceptance. The Portuguese dictatorship, in comparison, primarily used art exhibitions to foster cohesion within the colonial empire upon which its ideologically constructed legitimacy was based.
Keywords: art exhibition, cultural diplomacy, Francoist Spain, Salazarist Portugal

Nathalie Patricia Soursos
Perceiving Fascism in Photographs of a Benign General

Taking as its point of departure an iconic picture of the "4th of August regime" (1936–41) by the press photographer Petros Poulidis depicting the Greek dictator Ioannis Metaxas and his entourage, this article explores the visual implementation of the regime's main characteristics. While core elements – the leader cult, the *EON*, the Church, the military, censorship of the press and literature, and anti-communism – are depicted in this photograph, others are missing – for example, King George II and the royal family. In addition, the proximity to fascism is obvious on the visual level despite the fact that the

regime's foreign policy was surprisingly reserved towards Italian Fascism and National Socialism. When fascism is associated with perfectly constructed photographs of charismatic leaders, large-scale spectacles, and choreographed crowds, its banality beyond these pictures is ignored and it becomes difficult to classify imitators with more limited technical capabilities. Via this iconic photograph, the article analyses the difficulties of classifying "small dictatorships" within fascist studies.
Keywords: visual history, photography, authoritarianism, fascism, modern Greece, Metaxas-dictatorship

Johannes Thaler
Three Opposing Interpretations of Fascism and their Synthesis. Political Practice –
Ideology – Genesis

This article examines three very different attempts to circumscribe and define the phenomenon of fascism and their mutual complementarity. While some essential aspects of Sven Reichardt's praxeological definition of fascism, Roger Griffin's "fascist minimum" and Zeev Sternhell's historical derivation of the fascist ideology contradict each other, they each touch neuralgic spots that help provide a better understanding of fascism. Along with proposals for sharpening and expanding the individual theoretical attempts to explain the phenomenon, Sternhell's approach rooted in the history of ideology is presented as the missing link between those taken by Reichardt and Griffin.
Keywords: fascism, ideology, violence

Florian Wenninger
Social Polarization and Its Historical Analysis. The Example of the First Austrian
Republic

A dispute among historians in the early years of the Second Austrian Republic brought to light, for the first time in a public debate, completely divergent interpretations of what had happened in Austria between 1918 and 1938 and had ended in the liquidation of democracy and the establishment of a Catholic dictatorship. In the pillarized post-war society, these interpretations had strong identity-defining content. Against the background of the current state of research, the dissertation summarized in the article examines the tendencies towards polarization during those years and embeds them in a longer tradition of economic and socio-cultural clashes of interest.
Keywords: First Austrian Republic, Austrofascism, memory politics

Filip Zieliński
The "Golden Age" Narrative of Interwar Poland and Its Effects on Democratization in 1989. A Case Study in History Politics

Historic narratives create a horizon spanning the past, the present and the future; they are as much about the past as they are about what we do in the present in order to arrive at a future envisioned by the narrative. The "golden age" narrative – i. e. the idea that the Third Republic (since 1989) is a direct successor of the Second Republic (1918–45), which is perceived in highly positive terms, while dismissing or ignoring the People's Republic (1945–89) as a period of foreign rule – is a good example of the political effects of such narratives. On the one hand, the narrative was useful in "masking" the many factual continuities of pre- and post-1989 Poland by creating a clear but merely symbolic break. On the other hand, the dominant "golden age" narrative and the many other narratives that make up the history of history politics in Poland have not only legitimized, but actually informed many decisions of Polish lawmakers across all political issues of the time. Furthermore, they have influenced the construction and differentiation of identities of post-1989 political parties.
Keywords: democratization, history politics, Poland

Authors and Editors

Dr. Lucile Dreidemy is Maitre de Conférences at the University of Toulouse Jean Jaurès and currently a post-doctoral assistant at the Institute of Contemporary History at the University of Vienna.

Dr. Katharina Ebner is a freelance contemporary historian and was a fellow of the Vienna Doctoral College "European Historical Dictatorship and Transformation Research" at University of Vienna.

Dr. Linda Erker teaches and researches as a historian at the Institute for Contemporary History at the University of Vienna.

Dr. Eleni Kouki holds a PdF in Greek modern history. She teaches at the Open Greek University.

Dr. Florian Kührer-Wielach is a historian and director of the Institute for German Culture and History of Southeast Europe at LMU Munich.

Dr. Florian Musil studied in Vienna, Barcelona and Granada History and Communication Science and worked at the Universities of Vienna, Kassel, Klagenfurt, Salzburg, Haifa and Eichstätt as Researcher, Teacher, and Manager.

Dr. Inga Paslavičiūtė studied German Studies (Klaipėda, Rostock, Würzburg) and pursued her doctoral studies in Munich and Vienna.

Dr. Kathrin Raminger is a Romance scholar and contemporary historian with a focus on visual contemporary and cultural history.

Prof. DDr. Oliver Rathkolb is Professor of Modern History with focus on contemporary history. He is chairman of the Institute of Contemporary History at the University of Vienna and was spokesman of the Doctoral College "European Historical Dictatorship and Transformation Research" (2009–2013).

Dr. Nathalie Soursos is a lecturer in Modern Greek History and Gender Studies at the University of Vienna.

Dr. Johannes Thaler, formerly a doctoral student and research assistant at the Institute of Contemporary History at the University of Vienna, is a contemporary historian at the Austrian Federal Monuments Office.

Dr. Florian Wenninger heads the Institute for Historical Social Research in Vienna. In addition to Austrian contemporary history, his recent work focuses on police history.

Dr. Filip Zieliński, post-doctoral researcher at the Max-Weber-Institute of Sociology, Heidelberg University.